WISDOM'S WONDER

WISDOM'S WONDER

Character, Creation, and Crisis
in the Bible's Wisdom Literature

William P. Brown

WILLIAM B. EERDMANS PUBLISHING COMPANY
GRAND RAPIDS, MICHIGAN / CAMBRIDGE, U.K.

Published 2014 by

Wm. B. Eerdmans Publishing Co.

2140 Oak Industrial Drive N.E., Grand Rapids, Michigan 49505 /

P.O. Box 163, Cambridge CB3 9PU U.K.

Printed in the United States of America

20 19 18 17 16 15 14   7 6 5 4 3 2 1

Library of Congress Cataloging-in-Publication Data

Brown, William P., 1958-

   Wisdom's wonder: character, creation, and crisis in the

   Bible's wisdom literature / William P. Brown.

      pages   cm

   Includes bibliographical references and index.

   ISBN 978-0-8028-6793-3 (pbk.: alk. paper)

   1. Wisdom literature — Criticism, interpretation, etc. 2. Bible. Job —

   Criticism, interpretation, etc.   I. Title.

BS1455.B7625   2013

223'.06 — dc23

                                2013044665

www.eerdmans.com

Contents

CONTENTS

Preface

When I was invited by William B. Eerdmans to revise *Character in Crisis* (1996), my first reaction was to decline. Since its appearance in print, as well the publication of an edited volume on character ethics and biblical interpretation (1999), I have moved on to other areas of interest in biblical studies. Nevertheless, I have been surprised over the years how this modest book has enjoyed a long life in print.

My second, more reflective reaction fortunately won the day. I agreed to accept the invitation on the condition that I could rewrite it. I came to realize that the invitation afforded me the unique opportunity to take up my earlier interests and do something new, with the result of fostering all the more my love for biblical wisdom. It was a chance to struggle anew with the wisdom corpus and to offer, once again, a "fresh approach," as the subtitle of the original work claimed to do.

My motivation is now, as it was then, to provide an engaging reading of the wisdom literature that would set itself apart from standard introductory treatments. Most works of introduction maintain an appropriate level of detachment that comes from addressing a diverse array of issues and perspectives with some measure of "objectivity." Not here. As in *Character in Crisis,* I follow a particular perspective, one that I am particularly passionate about, and in doing so attempt to enliven the ancient words of the biblical sages for contemporary readers.

Rereading *Character in Crisis* as preparation for this new treatment was like reading a series of old sermons: while appreciating certain flashes of insight, I mostly cringed at the over-the-top manner in which I pressed my case, sometimes carelessly. My first foray into the wisdom corpus was passionately argued but largely lacked nuance and, at certain points, clarity. Indeed, I see myself in that book very much like the figure of Elihu in the book of Job: brash and utterly self-convinced of his argument, not to mention repetitive and occasionally turgid. (Make no mistake, I still respect Elihu.) The challenge with this new publication has been to forge a new direction without altogether abandoning the original argument, a delicate balance to be sure.

Since the publication of *Character in Crisis,* subsequent studies have profitably and critically used the language of moral formation or character to highlight a prominent feature of the wisdom corpus, though certainly not due to my book alone. Now, seventeen years later, I find this "fresh approach" to be stale and narrow. Other issues of sapiential significance include socioeconomic context, scribal development, education, gender roles, psychology, rhetoric, epistemology, spirituality, and even ecology. Yet character formation remains in the mix, as well it should.

My new "fresh approach" is more encompassing. It signals my attempt to go beneath and beyond issues of moral formation in sapiential discourse. Hence this "revision" builds on, corrects, and expands the earlier work while moving more broadly toward matters of epistemological and philosophical interest. In the process, I have come to identify a new lens through which to read and understand the wisdom corpus in its richness and diversity.

Seventeen years ago, I was interested in "character ethics" as a response to "the predominance of self-interest in corporate and private spheres" and "the violent fragmentation of American society," to quote from my original preface. I still am. A recent article in the *Journal of Positive Psychology* observes a steady decrease in the use of terms related to "moral excellence and virtue" in contemporary American literature (e.g., character, conscience, decency, dignity, rectitude, righteousness, uprightness, virtue).[1] Pelin and Selin Kesebir attribute this decline to the cultural trend in the United States toward "greater individualism." While not suggesting a causal relation, they note that accompanying the "downward trend in the cultural salience of morality terms" is an "upward trend in the salience of terms related to the self," such as *"unique, personalize, self,* and phrases like *all about me, I am special,* and *I'm the best."*[2]

1. Kesebir and Kesebir, "Cultural Salience of Moral Character."
2. Doll, "Moral Decline."

More anecdotally, the word "character" today has become associated with moralistic myopia, something associated more with Sunday school than with emotional and moral intelligence. (And as an avid Sunday school teacher myself, I take offense!) Since the notion of character is typically (and erroneously) relegated to the noncognitive realm of human development, it seems to have little place in formal education. On the other hand, the forced trend in American public education today to "teach to the test" seems, many feel, to miss crucial dimensions of academic development such as critical thinking, artistic expression, creative imagination, heightened curiosity, and resilience. Through his own research of successful and failing schools, journalist Paul Tough broadens the notion of "character" to include curiosity and the ability to overcome failure — prime ingredients for educational success.[3]

Beyond education, the American political scene thrives on the "rhetoric of divisiveness." Cultural fears continue to mount, particularly of the xenophobic variety, as America's demographic landscape undergoes seismic changes. Add to that economic uncertainty, deadlocked politics (at the time of this writing), gun massacres, public incivility, rampant cynicism, threats of terrorism, and loss of faith in public institutions, not to mention the "long emergency" now upon us — the convergence of economic and ecological pressures that portend disaster for much of the world.[4]

It is in this fraught context that I — a white, now older and, I hope, wiser male who teaches in a mainline, ethnically diverse seminary setting — reengage the wisdom corpus with clearer vision. This new engagement addresses the following deficiencies of the older work:

1. The nearly complete lack of attention given to the role of emotions and desire in moral formation, about which the sages had much to say and about which much is being written today.
2. A failure to appreciate fully the diversity (literary, existential, and theological) of the three biblical wisdom books.
3. A failure to explore more fully the "crises" that the sages addressed in their various writings.
4. A one-sided, moralistic emphasis on individual character at the expense of discussing biblical wisdom's larger scope, including the self's relationship to the world as the sages saw it.

3. Tough, *How Children Succeed.*
4. See Kunstler, *Long Emergency,* 147-234.

As the reader will soon discover, I regard the notion of wonder as an appropriate heuristic framework for understanding biblical wisdom more fully. Wonder, I believe, links the cognitive and noncognitive roots of wisdom into a seamless whole. One reason for reading the wisdom corpus through the lens of wonder is the countercultural implications it has in a North American, highly commercialized context. In the Methodist hymn penned by Charles Wesley (1747), "Love Divine, All Loves Excelling," the final stanza concludes with the arresting phrase "lost in wonder, love, and praise." Today, *losing* wonder is more the norm; fear and fatigue have all but displaced love and wonder.

Nevertheless, as bioanthropologist Melvin Konner notes, the capacity to wonder is "the hallmark of our species and the central feature of the human spirit."[5] Although *Homo sapiens* ("wise human") may be too self-congratulatory a classification, there is no doubt that we are *Homo admirans,* the "wondering human." Wonder is what unites the empiricist and the "contemplator," the psalmist and the scientist, the mythographer and the mathematician.[6] Indeed, an awareness that wonder lies at the heart of scientific investigation and aesthetic expression, as well as at the core of "faith seeking understanding" (à la St. Anselm), may be nothing short of liberating for persons of faith and lovers of wisdom.

Genuine wonder of the other, moreover, fosters mutual respect across racial, ethnic, religious, and cultural divides. It is no wonder that of all leadership figures profiled in the Hebrew Bible,[7] it is the sage who actively and positively engages other cultures, learning and appropriating the wisdom of other lands for the benefit of his or her own community. That alone would cast the wisdom corpus of the Hebrew Bible as the open door in an otherwise closed canon.

I have become convinced that the biblical wisdom corpus speaks deeply to our need for retrieving and nurturing wonder in consort with the necessity of cultivating wisdom for human flourishing. And so begins a new journey (for me at least) into the challenging complexities and puzzles of the sapiential corpus. This book is essentially a testimony to the rich and evocative language of the wisdom books, which continue to be a source of wonder and wondering for me. May it be so for the reader.

Requisite thanks go to the editors at Eerdmans for affording me the

---

5. Konner, *Tangled Wing,* 488.
6. Konner, *Tangled Wing,* 486.
7. For a cursory description of each, see Stevens, *Leadership Roles.*

opportunity to redeem an earlier work, particularly to Michael Thomson for his encouragement throughout. Thanks also to my teaching institution, Columbia Theological Seminary, for granting me sabbatical leave to start and finish the project. Heartfelt thanks go also to the sages that fill my academic life here in the Atlanta area, particularly Carol Newsom, Christine Roy Yoder, Kathleen O'Connor, and Brennan Breed, each of whom has written profoundly on biblical wisdom and from whom I have learned much. Beyond them (and beyond Atlanta), I am greatly indebted to the foundational scholarship of James Crenshaw, Michael Fox, †Roland Murphy, and Choon-Leong Seow. Also, I mention three former doctoral students whose recent dissertations I have found invaluable in the course of this study: Anne Stewart, Robert Williamson Jr., and Davis Hankins. I hope that by the time my work is published, theirs will be too.

Finally, thanks to my family: to our daughters Ella and Hannah, constant sources of wonder; and to my beloved partner, Gail, whose encouragement, support, *and* high expectations have been invaluable for this project. She has helped carry the burden and shared the joy of seeing this project through to its timely completion.

WILLIAM P. BROWN
December, 2013

Abbreviations

AB	Anchor Bible
ABRL	Anchor Bible Reference Library
ANET	James B. Pritchard, ed., *Ancient Near Eastern Texts.* 3rd ed. Princeton: Princeton University Press, 1969
AOTC	Abingdon Old Testament Commentaries
ATANT	Abhandlungen zur Theologie des Alten und Neuen Testaments
ATD	Das Alte Testament Deutsch
BBB	Bonner Biblische Beiträge
BDB	Francis Brown, S. R. Driver, and Charles A. Briggs, eds., *A Hebrew and English Lexicon of the Old Testament, with an Appendix Containing the Biblical Aramaic.* 1907. Repr. Oxford: Clarendon, 1962
BETL	Bibliotheca ephemeridum theologicarum lovaniensium
BHT	Beiträge zur historischen Theologie
BI	*Biblical Interpretation*
Bib	*Biblica*
BibRev	*Bible Review*
BIS	Biblical Interpretation Series
BJS	Brown Judaic Studies
BLS	Bible and Literature Series
BWL	W. G. Lambert, *Babylonian Wisdom Literature.* 1960. Repr. Winona Lake, IN: Eisenbrauns, 1996
BZAW	Beihefte zur Zeitschrift für die alttestamentliche Wissenschaft
CBQ	*Catholic Biblical Quarterly*
CBQMS	Catholic Biblical Quarterly Monograph Series
COS	William W. Hallo, ed., *The Context of Scripture.* 3 vols. Leiden: Brill, 1997-2003
DSD	*Dead Sea Discoveries*

Ebib	Etudes bibliques
FRLANT	Forschungen zur Religion und Literatur des Alten und Neuen Testaments
HALOT	Ludwig Koehler, Walter Baumgartner, and Johann Jakob Stamm, *The Hebrew and Aramaic Lexicon of the Old Testament.* Trans. and ed. under the supervision of M. E. J. Richardson. 5 vols. Leiden: Brill, 1994-1999
HAR	*Hebrew Annual Review*
HAT	Handbuch zum Alten Testament
HBM	Hebrew Bible Monographs
HBT	*Horizons in Biblical Theology*
HS	*Hebrew Studies*
HSM	Harvard Semitic Monographs
HTR	*Harvard Theological Review*
HTS	Harvard Theological Studies
HUCA	*Hebrew Union College Annual*
IBC	Interpretation: A Bible Commentary for Teaching and Preaching
Int	*Interpretation*
IRT	Issues in Religion and Theology
JAAR	*Journal of the American Academy of Religion*
JBL	*Journal of Biblical Literature*
JBR	*Journal of Bible and Religion*
JP	*Journal of Philosophy*
JRE	*Journal of Religious Ethics*
JSJSup	Supplements to the Journal for the Study of Judaism
JSOT	*Journal for the Study of the Old Testament*
JSOTSup	Journal for the Study of the Old Testament Supplement Series
KAT	Kommentar zum Alten Testament
LBS	Library of Biblical Studies
LCL	Loeb Classical Library
LD	Lectio divina
LHB/OTS	Library of Hebrew/Old Testament Studies
LLA	The Library of Liberal Arts
MBS	Message of Biblical Spirituality
NCBC	New Century Bible Commentary
NIB	Leander E. Keck, ed., *The New Interpreter's Bible.* 12 vols. Nashville: Abingdon, 1994-2002
NICOT	New International Biblical Commentary on the Old Testament
NRSV	New Revised Standard Version
OBO	Orbis biblicus et orientalis
OTL	Old Testament Library
OTP	James H. Charlesworth, ed., *Old Testament Pseudepigrapha.* 2 vols. Garden City, NY: Doubleday, 1983-1985
PSB	*Princeton Seminary Bulletin*

SBL	Society of Biblical Literature
SBLAIL	Society of Biblical Literature Ancient Israel and Its Literature
SBLBE	Society of Biblical Literature Biblical Encyclopedia
SBLDS	Society of Biblical Literature Dissertation Series
SBT	Studies in Biblical Theology
SJT	*Scottish Journal of Theology*
SPOT	Studies on Personalities of the Old Testament
ThViat	*Theologia Viatorum*
TS	Texts and Studies of the Jewish Theological Seminary of America
TUMSR	Trinity University Monograph Series
VT	*Vetus Testamentum*
VTSup	Supplements to Vetus Testamentum
WBC	Word Biblical Commentary
WMANT	Wissenschaftliche Monographien zum Alten und Neuen Testament
ZAW	*Zeitschrift für die alttestamentliche Wissenschaft*
ZTK	*Zeitschrift für Theologie und Kirche*

CHAPTER 1

Introduction: Character, Creation, and Wonder in Wisdom

[T]here is an intellectual desire, an eros of the mind. Without it there would arise no questioning, no inquiry, no wonder.

Bernard Lonergan[1]

Before the *cogito* is wonder.

Kelly Bulkeley[2]

In a 1994 popular publication, the Catholic biblical scholar Roland Murphy identified Prov. 30:18-19 as his favorite biblical proverb,[3] a numerical saying found among the "words of Agur."[4]

> Three things are too wonderful for me;
>   four things I do not understand:
> the way of an eagle in the sky,
>   the way of a snake on a rock,
> the way of a ship on the high seas,
>   and the way of a man with a woman.[5]

1. Lonergan, *Insight,* 97.
2. Bulkeley, *Wondering Brain,* 52.
3. Murphy, *Responses to 101 Questions,* 40-41.
4. "The words of Agur, son of Jakeh," is commonly taken as the canonical superscription to the chapter as a whole. See Yoder, "On the Threshold of Kingship," 255, 259-62.
5. Heb. *'almâ* is specifically "young woman." Note the unfortunate NRSV translation: "girl."

Murphy found Agur's celebration of the "mysteries of nature" irresistible, and rightly so. This artfully crafted saying is both a testimony and a puzzle, a testimony to wonder and an exercise in wondering. The proverb invites the reader, as it did the rabbis,[6] to ponder these four distinct "ways." How are they possible, these baffling means of movement? What do they share in common: soaring eagles, slithering snakes, floating ships, and love-making couples? Each example by itself arrests the attention, but together they conjure a world of wonder. The proverb's appeal derives from its power to elicit bewildered curiosity. To presume that a tidy solution lies behind these four disparate images would run counter to the sage's own confession of befuddled awe. These "four things," the sage testifies, will always retain an element of mystery regardless of how much is known about them, no matter how well each "way" can be explained. Such is the sage's testimony: there is nothing quite like ships, snakes, and sex (not to mention soaring raptors) to provoke a sense of wonder.

Like the four "ways" identified in Prov. 30, the three wisdom books of the Hebrew Bible are irreducibly distinct. If the wisdom corpus were a choir, melodious harmony would not be its forte. Dissonance would resound at almost every chord. While one is regarded as the strangest book in the Bible (Ecclesiastes), another is considered the one book of the Bible that is against the Bible (Job). And along with the strange and the subversive is the more traditional, didactic book of Proverbs.[7] What possibly holds these three books together? Is there a "way" to bring the whole of this corpus into coherent focus while also highlighting its diversity? Is there a way to convey the *mira profunditas,* or "wondrous depth," of these various so-called wisdom books without resorting only to form-critical or sociological abstractions? I wonder.

The wisdom literature of the Hebrew Bible remains an enigma. No other biblical corpus exhibits greater inner tension and diversity of perspective.[8] Wisdom's literary forms do not conform to the more prevalent forms of historical narrative, law, psalmic poetry, and prophecy. The same goes for its content: these three books resist all attempts at homogenization. Indeed, each wisdom book is itself a puzzle, given the variety of

---

6. The rabbis proposed that each "way" left no trace. Cf. Wisd. 5:9-14. See the discussion in Fox, *Proverbs 10–31,* 871.

7. But even Proverbs, we will see, has its share of internal dissonance.

8. This is particularly highlighted in Penchansky, *Understanding Wisdom Literature.* There are, moreover, the questions about excluding the book of Job from the wisdom corpus and including the Song of Songs (Song of Solomon, Canticles).

conflicting material present within each one. Moreover, whether apart or together, the wisdom books cannot be shoehorned into Israel's foundational historical narratives or covenantal traditions.

The wisdom literature occupies a distinctive niche within the canonical sweep of ancient Israelite literature. As often noted, the wisdom corpus makes no explicit mention of the paradigmatic events of ancient Israel's history, such as the exodus or the giving of the law at Sinai/Horeb. On the face of it, wisdom holds only modest interest in cultic activity.[9] Corporate history and cultic hymnody are not distinctly sapiential domains. Wisdom's home lies primarily outside the sanctuary of praise and petition that the God of the psalmist inhabits. An even more sweeping observation: nothing is explicitly said about God in the wisdom corpus that could be considered uniquely Israelite, Jewish, or Christian.[10] Indeed, ancient Israel's sages had no qualms incorporating the wisdom of other cultures.[11] Biblical wisdom seeks the common good along with the common God. Wisdom's international, indeed universal appeal constitutes its canonical uniqueness. The Bible's wisdom corpus is the open door in an otherwise closed canon.

Biblical wisdom has been, and continues to be, studied from a variety of approaches, from form-critical to feminist, from sociological to theological, in part because it is such an elusive yet uniquely accommodating body of literature. Questions have been raised whether biblical wisdom even constitutes a distinct tradition.[12] At the most abstract level, certain interpreters regard biblical wisdom as uniquely anthropocentric in character, as reflective of the human quest to secure wholeness and prosperity.[13]

---

9. The foundational study is Perdue, *Wisdom and Cult*. See also Brown, "Come, O Children."

10. The sages did, however, consider their God to be YHWH, the God of Israel.

11. As is well known, much of Prov. 22:17–24:22 is adapted from Egyptian didactic literature, specifically the Late Kingdom Instruction of Amenemope. See Miriam Lichtheim's translation in *COS* 1.47.

12. See, most recently, Sneed, "Is the 'Wisdom Tradition' a Tradition?" I agree with Sneed that the wisdom literature does not constitute a self-contained "alternative to Yahwism" or a "unified worldview," much less a genre, but rather reflects a distinctive "mode" or orientation (cf. p. 57).

13. Although most approaches to the study of wisdom literature differ only in degree, it is helpful to identify those that stress the anthropological or experiential side of wisdom in relation to those who highlight wisdom's cosmological or theological dimensions. To the former belong von Rad's earlier work on wisdom in *Old Testament Theology*, 1:418-41 (note particularly his definition on p. 418); Priest, "Where Is Wisdom?"; idem, "Humanism, Skepticism, and Pessimism"; Brueggemann, *In Man We Trust*; Towner, "Renewed Author-

Such an approach often focuses on the rhetorical, pragmatic, and ethical dimensions of sapiential discourse by identifying character formation as the central aim of the wisdom corpus.[14] Wisdom, after all, begins and ends with the self in recognition that knowledge of God is inseparably entwined with knowledge of the self. In the book of Proverbs, for example, knowledge of God and of creation is framed within human discourse and perception: it opens with parental discourse on proper conduct and attitude (Prov. 1:8) and ends in homage to the "woman of strength" (31:10-31). In Ecclesiastes the "Solomonic" speaker Qoheleth recounts his personal musings over God's inscrutability and the world's insensitivity to human plight. From Job's anguished cries to his final confession before God, the language of the self predominates.

For some interpreters, wisdom is fundamentally concerned with shaping moral character, with cultivating, for example, the values of "righteousness, justice, and equity," the cardinal virtues referenced in Prov. 1:3. Moreover, the common image of "path" or "way," found particularly in Proverbs and Job, highlights the critical importance of moral discernment and right conduct. Sapiential discourse, in short, has much to do with directing the will toward a vision of human flourishing.

Other interpreters, however, have observed that much of the wisdom corpus draws from the realm of creation for its didactic insights and thus find wisdom's *theocentric* side to provide the best entry point.[15] The world as created by God provides ostensible order and discernible structures from which one can readily learn. To be sure, both approaches, the anthropocentric and the theocentric, character and creation, highlight two fundamental sides of biblical wisdom.[16] Yet the question remains whether

---

ity." With appropriate acknowledgment of the role of cosmology in wisdom, see Zimmerli, "Concerning the Structure"; and idem, "Place and Limit." Although Crenshaw finds multiple levels of definition for wisdom in the sapiential corpus, it is noteworthy that he begins his introduction with a discussion of "sapiential ethics" in Job 31, Job's defense of his integrity (*Old Testament Wisdom*, 7-9).

14. This includes, of course, the first edition of this book (Brown, *Character in Crisis*, esp. 1-21). See also Crenshaw, *Education in Ancient Israel*, 1-11; Davis, "Preserving Virtues"; cf. idem, *Proverbs, Ecclesiastes, Song of Songs*, 1-7.

15. E.g., Gese, *Lehre und Wirklichkeit*; Hermisson, "Observations on Creation Theology"; Schmid, *Gerechtigkeit als Weltordnung*; idem, "Creation, Righteousness, and Salvation"; and Perdue, "Cosmology and Social Order." For more novel approaches see Terrien, "Play of Wisdom"; Murphy, "Wisdom and Creation."

16. Note, most recently, Dell's highlighting of both character and creation as two major, irreducible poles in proverbial wisdom (*Book of Proverbs*, 11, 91, 178-79).

there is an encompassing framework that can account for both. Leo Perdue has suggested what he calls a "dialectic of anthropology and cosmology."[17] But such a framework is of limited use, since it simply defines the issue as abstractly as possible rather than offering a concrete way forward. Determining the precise relationship between these two sides or dialectical poles bedevils any interpreter who wants to grasp the full range and depth of the wisdom corpus.

To summarize thus far: One proposed way for discerning the literature's coherence is to identify creation as wisdom's central theme and focus. The other highlights the issue of character formation with particular emphasis on the self as a developing moral agent in the world. Both views are pertinent but, I propose, at different levels. Attention to creation provides a generative *context* for sapiential insight, whereas character formation captures much of the rhetorical *aim* of the wisdom corpus. For the biblical sages, the world — both natural and international — was their classroom. The will, specifically its desire and formation, was their goal. They recognized that moral conduct was informed and shaped by the world's order and that the world's order, in turn, was established and sustained by right conduct. If one can discover the sapiential link between world and will, the nexus between creation and character, then one has come upon a common heuristic framework, a hermeneutical lens, by which to understand both wisdom's subtle coherence and its striking diversity. To discover that connection would, in my estimation, constitute nothing less than a *eureka* moment in the study of the wisdom literature.

Character and Creation

At the conclusion of his treatise *Critique of Practical Reason* (1788), Immanuel Kant famously stated, "Two things fill the mind with ever new and increasing admiration and reverence, the more often and more steadily I reflect upon them: the starry heaven above me and the moral law within

---

17. Perdue, *Wisdom in Revolt*, 20; idem, *Wisdom and Creation*, 48. The dialectic that Perdue draws from von Rad's classic treatment on wisdom functioned quite differently for von Rad. Von Rad repeatedly stressed the practical or experiential side of wisdom without subsuming it entirely under the overarching framework of creation theology the way Perdue has attempted to do (cf., e.g., von Rad, *Wisdom in Israel*, 3-5, 312-18; idem, *Old Testament Theology*, 1:418-41).

me."[18] Neither, Kant goes on to say, is veiled in obscurity or concealed within the realm of the transcendent; both are readily discernible through observation and reason. Put more succinctly, what gripped the eighteenth-century German philosopher with wonder were the distinct but interrelated notions of moral character and creation. So also the biblical sages. As I hope to demonstrate, the prominent themes of character and creation pervade much of their discourse in ways that are intended to elicit wonder and, consequently, cultivate wisdom. First, a word about both.

Character

In their now classic study on Christian ethics, Bruce Birch and Larry Rasmussen acknowledge two root meanings inherent in the notion of character, which for convenience can be labeled descriptive and prescriptive. From the Greek *charactēr,* originally meaning "engraving tool," the term has come to refer to certain qualities that distinguish one person from another.[19] Literarily speaking, character is a narrative construct: it refers to those figures (e.g., human beings, animals, communities, animate objects) that assume certain roles within a narrative and are designated by certain terms that denote characteristic traits.[20] The literary relationship between action and character in narrative is a matter of debate. Aristotle, for example, argued that character is subordinate to action.[21] However, as the contemporary literary critic Shlomith Rimmon-Kennan suggests, character and action must ultimately be construed as interdependent referents, in accordance with Henry James's famous dictum: "What is character but the determination of incident? What is incident but the illustration of character?"[22]

18. Kant, *Critique of Practical Reason,* 133. The original reads: "Zwei Dinge erfüllen das Gemüt mit immer neuer und zunehmender Bewunderung und Ehrfurcht, je öfter und anhaltender sich das Nachdenken damit beschäftigt: der bestirnte Himmel über mir und das moralische Gesetz in mir." These words were also inscribed on Kant's gravestone in Kaliningrad.

19. Birch and Rasmussen, *Bible and Ethics,* 75.

20. Rimmon-Kennan, *Narrative Fiction,* 33.

21. See particularly chs. 2 and 6 in the *Poetics.* See discussion in Chatman, *Story and Discourse,* 109.

22. Quoted from Rimmon-Kennan, *Narrative Fiction,* 35. See also Kermode's comments on the interrelationship between character and narration in *Genesis of Secrecy,* 75-77.

Literary Character

In literary studies, "character" refers to a "paradigm" or distinctive cluster of personal traits, a trait being a "relatively stable or abiding personal quality."[23] More than "ephemeral psychological phenomena,"[24] character traits are attributes or predicates that exhibit a degree of consistency with respect to the subject. As formulated by E. M. Forster, characters in fiction can either be "flat" or "round."[25] Flat characters do not develop in the course of the plot and are restricted in qualities. Round characters, by contrast, exhibit more than one quality or trait. Since Forster's pioneering distinction, literary critics have made further distinctions.

Biblical scholar Adele Berlin argues for three categories of narrative character: (1) the "full-fledged" or round character, (2) the type or flat character, and (3) the agent or functionary character.[26] Types are built around a single trait. To this category Berlin assigns the character of Abigail, "the perfect wife," and Nabal, the proverbial fool (1 Sam. 25).[27] An agent is a character that is merely functional and thus cannot be characterized.[28] The character of Abishag, the Shunammite who ministered to the ailing David and was the object of political intrigue, falls under this character type (1 Kgs. 1–2).[29] As for the full-fledged character, Berlin finds Michal and Bathsheba to be "realistically portrayed" and their emotions made explicit.[30]

The problem with such a classification schema is the danger of forcing every literary character into a single category, a move that invariably requires some amount of shoehorning.[31] More helpful is Joseph Ewen's classification of characters along three axes: complexity, development, and penetration into the "inner life."[32] To one end of the pole belong allegorical figures, caricatures, and types — in other words, characters that exhibit a single or dominant trait. Such characters in narrative are essentially static

23. Chatman, *Story and Discourse,* 126.
24. Chatman, *Story and Discourse,* 126.
25. Forster, *Aspects of the Novel,* 75.
26. Berlin, *Poetics and Interpretation,* 23.
27. Berlin, *Poetics and Interpretation,* 30-31.
28. This category is taken from Abrams, *Glossary of Literary Terms,* 21.
29. Berlin, *Poetics and Interpretation,* 30-32.
30. Berlin, *Poetics and Interpretation,* 31-32.
31. It is a problem that Berlin also recognizes in stressing that character types differ in degree (*Poetics and Interpretation,* 32).
32. Rimmon-Kennan, *Narrative Fiction,* 41-42.

and viewed from the outside. Fully developed characters, on the other hand, exhibit complexity and development, revealing themselves from the inside out. In between the poles on each axis is an infinite degree of variation. As Adele Berlin, Robert Alter, David Gunn, and others have fruitfully pointed out, biblical narrative is replete with characters that range from the remarkably complex to the uniformly simple.[33] What remains for further study are characters that do not have their primary home in biblical narrative proper but nonetheless exhibit a range of complexity and variation, such as those profiled in the wisdom literature. Or to put it another way, do the "characters" featured in the wisdom corpus point to subtle narrative dynamics within the literature? Regardless of the answer, what is clear is that the wisdom corpus is particularly interested in moral character, whether its formation or its deformation.

Moral Character

Ethicists speak of character in a different but not wholly unrelated sense. Both definitions of character — literary and moral — acknowledge that the shape of the self, whether individual or collective, is expressed by certain configurations of action, affect, and responsibility within situational contexts.[34] Character is reflected in the tendency to act, feel, and think in certain describable ways. Generally speaking, moral character refers to the sum and range of specifically *ethical* qualities or traits the individual or community possesses.[35] One can speak of a person as having exemplary, credible, or unassailable character, or simply possessing character, or having integrity.[36] Such language invests normative significance in certain aspects of a person's morphology, traits that are positively esteemed and

33. E.g., Alter, *Art of Biblical Narrative*; Gunn, *Story of King David*; idem, *Fate of King Saul*; Bar-Efrat, *Art of the Biblical Story*, 73-112; Sternberg, *Poetics of Biblical Narrative*, 321-64.

34. From Platonic and Aristotelian ethics, the elements of character include "desires, goods, and reasons." For discussion and critique, see van der Ven, *Formation of Moral Self*, 346-64. Building on classical notions, van der Ven develops a notion of character that is "interactive, dynamic, unique, and open-ended," a matter of formation and narration (355, 358-60).

35. See the common definition given in *The Oxford English Dictionary* (2nd ed.; Oxford: Clarendon, 1989), 3:31, no. 11, where the normative and descriptive dimensions of character are mentioned together.

36. To be distinguished from the colloquially ambiguous claim that a certain person "is (such) a character," which typically has nothing to do with the person as a moral agent.

therefore serve as a model for others. More specifically, someone who has character is one who exercises sound judgment, knows what is right, and has the courage to act on it,[37] which sounds a lot like having wisdom. When compared to the literary qualities that highlight a character's uniqueness, ethical character represents a *generalizing* aspect: particular values and virtues are highlighted that bear a normative status for others.

Ethicists identify several constitutive elements to the moral life, various factors that account for a person's moral character. Among them, Birch and Rasmussen posit three that constitute the profile of moral character: perception, intention, and virtue,[38] to which a fourth needs to be added: emotion.

Perception   In ethical discourse, perception is considered more than observation; it involves the selective internalization and integration of events and aspects of life, thereby giving shape to the way people experience events and render them meaningful. Perception involves the way one selects, interprets, and evaluates events by means of certain fundamental symbols.[39] The role of perception in the formation of character cannot be overemphasized, for the subject matter of character is in essence the *self in relation,* in relation to the perceived Other (e.g., the world, God, another subject) as well as to the history and pattern of one's choices.[40]

The biblical sages viewed the world from the perspective of all things sustained by God's will and wisdom. It is within the context of perception — how the self apprehends the world — that creation, from the starry heavens to the industrious ant, played such a vitally important role for the ancient sages.

Intention   The second element of moral character, intention, needs only brief mention. Intentions consist of "expressions of character which show aim, direction, purpose; they express the volitional side of character."[41] Presupposing a degree of self-determination, intention expresses purpose and gives direction to choice.[42] It builds upon free choice and thus pro-

37. Birch and Rasmussen, *Bible and Ethics,* 75.

38. Birch and Rasmussen, *Bible and Ethics,* 74-81.

39. Birch and Rasmussen, *Bible and Ethics,* 77. See also Hauerwas, *Character and Christian Life,* 203.

40. Bondi, "Elements of Character," 204; idem, "Character," 83.

41. Birch and Rasmussen, *Bible and Ethics,* 79.

42. Birch and Rasmussen, *Bible and Ethics,* 80.

vides a basis for ethical accountability. More than discrete acts of the will, intentions provide coherence to the decisions and actions of an individual or community. They are by nature "goal-oriented determinations."[43] Through intention, the language of character casts the self as having duration and growth, the self in formation.[44] Intention thus points to the narrative dimension of moral character.

Emotion and Desire Emotions, too, play an indispensable role in the growth of character, indeed in the gaining and exercise of wisdom.[45] Moral maturity is not only a matter of cognitive development; it is also an indication of emotional sensibility. Pushed further, emotions are themselves "part and parcel of the system of ethical reasoning."[46] As essential elements of human intelligence, emotions figure indispensably in making judgments about what is important; they indicate "appraisals or value judgments" made for the sake of the self's flourishing.[47] In short, emotions shape how we perceive the world. They embody a "way of seeing."[48] Fear finds the world filled with threat; depression overlooks the good things in life; bliss neglects the storm clouds on the horizon.[49] "Simply put, emotions are there in order to tell us what to think about; our hearts not only try to rule our heads, but should perhaps be allowed to do so."[50] Drawing from Aristotle and contemporary moral theory, Nancy Sherman identifies various interrelated roles that emotions play in the development of the self: they serve as "moral antennae," "modes of broadcast," and motivations for action.[51] Emotions are "intentional states"; they form part of the individual's character as much as do belief and reason.[52] Emotion thus takes its rightful place alongside and inextricably tied to cognition as a critical component of wisdom and character. Forming character and growth in wisdom, in other words, have all to do with emotional learning.[53] A crowning example

43. Birch and Rasmussen, *Bible and Ethics,* 80.

44. Hauerwas, *Character and Christian Life,* 3-4.

45. Indeed, some psychologists define wisdom as "emotional intelligence" (Hall, *Wisdom,* 43). See below.

46. Nussbaum, *Upheavals of Thought,* 1.

47. Nussbaum, *Upheavals of Thought,* 4.

48. Nussbaum, *Upheavals of Thought,* 27.

49. Hinman, "Seeing Wisely," 414.

50. Plotkin, *Darwin Machines,* 207.

51. Sherman, "Wise Emotions," 324-27.

52. Sherman, "Wise Emotions," 328.

53. See the discussion of "emotional learning" in van der Ven, *Formation of Moral*

is justice: in moral discourse justice is not simply a notion or a concept; it is also an emotion.[54] For someone to have a "sense of justice" means that one has a desire, indeed a passion, for justice.

Related to but not entirely identifiable with emotion, desire — its shaping and direction — is also fundamental to the formation of character. While desire can highlight the emotional side of intention,[55] it also signals something deeper: a yearning, a hunger to act in a particular way. Fear, for example, may prompt the desire to flee; anger, the desire to retaliate; love, the desire to protect and affiliate with a loved one.[56] Desire can constitute the bridge between emotion and act; it "contains considerable intentionality and selectivity."[57] That is, other matters of concern fall by the wayside before the object of one's desire. But deeper than emotion, desire is akin to appetite, a bodily "drive" that "pushes" the self toward the object of desire.[58] When we speak of more complex desires, such as sexual desire, objects themselves seem to exert an irresistible "pull" on the perceiving subject,[59] a compulsion to affiliate with, rather than to avoid, the Other. Desire is not simply what the individual does; it also happens to the individual, something that may awaken desire for the other.[60] Desire captures well something of the visceral side of character formation.

Virtue or Disposition   The element of character that has received the most attention in classical discussions is virtue. Virtue is a disposition that denotes the pattern of choices an individual or community makes. Dispositions comprise persistent attitudes or "habits"[61] that dispose one to a consistency of action and expression.[62] Bound up with perception, dispositions constitute the traits of character that are demonstrated in customary patterns of ethical behavior. Classically, such dispositions have been called "virtues."

Self, 331-37, who identifies three modes of emotional learning: observation, experience, and concept.

54. Van der Ven, *Formation of Moral Self,* 315-18.

55. Roberts, *Emotions,* 160-67; Nussbaum, *Upheavals of Thought,* 135-36.

56. Yoder, "Shaping of Erotic Desire," 150.

57. Nussbaum, *Upheavals of Thought,* 136.

58. Nussbaum, *Upheavals of Thought,* 130-31.

59. Nussbaum, *Upheavals of Thought,* 131.

60. Henriksen, "Desire: Gift and Giving," 2.

61. Properly speaking, *habitus* in Latin or *hexis* in Greek.

62. Birch and Rasmussen, *Bible and Ethics,* 79-80.

Aristotle defined virtue[63] as "a deliberated and permanent disposition, based on a standard applied to ourselves and defined by the reason displayed by the man of good sense."[64] Similarly, Thomas Aquinas described virtue as "that which makes good he who has it and renders good his work."[65] Together, these two definitions highlight several elements: Virtue is both a disposition and a standard; it is based on reason and is the source of good conduct.[66] As dispositions that involve a tendency to do certain sorts of action in particular situations, virtues are by no means static qualities. They are dynamic and hence "determinable" as opposed to determinate.[67] Not wholly inborn, virtues are acquired through education and practice.[68] Once a particular virtue is developed, it is ever present, at least in potential form.

Like character itself, the element of virtue cannot be identified with any moral principle. In contrast to the ethics of duty, virtue points to an ethic of being, a way of being in the world, of being in relation. Rules can never be comprehensively specified so as to preclude the need for personal and collective judgment.[69] Even when moral rules serve as adequate guides for conduct, they merely constitute the form of morality, not its point.[70]

As determinable dispositions, virtues imply self-conscious, intentional behavior and thus provide the means for assessing a person's charac-

---

63. The Greek term *aretē* exhibits a tremendous range of meaning. For Homer, *aretē* was synonymous with courage. Later the term came to signify "civic virtue" and moral qualities other than courage (see Ostwald's annotation in Aristotle's *Nicomachean Ethics*, 303). The basic root meaning of the term was power or ability to do something; hence, it could denote whatever caused someone to perform a function well in relation to particular tasks. For a thorough and comprehensive history of the term in Greek literature, see Jaeger, *Paideia*, vol. 1, esp. 3-14.

64. *Nicomachean Ethics* 2.6.15 (quoted from Jean Baechler, "Virtue," 27). Aristotle's theory of the median between the extremes of excess and deficiency as it relates to defining the virtues (*Nicomachean Ethics* 2.6) is beyond the scope of this study. Suffice it to say that Aristotle makes the claim that the median is always "relative to us" (2.6.7), and hence is a matter of perception (see Hauerwas, *Character and Christian Life,* 72).

65. Baechler, "Virtue," 27.

66. Baechler, "Virtue," 27.

67. Pincoffs, *Quandaries and Virtues,* 77.

68. See MacIntyre's definition of virtue in *After Virtue,* 178.

69. Budziszewski, "Religion and Civic Virtue," 57.

70. Budziszewski, "Religion and Civic Virtue," 57. For a radical statement of the primacy of moral virtue over value, see Pincoffs's criticism of MacIntyre's definition of virtue in *Quandaries and Virtues,* 97.

ter.[71] Unlike the modern sense of "habit," which denotes a psychologically automatic response, virtue is a "quality which permits the reason and will . . . to achieve their maximum capacity on the moral plane."[72] Moral virtues are virtues of character (Greek *ēthos*) and thus distinguishable from abilities. One can possess the ability to think intelligently without having the disposition to use it.[73] Dispositions imply a lasting "readiness for action."[74] Furthermore, moral virtues must be distinguished from "skills for success" or "instrumental virtues."[75] But the appeal of popular literature is in large measure due to a blurring of the boundaries between moral virtues and instrumental skills.[76] According to the classical ethicists, moral virtue is no guarantee of success, and success is not necessarily a sign of moral integrity. The appeal of the virtuous life is intrinsic. Distinct from professional skills or expertise, moral virtue is characteristic of a "unitary life."[77]

The history of ethical discourse has attempted in various ways to prioritize or reduce the "swarm of virtues," to borrow a phrase from Plato's *Meno*. The most basic and highly esteemed virtues are designated "cardinal" virtues. Plato and Aristotle identified four: prudence, justice, fortitude, and temperance. For Aristotle, prudence or practical wisdom[78] was primary, since it is both a moral virtue and one of the five intellectual virtues (the others being understanding, science, wisdom, and art).[79] As practical wisdom, prudence embodies wisdom in practice and in judging right action in particular situations.[80] By bringing the mind and heart,

71. So Pincoffs (*Quandaries and Virtues,* 77). Pincoffs goes on to define virtues and vices in purely functional terms as "dispositional properties that provide grounds for preference or avoidance of persons" (p. 82). Although Pincoff's concern to find a nonreductive basis for virtue is commendable, establishing it in terms of rationales given for the preference of individuals is much too broad. Certain reasons given for preferring, as opposed to avoiding, someone do not necessarily imply that such a person possesses particularly normative qualities. Consistent with his approach, however, Pincoffs's chart of virtues makes moral virtues merely one category among other kinds of virtue (p. 85).

72. Pinckaers, "Virtue Is Not a Habit," 71.

73. Frankena, *Ethics,* 68.

74. Hauerwas, *Character and Christian Life,* 71. Hauerwas, however, does suggest that it is an ability, but see *Nicomachean Ethics* 2.5.7-12.

75. Pincoffs, *Quandaries and Virtues,* 84-86.

76. E.g., Covey, *Seven Habits*; Blanchard and Peale, *Power of Ethical Management*; Peters and Waterman Jr., *In Search of Excellence.*

77. MacIntyre, *After Virtue,* 191.

78. See Ostwald's annotation in Aristotle, *Nicomachean Ethics,* 312.

79. Aristotle, *Nicomachean Ethics* 6.3-7.

80. As a moral virtue, Aristotle defined prudence as "a reasoned and true state of

reason and inclination or desire together, prudence enables the person to determine what is and how to do the right thing in every situation.[81]

Thomas Aquinas's contribution was his addition of three theological virtues to the cardinal list: faith, hope, and charity. A quick glance at his configuration of ethical character is important for the study of character in biblical wisdom literature, since Thomas was able to establish a distinctly *theological* context for *habitus* or virtue.[82] Like Aristotle, Thomas highlighted prudence for its unitive function of integrating practical reason and desires toward making moral judgments.[83] As the bridge between moral knowledge and virtuous action, prudence precedes choice and coordinates the activity of the other virtues.[84] For Thomas, however, a virtue other than prudence was to assume the head position, and that was the theological virtue of charity or love. Charity, along with faith and hope, was infused in human beings in order to direct them to God.[85] "Charity is the mother and the root of all the virtues, inasmuch as it is the form of them all."[86] In other words, charity is the default drive in the exercise of any virtue for Thomas.

Much more recently, ethicists such as Arthur Schopenhauer and William Frankena have either reduced the cardinal virtues to two (benevolence and justice)[87] or, like Edmund Pincoffs, have refused to limit the "swarm" altogether.[88] Common to most attempts at delineating and specifying the collage of virtues is the recognition that character is more than the sum of its constituent moral parts. The shape of character entails a unity by which "the total determination of the self . . . is present through each particular virtue and habit."[89] From Aristotle's perspective, the exercise of the virtues requires a unity of the soul in its three elements — perception, intelligence, and desire.[90] Cast another way, ethical character has

---

capacity to act with regard to human goods." See *Nicomachean Ethics* 6.5.20 (as quoted from Ross's translation with slight alteration [i.e., the translation for *hexis*] in Yves R. Simon, *Definition of Moral Virtue*, 96).

81. See Simon's discussion in *Definition of Moral Virtue*, 96.
82. See Cessario, *Moral Virtues and Theological Ethics*, 7.
83. Cessario, *Moral Virtues and Theological Ethics*, 82-95.
84. Nelson, *Priority of Prudence*, 52.
85. Thomas Aquinas, *Summa Theologiae*, I-II, q. 62, a. 1.
86. Thomas Aquinas, *Summa Theologiae*, I-II, q. 62, a. 4.
87. Frankena, *Ethics*, 64-65.
88. Pincoffs lists a total of sixty-seven virtues (*Quandaries and Virtues*, 85).
89. Hauerwas, *Character and Christian Life*, 78.
90. *Nicomachean Ethics*, 6.1-2.

all to do with moral integrity, a wholeness or completeness regarding the exercise of virtue. Integrity ultimately points to the moral posture of the self, a posture vis-à-vis the Other. Such a holistic understanding is crucial to biblical wisdom, since, as we shall see, the sapiential notion of integrity is typically rooted in humility to God and other subjects.

In summary, the elements of perception, intention, emotion, desire, and virtue together provide a holistic model by which to understand the morphology of the moral life. Although the relationship between moral principle and virtue is an interdependent one, virtue finds its primacy in situations of conflicting rules, in circumstances unaccounted for by existing rules, and thus in the community's need to continually revise rules. Moral rules and principles, consequently, cannot operate apart from the formation of character. Rather, they remain an integral part of the complex dynamic of moral formation by contributing to the community's task of constructing particular conceptions of the good by which character is formed.[91] Ever subject to and in need of revision, moral rules and principles mark the achievement of the community, which seeks to appropriate the wisdom of the past for every new social context and challenge.[92]

Literary and Moral Character

The relationship between descriptive and prescriptive character is of critical importance in the wisdom corpus, since much of the literature conveys or models the contours of normative character through literary characterization. The book of Proverbs, for instance, introduces the reader to a veritable cavalcade of competing characters in lively discourse: parental figures, rebellious youth, Wisdom, the "strange" woman, the fool, the wise, the righteous, and the wicked, just to name a few. The book of Job profiles Job, his friends, and God, all in passionate interchange. Ecclesiastes portrays its main and only character, Qoheleth, in revealing autobiographical fashion.

All characters are defined primarily by their discourse. Some bare their souls while others remain relatively flat and one-dimensional. Flat characterizations, such as the parental figures in Proverbs, recall traditional values in the face of challenge and conflict. More complex or "round" literary characters exhibit a mixture of estimable and not-so-estimable quali-

---

91. Fowl and Jones, *Reading in Communion*, 10.
92. Fowl and Jones, *Reading in Communion*, 10.

ties, a delicate balance of conservative and unorthodox traits. In addition, full-fledged characters demonstrate a candid development of character, displaying their complex "inner life," because their integrity has become an open question. They are enfleshed with ambiguity. Round or complex characters connote a sense of personal realism. Their task is to deconstruct and reform traditional contours of ethical character — in short, bring about transformation. In the biblical wisdom literature, the way in which a literary character is portrayed is relevant to the way in which normative character is profiled. Such is the rhetoric of wisdom, a mode of discourse that features various characters, both flat and full, simple and complex, absent tidy narratives.

Creation

Various characters see the world in various ways. As noted above, perception plays an integral role in moral formation. How the subject perceives the world is critical to how he or she lives and acts in the world. It is no coincidence, then, that the wisdom corpus is filled with references to the world, to creation, ranging from vast cosmologies to concrete images drawn from the natural realm. Each book, moreover, offers its own evocative tableau of creation. In Prov. 8:22-31 Wisdom bears witness to God's creation, fashioned for the sake of her "play." YHWH's answer to Job presents a cosmic panorama, focusing specifically on what is considered alien to human perception (Job 38–41). Qoheleth, particularly in Eccl. 1:4-11 and 3:1-8, beholds a world of perpetual activity devoid of change and discernible direction. Each creation text, as we shall see, is inextricably connected to the sage's perspective on the self. Each, moreover, arouses a certain kind of wonder.

The emphasis on creation in the wisdom corpus has long been recognized in scholarship.[93] Over forty years ago, Gerhard von Rad boldly claimed that biblical wisdom was, in essence, "the self-revelation of creation" (*die Selbstoffenbarung der Schöpfung*).[94] More recently, Leo Perdue advanced this view by identifying a host of theological precursors to biblical wisdom found among the cosmogonic myths of the ancient Near

---

93. See the brief review of scholarship in Dell supplemented by her own insights, *Book of Proverbs*, 130-46.

94. Von Rad, *Wisdom in Israel*, 144-76 (*Weisheit in Israel*, 189-228).

East.[95] Such studies emphasize the importance of order and structure in creation.[96] The ancient sages discerned a natural world that was orderly and hence meaningful and instructive.[97] They, along with the psalmists and other cosmogonists of the ancient world, viewed creation as both a matter of primordial beginnings and the arena of present experience.[98]

What the wisdom corpus lacks in terms of the *magnalia dei*, the salvific acts of God associated with ancient Israel's national identity, it more than makes up in orienting readers to God's work of creation, past and present. "Creation theology and its correlative affirmation, providence, were at the center of the sages' understanding of God, the world, and humanity," observes Perdue.[99] In wisdom, cosmic order and social order find a clear convergence.[100] One could say that Prov. 3:19-20 provides the cornerstone to sapiential creation theology:

> YHWH founded the earth by wisdom;
>   he secured the heavens by understanding;
> by his knowledge the deeps split open,
>   and the clouds dripped dew.

Because God fashioned creation through wisdom, creation in turn reflects God's wisdom. The cosmos is deemed comprehensibly didactic.[101] Creation's regularity allows for discerning observable patterns in which human actions have predictable consequences, and knowing these consequences leads to an informed life.[102] The following two sayings recognize exceptions, but they too have moral import:

> Like snow in summer or rain at harvest,
>   so honor does not befit a fool. (26:1)

---

95. E.g., Perdue, *Wisdom and Creation*; idem, *Wisdom Literature,* esp. 15-36. The theme of creation also finds special prominence even in his more sociohistorically oriented study, *Sword and Stylus,* 4-6, 11-12, 109-16, 131-33, 148-51.

96. See Perdue, "Cosmology and Social Order," 457-78.

97. In other words, character and creation are inseparably related in the wisdom corpus, contra Dell's claim that the creation emphasis in wisdom "is an extra dimension beyond the moral context" (*Book of Proverbs*, 91).

98. See Fretheim, *God and World,* 5-9; Murphy, "Wisdom and Creation," 5-6.

99. Perdue, *Wisdom and Creation,* 20; see also idem, *Proverbs,* 7.

100. See Perdue, "Cosmology and the Social Order," 458-61.

101. See Perdue, *Wisdom and Creation,* 82; idem, *Proverbs,* 103.

102. Most famously (and abstractly) stated by Koch in "Doctrine of Retribution." For a critique see Murphy, *Tree of Life,* 115-17; S. Adams, *Wisdom in Transition,* 1-6.

> Under three things the earth convulses;
>> under four it cannot bear up:
> a slave becoming king,
>> a fool glutted with food;
> an unloved woman getting a husband,
>> a female slave succeeding her mistress. (30:21-23)

The second saying vividly testifies that the cosmic order depends upon the proper ordering of the social realm, specifically in terms of the latter's hierarchical structure. The way of the ant yields a pointed lesson on the necessity of diligence, provoking a sense of wonder over its lack of leadership (6:6-11). For the sages, the bond between the natural and the social supplied rich possibilities for constructing analogies.

> Eating (too) much honey is not good,
>> so also searching for excessive honor.[103] (25:27)

> Like somebody who grabs the ears of a passing dog
>> is one who meddles in another's quarrel. (26:17)

> Like a dog that returns to its vomit
>> is a fool who replicates his folly. (26:11)

> Like a muddied spring or polluted fountain
>> is a righteous person who gives way before the wicked. (25:26)

> The north wind produces rain,
>> and a backbiting tongue [produces] angry looks. (25:23)

> For as pressing milk yields curds,
>> pressing the nose yields blood,
>> and pressing anger yields strife. (30:33)

Such sayings testify to the sages' perception that the natural and social realms are an interconnected whole. The world was created wisely for human instruction. With the wealth of images and analogies they drew from nature and their cosmological outlook, the sages beckoned their audience to behold and become wise.

---

103. The second line is corrupt. The consonantal spelling could be the result of a misdivision of words, originally meaning "honor after honor." Or the final *mem* of the penultimate word may be enclitic.

Wisdom's Wonder

Creation and character: both are tightly interwoven within the fabric of sapiential rhetoric even as they point outward to broader frames of reference that characterize biblical wisdom as a whole. But for all the abstract talk of "dialectical" notions of anthropocentric and theocentric frameworks, something remains missing from current discussions regarding biblical wisdom's basis and aim.[104] Specifically, where do the central foci of creation and character in sapiential discourse converge? What grants them their rhetorical allure, their power to arouse and compel those who have ears to hear and eyes to see? Or put differently, where is the sense of encounter between Wisdom and the subjective self? Where is the *eros* in the inquiring?

I believe such questions come down to asking, Where is wisdom's wonder? The notion of wonder builds on what scholars have long held about the epistemological distinctiveness of biblical wisdom, namely its appeal to experience. The sages considered themselves keen observers of the world around them, the world filtered through and informed by their theological convictions (and their theological convictions informed by their experiences).[105] The sages, in short, excelled in the art of perception. "I saw and took it to heart; I looked and received instruction," begins a new lesson in Prov. 24:32. "I turned my mind to know and investigate and seek out wisdom and an accounting (of everything)," Qoheleth testifies about his quest (Eccl. 7:25; cf. 1:13). "See, we have searched this out, and it is true. Hear and know it for yourself," Eliphaz declares to Job (5:27). Seeing and searching, perceiving and inquiring, are what the sages do.[106] If Wisdom is considered the quintessential object of inquiry (Prov. 8:17), then the sages are her quintessential seekers.

The sages are also "fearers." The poetic pairing of "fear" and "knowledge" in Prov. 1:7a gives, as we shall see, the "fear of the LORD" a distinctly

---

104. See, e.g., Murphy's critique of wisdom as merely the search for order in creation in "Wisdom and Creation," 9-11. Murphy finds the appeal to order to be too abstract in comparison to the lyrical rhetoric used to describe the lively character of Wisdom in Prov. 8:22-31.

105. If not empiricists, the sages were, to coin a new word, "perceptionists," as one would expect from educators of character. In warning against the label of empiricism in Proverbs, Michael Fox unnecessarily minimizes the role of perception, which is by nature slanted and selective, in the acquisition of knowledge. See Fox, *Proverbs 10–31,* 963-67, 973. For his discussion of Qoheleth as a bona fide empiricist, see Fox, "Wisdom in Qoheleth," 121.

106. See, e.g., Prov. 11:27; 15:14; 18:15; 25:2 [kings]; Job 5:27; 12:7-9; 13:1; 27:11-12; 35:5; Eccl. 1:13-14; 2:13; 3:10, 16, 22; 4:1, 4, 7, 15; 5:18; 7:15, 25; 8:10, 17; 9:11.

experiential, if not epistemological, grounding: "fear" becomes a way of knowing, the way of wisdom. It is the awe-filled and awful wonder of God and creation — the wonder of the Other — that constitutes nothing less than the epistemological foundation and aim of biblical wisdom.[107] Wisdom, in all its richness, aims to cultivate such wonder, and such wonder, in turn, is fostered to sustain wisdom.

But all this is jumping ahead. What is wonder? The *Oxford English Dictionary* defines it as: "the emotion excited by the perception of something novel and unexpected, or inexplicable; astonishment mingled with perplexity or bewildered curiosity." Most suggestive are the last two words, "bewildered curiosity," which convey a double aspect to wonder. There is the unsettling element of perplexity, but add to it the element of curiosity, the desire to know more, and, voilà, wonder!

A sapiential orientation to wonder pushes the double aspect of perplexity and curiosity in powerful ways. In her discussion regarding the relation between wonder and wisdom, Celia Deane-Drummond describes two different experiences of wonder. First, wonder is frequently prompted by experiences that "destabilize the existing order of things,"[108] an experience of disorientation in which the unknown breaks into one's world of familiarity, throwing everything into question — in short, a crisis. The beginning point of wonder thus can elicit fear, contrary to current sanitized notions. Mary-Jane Rubenstein laments that:

> wonder loses much of the sugarcoating it has acquired in contemporary usage. . . . Wonder . . . responds to a destabilizing and unassimilable interruption in the ordinary course of things, an uncanny opening, rift, or wound in the everyday. . . . [W]onder's capacity to arouse and inflict terror, worship, and grief is utterly decimated — or, more precisely, fervently repressed — by the modern brand of wonder that connotes white bread, lunchbox superheroes, and fifties sitcoms.[109]

Wonder, in short, can be "a profoundly unsettling pathos," an "open sea of endless questioning, strangeness, and impossibility."[110] Such is the dis-

---

107. See, e.g., Perdue's definition of the "fear of the LORD" as "wonder evoked by the marvelous acts of creation and providence that awakens human mimesis and allegiance" (*Sword and Stylus*, 6).

108. Deane-Drummond, *Wonder and Wisdom*, 1.

109. Rubenstein, *Strange Wonder*, 10.

110. Rubenstein, *Strange Wonder*, 4, 5.

orienting, fearful, questioning side of wonder.[111] Wonder is kin to fear. But there is more.

The other experience of wonder identified by Dean-Drummond is a "sense of perfection in the ordering of the world,"[112] not unlike the way some scholars have described creation's significance in sapiential discourse, a sense of order and regularity in creation that invites cognitive assent. One could even claim that the progress of science, from Francis Bacon to Albert Einstein, has been driven by an insatiable sense of wonder about the natural realm.[113] Wonder is the "vital spark . . . that drives the best science."[114]

Wonder thus oscillates freely between experiences of order and novelty, between fear and fascination.[115] With such divergence one might conclude that the notion of wonder is fundamentally incoherent. Nevertheless, common to all bona fide experiences of wonder is their proclivity toward "approach and affiliation rather than avoidance."[116] As Abraham Heschel famously stated about wonder's closest sibling, awe: "Unlike fear, [awe] does not make us shrink from the awe-inspiring object, but on the contrary draws us near to it."[117] It is this affiliative, luring side of wonder that the *Oxford English Dictionary* lamely associates with "curiosity." In its fullness, wonder exhibits an irresistible pull that may begin with a centrifugal push of fear, the push away from the perceived source or object of ear, but ultimately wonder attracts rather than repels. In wonder, fascination overcomes fear, desire overcomes dread. Desire captures well the affiliative power of wonder: wonder awakens desire, and with desire comes a new attentiveness, a freshness of perception that "imbues the world with a certain 'luring' quality."[118] Wonder "imparts a heuristic quality to cognition. It leads us forward,

---

111. See also Jerome Miller, who describes wonder as "falling in love with questioning" (*In the Throe of Wonder*, 59).

112. Deane-Drummond, *Wisdom and Wonder*, 2.

113. See, e.g., Holmes, *Age of Wonder;* Campbell, *Wonder and Science;* Daston and Park, *Wonders and Order,* esp. 303-28.

114. Impey, *Living Cosmos*, 212.

115. It is no accident that wonder's double-sidedness parallels Rudolf Otto's notion of the "holy," which he encapsulated as *mysterium tremendum et fascinans,* i.e., an experience of mystery marked by both fear and fascination (*Idea of the Holy,* esp. 12-40). This dialectic is by no means limited to the experience of divine holiness.

116. Fuller, *Wonder,* 60.

117. Heschel, *God in Search of Man,* 77.

118. Fuller, *Wonder,* 66.

inviting us to discern more."[119] Call it a noetic emotion, a visceral cognitive emotion that is revelatory of otherness. Moments of wonder "forcibly propel us outside the normal range of experience, shattering our preconceptions, disclosing new possibilities, and revealing previously unknown dimensions of reality."[120] Simply put, wonder "projects us toward the unknown and animates our desire to know it."[121] To know something in wonder is not to control or use but to know passionately, ever provisionally, and always reverently (if not fearfully). While the object or source of wonder is knowable, it can never be exhausted by our knowing. Mystery remains.

Although wonder has to do with encountering mystery, it is never to be confused with ignorance. Far from it. As the philosopher Jerome A. Miller notes, "It is not we who break through to the unknown. It is the unknown which breaks through to us, ignites in us the eros of the desire to know, and so transforms us into questioners."[122] Wonder, like desire, cannot be forced; it is not something one can produce or possess by dint of sheer effort. Rather, wonder is prompted by something beyond the self, by something other. Wonder is a sense of being touched by otherness. It comes unbidden, much like a gift, and yet it exercises the self's emotional and rational faculties.

Philosophers, both ancient and modern, have identified wonder as the basis for deep inquiry. Socrates claims that "wonder *(to thaumazein)* is the only beginning of philosophy," the love of wisdom (*Theaetetus* 155d).[123] Put more provocatively by Miller, wonder is "surrendering ourselves to the *eros* of inquiry."[124] If, according to von Rad, biblical wisdom is *der geistige Eros* (translated "intellectual love"),[125] then such love becomes insatiable in the throe of wonder. It is this dynamic, "seeking," open-ended, affiliative nature of wonder that accounts for biblical wisdom's basis and remarkable diversity. It is wonder's gravitational pull and "frightening indeterminacy," as Rubenstein puts it, that keeps wisdom ever changing and self-sustaining, ever generative and open to the new.[126]

119. Fuller, *Wonder*, 156.
120. Bulkeley, *Wondering Brain*, 17.
121. Miller, *In the Throe of Wonder*, 130.
122. Miller, *In the Throe of Wonder*, 4.
123. Plato, *Theaetetus, Sophist*, trans. Fowler, 54-55. For fuller discussion of Plato's *Theaetetus*, see chapter 6 below.
124. Miller, *In the Throe of Wonder*, 15, 53.
125. Von Rad, *Weisheit in Israel*, 217-28 (*Wisdom in Israel*, 166-76).
126. Rubenstein, *Strange Wonder*, 7.

Such is wonder's paradox: wonder instills a reverent, even fearful, receptivity toward the Other, a posture of standing back or bending the knee. Such is wonder's affinity with awe, even fear. At the same time, wonder also quickens the desire to venture forth to know more, to know the Other. Wonder ignites the "*eros* of inquiry," the love of knowing.[127] Or, as Martha Nussbaum puts it: wonder is "outward-moving, exuberant. . . . In wonder I want to leap or run, in awe to kneel."[128] Born of awe, wonder is more active than awe. Wonder "generates cognitive openness."[129] In the throe of wonder, epistemological barriers break down and an awareness of deep connectedness emerges. If, as Proverbs claims, wisdom is a matter of pursuit, then wonder is the animating drive behind the pursuit. Such are the two sides of wonder: awe and inquiry.

Wonder marks the awakening of desire, the desire to inquire and understand. To return to Murphy's favorite proverb: marveling at the "way of the eagle in the sky" and that of "the snake on a rock" awakens the desire to know more about the eagle and the snake, their nature and habits, their means of movement. The images may also prompt one to wonder about what it is like to be able to glide, nearly motionless, upon updrafts of warm air, scanning the landscape with near telescopic vision, or to slither so gracefully upon the smooth, warm surface of a rock (despite one's fear of snakes). To marvel at ships plying the sea provokes a sense of awe at the ingenuity of human technology; it awakens the desire to know how ships work as well as to imagine the thrill of life on the high seas. And then there are the myriad ways of sexual intimacy. . . . The point is that this evocative proverb awakens the desire to know and at the same time transports readers into the realm of mystery. Such, one could say along with Murphy's favorite sage, is "the way of a proverb in the mind and heart of a reader."

As for wonder's connection to character, there is a developmental and ethical side to wonder. Among certain moral philosophers, wonder is considered a foundational emotion, indeed the first of all passions, according to Descartes.[130] A life shaped by wonder is one that cultivates both "intellectual and moral sensibilities."[131] For Nussbaum, wonder is funda-

---

127. Miller, *In the Throe of Wonder*, 16.

128. Nussbaum, *Upheavals of Thought*, 54 n. 53. Again, Otto's parallel notion of *mysterium tremendum et fascinans* contains both senses (see n. 115 above).

129. Fuller, *Wonder*, 156.

130. See Bulkeley, *Wondering Brain*, 52.

131. Fuller, *Wonder*, viii.

mental for the cultivation of love and compassion.[132] Wonder thus plays an indispensable role in the formation of the moral self in part because wonder has all to do with perception, as much as perception has all to do with the formation of character. Wonder prompts fresh ways of seeing. In wonder, eyes are opened and the world looks different. In wonder, the self pays attention in a new way. As Job remarked of God's revelation, "I declared what I did not perceive, things too wonderful for me" (42:3).

To sum up, I offer my own tentative definition of wonder: *an emotion born of awe that engenders a perpetually attentive, reverently receptive orientation toward the Other by awakening both emotional and cognitive resources for contemplation and conduct — in short, for wisdom.* As awe begins with a primal, even fearful response to the novelty of the Other, so wonder follows awe in the awakening of desire to know the world (and beyond) as Other,[133] to contemplate and reorient the self around that which is deemed worthy of wonder. Call it "inquisitive awe" or the "*eros* of inquiry." Cast in a more biblically grounded idiom inspired by Proverbs (and with a little help from St. Anselm), wonder is "fear seeking understanding," the beginning of wisdom.

Wisdom and the Wisdom Literature

What, then, is wisdom, biblically speaking? That is hard to say, since wisdom is a constantly moving target throughout the three biblical books. Indeed, wisdom, as the sages well attest, abounds in paradoxes and tensions, "wonderings" one might say. Wisdom embraces knowledge yet admits to uncertainty and severe limits. Wisdom is both eminently practical and rigorously intellectual. It draws from the natural order yet is also open to the unexpected, including the shock of divine revelation. Wisdom is a product of the community with its venerable traditions forged across generations, yet it also champions personal experience. Wisdom's appeal is universal, yet its advice can be highly contextual: a judicious course of action in one context can be sheer folly in another.[134] But perhaps most

132. Nussbaum, *Upheavals of Thought*, 54-55, 321.

133. I define "Other" as that which is unknown but not entirely unknowable to the perceiving self. The "Other" ensures that the world is not the solipsistic projection of the self but a place of genuine encounter, whether with the world, God, or another subject, even the self in a new way.

134. Cf. the contradictions Hall lists about wisdom in general (*Wisdom*, 11).

paradoxical of all, wisdom is deemed both a gift from God and an object of human striving, divinely endowed and humanly sought and practiced.[135] All in all, there remains something intractably mysterious about the very nature of wisdom, how it works, how it is gained, how it is given. Wisdom is itself a wonder.[136]

Nevertheless, some further rubric about wisdom might be helpful, at least as a point of departure. Biblical scholars have marveled over the wide range of nuances covered by biblical *ḥokmâ* ("wisdom"), from artistic technique and military skill to prudence and sound governance to erudition and esoteria.[137] From (or despite) its wide variety, some have boldly offered tidy definitions. R. N. Whybray, for example, prefers the simple, broad-based definition of "life-skill,"[138] whereas Michael Fox suggests "expertise."[139] Such definitions fit well with Proverbs, but less so with Job and Ecclesiastes, as we shall see. Moreover, missing from such definitions is the theological dimension, which is prominently featured even in Proverbs.[140] Without offering a pithy definition of wisdom (an impossible feat in my opinion), let me identify some sapiential contours that will need to be reexamined as each of the three wisdom books is addressed in the course of this study.

Wisdom is more than knowledge; it involves making sound judgments and doing the right thing. Knowledge is knowing that a tomato is a fruit; wisdom knows not to put it in a fruit salad. Wisdom is more than "know-how." Whereas knowledge or intelligence indicates *how* something should be done, wisdom points to what *should* be done, hence wisdom's tie to moral conduct. Wisdom grapples with questions of justice and equity; bring in God, and wisdom invariably addresses issues of theodicy. At the same time, wisdom can promote individual success and prosperity. Wisdom is both guide to and practice of moral character. In wisdom the moral

---

135. It is, in fact, this paradox or double-sidedness to wisdom that Katharine Dell lifts up as definitive of biblical wisdom: "[I]t is the meeting of the two aspects [i.e., the practical and the theological] that gives wisdom its distinctiveness" (*Get Wisdom, Get Insight,* 168; see also 6, 170-72).

136. Indeed, it is no accident that wonder's paradox parallels biblical wisdom's paradox.

137. See, e.g., Weeks, *Early Israelite Wisdom,* 74-75; Dell, *Get Wisdom, Get Insight,* 1.

138. Whybray, *Proverbs,* 32-33.

139. Fox, *Proverbs 1–9,* 32-33.

140. As also pointed out by Dell, *Get Wisdom, Get Insight,* 6-7. Missing, however, in Dell's otherwise nuanced treatment is wisdom's ethical dimension.

subject is acutely aware, both self-aware and outwardly aware of others as subjects in their own right. Fundamentally, wisdom is about making sense of God, the self, and the world, and acting accordingly. It cuts to what is truly important in life. Wisdom is the art of living fully, acting justly, and venturing forth reverently.

> The fear of the LORD is the beginning of wisdom;
>   comprehension of the good is for all who perform them.[141]
>
> (Ps. 111:10a; cf. Prov. 1:7)

Perhaps nothing more needs to be said.

As a phenomenon, biblical or otherwise, wisdom has a broader scope than wisdom as a body of literature. It is common to describe the wisdom literature of the Hebrew Bible as "advice" or "instructional" literature, a classification resulting in part from illuminating comparisons with the didactic literature of the ancient Near East, from Egypt to Mesopotamia, as well as from Qumran.[142] The biblical corpus, it is claimed, bears two defining features, "didacticism and moralizing," and has as its primary aim the moral and practical "enculturation of elite youth,"[143] including Scribal Skills 101.[144] This seems clear in Proverbs, whose first nine chapters are cast primarily as "lectures" addressed by a parent to a "son" *(bēn)*.[145] Nevertheless, as Katharine Dell rightly contends, "the varied backgrounds reflected by the proverbs [in Proverbs] suggest that this collection is much more than a manual for would-be administrators or a school textbook."[146] Indeed, Prov. 1:5 counts "the wise" also among the book's implied readers. This is all to say that a strictly generic or sociohistorical approach, if left to itself along with its sweeping generalizations, tends to flatten the rich and varied content of this diverse body of literature.[147]

---

141. *lĕkol-'ōśêhem.* The antecedent of the masculine plural suffix in the MT is a crux. LXX and Peshitta feature a feminine singular, presupposing "wisdom." The MT, however, bears the more difficult reading, whose antecedent is "precepts" in v. 7b.

142. See, e.g., Weeks, *Introduction,* 1-5; Collins, "Wisdom Reconsidered," 281.

143. Sneed, "Is the 'Wisdom Tradition' a Tradition?" 68-69.

144. Sneed, "Is the 'Wisdom Tradition' a Tradition?" 65.

145. This paternal setting is common to ancient Near Eastern sapiential discourse, as in the Egyptian Instruction of Anii (or Any; see Miriam Lichtheim, *Ancient Egyptian Literature,* 2:144-45) and in the Sumerian Instructions of Shuruppak, in *BWL,* 92-94.

146. Dell, *Get Wisdom, Get Insight,* 26.

147. Such generalizations apply primarily to Proverbs. It is hard to imagine the books of Job and Ecclesiastes designed for youth in the way that Proverbs is.

Also crucial is elucidating the rhetorical aims of the wisdom corpus. If wisdom has anything to do with knowing one's proper way in life (i.e., the formation of right character), then one needs to ask how sapiential discourse shapes and forms the reader to that end. This is a question that involves, among other things, exploring the literature's rhetorical richness. If the (trans)formation of character is wisdom's overarching goal, then the means to that goal involves, I hope to show, the cultivation of wonder.

And so I propose wonder as an appropriate, indeed necessary hermeneutical lens for discerning the integrity of the wisdom corpus, on the one hand, and highlighting wisdom's diversity, on the other. Each book exhibits an irreducibly different take on wisdom — one reason why I have not formally defined wisdom *(ḥokmâ)* in this study. But through the lens of wonder, disparate thematic accents found throughout the corpus come to be seen as interrelated wholes: character and creation, the anthropocentric and the theocentric, fear and joy, mystery and knowledge, beauty and strangeness, feeling and thought, contentment and desire, the mundane and the extraordinary, intimacy and transcendence, to name a few. For the sages, it is wonder that holds together the "fear of the LORD" (Prov. 1:7), on the one hand, and Wisdom's exuberant delight (8:30-31), on the other.

Encompassing both disorientation and delight, wonder accounts best for the sustaining power of wisdom, specifically of wisdom's "cognitive openness" to an ever-changing world. Without wonder, wisdom withers; its journey is cut short. Without wisdom, wonder wanders, aimlessly so. By (re)reading the biblical corpus through the lens of wonder, ancient wisdom comes to life for a new generation of readers.

Modus Operandi

These preliminary probes into the nature of wisdom, character, and wonder are meant to develop a heuristic framework in which a fresh approach to the wisdom traditions in the Hebrew Scriptures can be explored. The goal of this study is to demonstrate that the wisdom corpus is more than simply "advice literature." It is to demonstrate that wisdom has as its goal the (trans)formation of the self and that the cultivation of wonder is central to the self's growth in wisdom. And so the following interrelated questions, with variations appropriate to each book, will be addressed within the wisdom corpus:

27

1. How does each book construe the human self, creation, and God in such a way as to foster wonder and thereby form character?
2. What crises or sources of disorientation does each book address?
3. Given wonder's affinity to fear, how is fear profiled in relation to wisdom? What are the objects of terror identified in each book?
4. What objects are deemed worthy of wonder? Who or what is considered quintessentially Other? How does each book arouse desire for the Other?

This study is itself a journey through the changing ethos of biblical wisdom, as the contours of character and creation are shaped and reshaped through the multifaceted lens of wonder. As will become clear, the three wisdom books by no means present a homogeneous view of character or, for that matter, wisdom. Each draws from different aspects of wonder; each reveals a different face of wisdom; each constructs a different view of the self. Yet the fact that there is shared terminology and a common focus on the self in relation to God and the world suggests certain lines of dialogue among these works, all part of the journey of "fear seeking understanding."

CHAPTER 2

Wonder, Desire, and the Art of Character Formation in Proverbs

Appetite or desire, not DNA, is the deepest principle of life.

Leon R. Kass[1]

In his best-seller *The Book of Virtues,* William J. Bennett writes, "We must not permit our disputes over thorny political questions to obscure the obligation we have to offer instruction to all our young people in the area in which we have, as a society, reached a consensus: namely, on the importance of good character."[2] Bennett's words reflect a sense of urgency.

On the surface, the book of Proverbs looks a lot like a book of virtues, an ancient one written primarily for (but not limited to) males on the cusp of adulthood.[3] At least that seems clear in the first nine chapters, which provide the prolegomena for this rather complex book.[4] Whereas most of the book consists of myriad proverbs, somewhat haphazardly arranged (chs. 10–29),[5] chs. 1–9 contain at least ten "lectures" of varying lengths delivered

---

1. Kass, *Hungry Soul,* 48.

2. Bennett, *Book of Virtues,* 13.

3. See Whybray, *Composition of Proverbs,* 11-12.

4. See Camp's discussion on the thematic relations between Prov. 1–9 and the subsequent chapters in *Wisdom and the Feminine,* 183-208; cf. Yoder, *Wisdom as Woman of Substance,* esp. 91-101. Dell has discerned numerous connections along more theological lines in *Book of Proverbs,* esp. 18-50, 72-75, 88-89, 90-124.

5. With an emphasis on "somewhat." The section "The Words of the Wise" (Prov. 22:17–24:22) is an exception, but even so, it consists of a mixture of brief and not-so-brief

by a parental figure to a "son,"[6] interspersed with several "interludes."[7] In their final form, chs. 1–9, along with ch. 31, provide a programmatic framework for the book as a whole, a meta-narratival arc, as we shall see. Proverbs begins on a journey that finds its destination in the last chapter, the journey of the self toward maturation, and along that journey various voices are encountered representing a variety of values. But not all voices are given equal weight. Some are commended for the reader's appropriation, others prescribed for rejection. One voice in particular is deemed worthy of edifying wonder, while another is considered an object of horror and revulsion. Wonder and terror, attraction and revulsion: each has its pedagogical value in the cultivation of wisdom.[8] The journey of Proverbs is fraught with conflict played out at the directive hands of the book's final editors. Resistance and desire, avoidance and affiliation, challenge and affirmation all have a hand in the rough-and-tumble arena of character formation, the sages testify.

By way of introduction, the journey begins with a signpost of sorts, a densely packed prologue (1:1-7) that does not signal warning or shout "beware!" concerning the challenges that lie ahead. Instead, it beckons the reader to take the first step toward wisdom in wonder, with great promise and high expectations. Enter, it says, not at your own risk but for your utmost benefit. Wisdom, the sages hope to demonstrate, is good for you.

The Prologue of Proverbs

As is often noted, the first seven verses of Proverbs provide the hermeneutical key to the book as a whole.[9] They delineate not only the objective of the book — to appropriate wisdom in its manifold character — but in

---

commands. See Whybray, *Wisdom in Proverbs,* 31. Heim notes evidence of editorial arrangement among certain clusters of proverbs *(Like Grapes of Gold).*

6. As labeled by Fox (*Proverbs 1–9,* 44-47). The parental lectures include 1:8-19; 2:1-22; 3:1-12; 3:21-35; 4:1-9; 4:10-19; 4:20-27; 5:1-23; 6:20-35; 7:1-27. Although more varied in content and form than the other lectures, 6:1-19 is also introduced with a parental address ("my son"), and so I would include this passage under parental discourse, but not necessarily as a "lecture."

7. The "interludes" of significance for this discussion have to do with Wisdom, both her counsel and her character: 1:20-33; 3:13-20; 8:1-36; 9:1-18.

8. Indeed, recent brain research has highlighted the sensation of revulsion or repugnance as integral to moral reasoning (Hall, *Wisdom,* 102-3; Kass, "Wisdom of Repugnance").

9. See Sandoval, "Revisiting the Prologue." The distinction Sandoval makes between purpose (vv. 2-4) and invitation (vv. 5-6), however, is artificial. The whole of the prologue, I would argue, is both invitational and purpose-filled.

so doing awaken the desire for wisdom, specifically the desire to read the book in anticipation of all that will be gained in doing so. To discern more fully the function of this prologue, I offer a translation.

> [1]The Proverbs of Solomon, Son of David, King of Israel:
> [2]To know wisdom and instruction;
>   to understand insightful sayings;
> [3]To gain efficacious instruction,
>   righteousness, justice, and equity.
> [4]To teach prudence to the immature,
>   and knowledge in discretion to the young.
> [5]Let the wise (also) attend and gain erudition,
>   and the discerning acquire skill.
> [6]To understand a proverb, a figure,
>   words of the wise, and their enigmas.
> [7]The fear of YHWH is the beginning of knowledge;
>   fools despise wisdom and instruction.[10]

Following the Solomonic superscription, these verses present an all-embracing purpose statement.[11] This ancient "course objective" is terminologically dense, featuring a veritable catalogue of sapiential terms that achieves an accumulative effect upon the reader, such that, as von Rad aptly notes, "the text seems to aim at something larger, something more comprehensive [*etwas Umfassenderes, Grösseres*], which could not be expressed satisfactorily by means of any one of the terms used."[12]

That "something larger" is a coherent profile of estimable character. One who possesses character is one who embodies all the virtues and values featured in the prologue, a complete package. Such is the shape of integrity. Although von Rad may be correct in noting that the plethora of terms cannot be precisely delineated, there is undeniably a range of values conveyed in the introduction that can be described, extending from concrete skill and resourcefulness to the more abstract qualities of righteousness and justice. The list is more than a smorgasbord

10. Some have argued that Prov. 1:7 is secondary, yet such judgment in the end is subjective and involves a complex model of development in which overtly religious themes are introduced into the corpus only at its latest stage. See Dell, *Book of Proverbs*, 94-124.

11. On the significance of attributing the book of Proverbs to the royal figure of Solomon, see Brueggemann, "Social Significance of Solomon."

12. Von Rad, *Wisdom in Israel*, 13 (*Weisheit in Israel*, 26).

of values; it is systematically arranged to highlight their distinctions and interrelations. The prologue opens and concludes with reference to the comprehensive values of wisdom and instruction (vv. 2a and 7b), as well as to their literary conventions: "words of insight" (v. 2a) and their forms (v. 6). Sandwiched in between are particular distinctions in virtues. Efficacious instruction, skill, prudence, and discretion (vv. 3a and 5b) point to practical or instrumental virtues that enable the person to successfully pursue certain goals.[13] By definition, instrumental virtues are pragmatic and practical; they are skills for life. At the strategic center of this constellation, however, are the distinctly moral traits of "righteousness, justice, and equity," which constitute normative communal relations and conduct (v. 3b).[14] All in all, the systematic arrangement of terms embedded in these six verses exhibits a tight concentric structure.

> A   Comprehensive, intellectual values: 2a
>   B   Literary expression of wisdom: 2b
>   C   Instrumental virtue: 3a
> _____
>   **D   Moral, communal virtues: 3b**
> _____
>   C′   Instrumental virtues: 4-5
>   B′   Literary expressions of wisdom: 6
> A′   Comprehensive, intellectual virtues: 7

Through its well-structured collage of values and virtues, the prologue imbues the book of Proverbs with great promise and high purpose. It heightens anticipation of what this book is able to deliver, from instilling prudence to cultivating righteousness, from navigating life's challenges to establishing justice. Although the primary implied audience is an adolescent, someone on the verge of becoming an adult, v. 5 claims that even the wise have much to gain from (re)reading the book. There remains always something new to appropriate in Proverbs. With the inclusion of v. 5, which breaks the poetic and syntactical pattern,[15] the prologue claims

---

13. This method of classification is based on Pincoffs, *Quandaries and Virtues,* 84.

14. In similar fashion, Schäfer sees in v. 3 the ultimate goal of sapiential instruction (*Poesie der Weisen,* 14-15).

15. I am tempted, along with others, to identify v. 5 as a secondary insertion, but I find a correlation with 9:7-12, which also addresses the wise, perhaps inserted in order to separate more fully Wisdom's invitation (9:1-6) from that of the "foolish woman" (vv. 13-17). See below.

the book as an inexhaustible source of wisdom and highlights in its own taxonomic way wisdom's universal and irresistible appeal. Who would not want insight, prudence, and skill? Who would not want to practice justice and righteousness? Who would not want to understand the enigmatic words of the wise? Who would not aspire to become wise? Only a fool. With its collage of sapiential terms, the prologue evokes a sense of wonder about the book and the values it espouses. By promising so much in its own calculated way, the prologue kindles the reader's desire to know wisdom.

But for all its invitational appeal, the prologue also issues a challenge in v. 6. As Timothy Sandoval rightly observes, "The verse . . . alerts the reader of Proverbs, at the outset of the reading project, that an understanding of this text will require a significant interpretive effort."[16] The three discrete references to literary discourse in v. 6 suggest that all subsequent material in Proverbs will challenge as much as it will sharpen the reader's interpretive skills. To state the obvious, Proverbs is full of "complicated literary discourse,"[17] discourse that will both edify and stupefy the reader in the course of reading. In addition to achieving a successful and impeccably moral life, the reader will gain skill in interpreting the occasionally obscure language of the sages, including the "figures" and "riddles" contained in the book. Perplexity, Proverbs promises, leads to discernment.

With the prologue's programmatic arrangement clarified, it is now necessary to examine briefly some of the individual terms featured therein, the parts of the greater sum.

Efficacious Instruction (mûsar haśkēl)

In Prov. 1:3a *haśkēl*[18] demonstrates a wide range of meaning. In both its verbal and nominal forms, it can connote prosperity (17:8; 1 Sam. 18:15; Jer. 10:21; 20:11) as well as that which brings about prosperity, such as reputation and good sense (Prov. 3:4; 12:8; 13:15). The term is outcome-oriented.[19] In its broadest sense, *haśkēl* denotes action that ensures the

---

16. Sandoval, "Revisiting the Prologue," 457.

17. Sandoval, "Revisiting the Prologue," 472.

18. NRSV translates this phrase as "instruction in wise dealing." The form *haśkēl* is verbal (infinitive absolute) but is used here as a substantive (see also Prov. 21:16; Jer. 9:23).

19. For example, the one who is restrained in speech and has the foresight to gather in the summer is a *maśkîl* (Prov. 10:5, 19; 16:23).

successful pursuit of desired objectives.[20] Not inherently moral, its range of meaning suggests more a category or type of virtue,[21] specifically a class of instrumental virtues that would include prudence, resourcefulness, cool-headedness, caution, courage, good sense, and persistence, to name a few.[22] The virtue of *haśkēl* is essentially pragmatic, fashioned from well-tested experience and conduct.

Righteousness (ṣedeq), Justice (mišpāṭ), and Equity (mêšārîm)

"Righteousness" and "justice" are frequently paired in prophetic and psalmic literature. They carry a distinctly moral as well as communal connotation, particularly in the context of governance. The Hebrew term for "justice" can refer to any aspect of justice, from the process of litigation (Isa. 3:14) to the actual sentence of judgment (1 Kgs. 20:40) to defending the rights of the poor (Ps. 72:2; Prov. 31:9). "Righteousness" similarly involves ethical relations between individuals and communities (e.g., Isa. 1:21). The righteous person is one who demonstrates *Gemeinschaftstreue* or "community loyalty."[23] The Hebrew term for "equity," whose basic meaning is "straight" or "even," is also closely bound up with justice and judicious speech. In the Psalter, "equity" is used exclusively as a qualification of the way in which God judges the people Israel.[24] God is praised for rendering justice equitably. In short, all three virtues deal explicitly with the way social relations are to be structured and justice is to be executed.

These three distinctly ethical virtues, virtues indispensable for the maintenance and governance of the community, occupy the center of this concentric structure. Taken together, the plethora of terms featured in the prologue seems to be weighted on the side of intellectual and instrumental categories. It is such an observation that prompts William McKane

20. Ringgren, *Sprüche/Prediger*, 13; McKane, *Proverbs*, 265. Fox notes that the nominal form *śekel* denotes "the ability to understand in practical matters and interpersonal relations and make beneficial decisions" (Fox, *Proverbs 1–9*, 36).

21. Note, e.g., the diversity of translations for the term and its cognates in various contexts in Proverbs according to NRSV: "good sense" (13:15), "repute" (3:4), "judicious" (16:23), "wisdom" (16:22; 23:9), "prudence" (10:5, 19), and "deals wisely" (14:35; 17:2).

22. This is to be distinguished from exclusively task-oriented virtues (see the discussion of instrumental versus task virtues in Pincoffs, *Quandaries and Virtues*, 84).

23. Schmid, *Gerechtigkeit als Weltordnung*, 185-86.

24. Pss. 9:9 (Eng. 8); 58:2 (Eng. 1); 75:3 (Eng. 2); 96:10; 98:9; 99:4.

to claim that "the educational process [outlined in Prov. 1:1-6] was more occupied with developing mature intellectual attitudes than with morality."[25] By sheer numbers alone, it would appear that the distinctly moral or communal virtues are in the minority. Yet they constitute nothing less than the prologue's centerpiece. Their strategic placement carries the prologue's rhetorical weight.

Prudence ('ormâ) *and Discretion* (mĕzimmâ)

"Prudence" finds its opposite in those vices that are embodied by the "simple" (*petî;* Prov. 1:4; 19:25; 27:12). The prudent person heeds admonition (15:5), is cautious, and does not believe everything (14:15). The prudent individual ignores insults rather than becomes inflamed with anger (12:16); understands and avoids danger (22:3; 27:12); and is endowed with knowledge but does not flaunt it (14:18; 12:23). The opposite of naïveté, prudence is founded upon caution and discretion (1:4b). It is precisely what youth lack, for it is founded upon well-tested experience and developed in practice. Prudence is the paramount pragmatic virtue. That the Hebrew term can be used pejoratively to denote craftiness (Job 5:12; 15:5; Gen. 3:1; Ps. 83:4 [Eng. 3]) highlights the instrumental force of this potential virtue-turned-vice.

Paired with prudence, "discretion" *(mĕzimmâ)* is similar to prudence (see also Prov. 8:12).[26] It is paired elsewhere with "good sense" or resourcefulness (*tušîyâ;* 3:21) and knowledge (5:2). Discretion can also turn sour in certain contexts by connoting excessive scheming (12:2; 14:17; 24:8). Hence this virtue is instrumental: it gains its moral force from moral objectives.

Skill (taḥbulôt)

Etymologically this term conveys the concrete image of rope pulling for the purpose of steering a ship.[27] Hence the term perhaps means some-

---

25. McKane, *Proverbs,* 265.

26. Indeed, NRSV renders the term "prudence" in 3:21 and 5:2.

27. Note the cognates: *ḥebel* (cord or rope) *ḥōbēl* (sailor), and *ḥibbel,* which refers to the mast of a ship.

thing akin to "the art of steering," as suggested by Walther Zimmerli, or what could be colloquially translated "learning the ropes."[28] Elsewhere in Proverbs the term refers concretely to the good advice given by royal counselors in the context of the nation's livelihood (11:14; 20:18; 24:6). Here the original sense of nautical expertise is transposed to the political domain. In the context of sagacious discourse, the term designates the art of solving problems and addressing challenges that face the community, requiring experience and intuition in various matters, such as battle strategy, diplomacy, and negotiation. Such counsel coming from the wicked, however, can be treacherous (12:5), thereby bringing about disaster and ruin. That this term in the prologue applies to the "wise" suggests a high degree of sophistication involving skill and insight in finding solutions and rendering advice in leadership capacities.

Wisdom (ḥokmâ) and Instruction (mûsār)

As the umbrella term for the prologue's extensive cluster, "wisdom" (ḥokmâ) incorporates all the virtues and values listed, from the instrumental and intellectual to the ethical and communal. Fox translates the term as "expertise," that is, expertise in "right living and good character."[29] However, in popular discourse "expertise" leans more toward specialization, whereas "wisdom" is clearly more generalist, indeed comprehensive and versatile, in orientation. Ḥokmâ is "wisdom": more than knowledge, more than ability, more than skill and expertise. It is all of the above and then some: it captures the sum and substance of "virtue-osity."

Because it can be learned, so the sages claim, wisdom is paired with "instruction" *(mûsār)* in the first and final verses of the prologue (1:2, 7). Call it *directive* instruction, for *mûsār* can also be translated "discipline" or "correction," even connoting punishment.[30] It is frequently paired with "reproof" and "rebuke" *(tôkaḥat)* in Proverbs and elsewhere (e.g., 9:8-9; 10:17; 12:1; 13:1). Wisdom thus is not easily acquired; it can be a painful pursuit. But then Proverbs is no easy book, and Wisdom, as we shall see, can be a harsh taskmaster.

---

28. See Zimmerli, "Place and Limit of Wisdom," 149; McKane, *Proverbs*, 265-66.
29. Fox, *Proverbs 1–9*, 33.
30. Fox, *Proverbs 1–9*, 34-35. See Prov. 13:24; 22:15; 23:13.

Fear of the Lord (yir'at YHWH)

The prologue finds its culmination in its penultimate line: "the fear of the Lord is the beginning of knowledge" (v. 7a; cf. 9:10; Ps. 111:10). As the prologue's theological capstone, "the fear of the Lord" is clearly not the kind of fear that paralyzes but, as the sages testify, the kind that mobilizes the self for the pursuit of wisdom. In Proverbs "fear" is a matter of choice (1:29). It is empowering and evocative, so much so as to motivate the reader onward in the pursuit of wisdom. Godly "fear" is the object of understanding and the basis of confidence; it is the source ("fountain") of a long and fruitful life, life in all its richness (2:5; 10:27; 14:26-27; 19:23).

In this so-called motto of the book, the "fear of the Lord" takes on a distinctly pedagogical, even epistemological character. Such "fear" is presented as a comprehensive intellectual or cognitive virtue.[31] It marks the starting point, as well as the end point, of gaining wisdom (2:3-5). Paired with humility and trust, "fear" counts as "instruction in wisdom" (15:33; 22:4a). It is both an object and an instrument of understanding (2:5). "Fear," in other words, serves as the impetus for gaining wisdom, and it leads to a life of integrity (see 9:10). Holy reverence provides nothing less than the epistemological base ("the beginning of [$rē'šît$] ...") for appropriating wisdom. Yet perhaps even more basic, "the fear of the Lord" introduces a relational dimension to the list of virtues that grounds this catalogue squarely within the parameters of normative character. Whereas the list of virtues delineates the external contours of ethical character, "fear" of God deals fundamentally with the heart and center of character, namely the position of the self *in relation* to God.[32] It indicates the requisite posture *coram Deo* for developing and broadening the repertoire of virtues. A posture of humble, receptive reverence, an acknowledgment that all wisdom is divinely rooted: this is not the kind of fear that walks on eggshells.[33] Such "fear" is to be embraced, not avoided. It is affiliative, not

---

31. See also Becker, *Gottesfurcht im Alten Testament*, 217-18; Fox, "Pedagogy of Proverbs 2," 238. Yoder notes that while "fear of the Lord" is primarily cognitive in Prov. 1–9, the expression can connote "dread of certain consequences" in certain proverbs, such as 15:16; 19:23 (*Proverbs*, 6). See also her excellent overview in "Forming 'Fearers of Yahweh,'" 183. Fox equates such fear with "conscience" (*Proverbs 1–9*, 70).

32. See chapter 1 above and Bondi's definition of character as "the self in relation" in "Elements of Character," 204.

33. It is such a perspective that prompts Jesus ben Sira, a Hellenistic Jewish sage, to proclaim, "the fear of the Lord delights the heart, and gives gladness and joy" (Sir. 1:12).

flight-provoking. Given its predominantly positive nuance in Proverbs, sapiential "fear" is akin to wonder. It is "fear seeking understanding."[34]

Proverbs, in short, takes pains to claim that wisdom begins in "fearful" wonder, in awe and reverence of God. Such wonder is distinct, though not categorically so, from the holy fear featured in historical narratives. The God of Proverbs is not the God of "signs and wonders," the *magnalia dei*, as one finds, for example, narrated in the book of Exodus. At the foothills of Sinai, the people tremble in terror. The mountaintop theophany, vividly described in Exod. 19, requires stringent preparations: the people are consecrated and boundaries are established. God's holy presence tolerates no contact with the impure. Sex is prohibited (v. 15), and touching the mountain is proscribed (vv. 12-13). On the third day, cloud and smoke envelop the mountain accompanied by thunder, earthquake, and blasts of the shofar. Deuteronomy recalls the mountain "ablaze with fire to the heart of heaven, shrouded in darkness, cloud, and gloom" (Deut 4:11). The theophany provokes such fear, such numinous awe, that the people can endure only so much, and so they select Moses as their intermediary. In his elected role, Moses himself becomes a figure of fear when his face turns effulgent with divine radiance (Exod. 34:29-30).

There are no pyrotechnical displays of divine glory recounted in Proverbs. The God of Proverbs is not the God of thunder and earthquake in Exodus. Wisdom's God in Proverbs lacks the theophanic trappings of holy terror. Proverb's God is more subtle yet no less worthy of wonder than the mighty God of torah and travail. Wisdom's God prefers generative wonder over raw fear. In wisdom, the "fear of the LORD" awakens rather than convulses body and soul. The God of Proverbs does not descend from on high in cloud and fire to thunder commands that elicit trembling obedience. No, wisdom's God both lures and leads, setting the reader squarely on the path of life that "shines ever brighter until full day" (Prov. 4:18).

To sum up so far, the prologue of Proverbs is structured deliberately to cover a variety of virtue types, from cognitive[35] to instrumental to inherently moral dispositions, a vast and varied repertoire arranged chiastically. But within this constellation is a movement that underlies the concentric structure. The language becomes more specific. The "insightful words"

---

34. See chapter 1 above.

35. The cognitive or intellectual values of wisdom, instruction, understanding, and insight presuppose a host of intellectual virtues such as attention, focus, imagination, discernment, and sound judgment.

mentioned in v. 2b are specified in v. 6. Efficacious instruction in v. 3 is exemplified in vv. 4 and 5. More striking is that beginning in v. 4 certain characters are introduced: youths, who in their immaturity stand in critical need of guidance (v. 4); sages, who continue to need instruction (v. 5); and those who delude themselves by thinking they have no need for wisdom; fearless fools they are (v. 7b).[36] Put another way, the constellation of values introduced in the first two verses is given personal rootage in the final four. The reader is thereby introduced to the kinds of characters who either appropriate or reject such values. The language, in short, moves from value to virtue: youths become prudent and shrewd; the wise become ever more resourceful, all the while fools remain intractably set in their ways. The movement toward specificity in the prologue is a movement toward "virtue-osity," the language of appropriation, and the first step toward appropriating wisdom is marked by fearful wonder.

In the "lectures" and "interludes" that follow, these virtues take on rhetorical, including metaphorical, depth, almost a life of their own. No longer simply categories and traits listed together, the prologue's values and virtues now become capitalized, richly reified, if not personified, as guardians, adornments, paths, street preachers, conversationalists, and intimate friends, all woven together into a rich tapestry of sapiential instruction. And Wisdom becomes fully characterized, fully personified. No longer laid out on a flat canvas in the prologue, these delineated virtues assume three-dimensional relief designed to heighten their rhetorical hold upon the reader. With added depth and color these virtues reflect a creative urgency on the part of the scribal sages. For the final editors of Proverbs, it did not suffice simply to compile and codify various aphorisms and admonitions, one after another, as one finds throughout chs. 10–29. Instead, the sages infused these values and virtues with wonder, wonder born of crisis.

Context and Crisis

The *book* of Proverbs was likely finalized sometime during the Persian period of Israel's history, that is, during the time of restoration after the exile.

---

36. As Yoder aptly points out, fools in Prov. 1–9 are defined by their misperception of the world: "their moral universe is upside down, characterized by *antipathy* toward God, wisdom, other people, and even themselves" ("Objects of Our Affections," 76).

The framing units of chs. 1–9 (the "Prolegomena") and 31:10-31 (the ode to the "woman of strength") reflect an urban setting filled with crowded street corners, marketplaces, and city gates. Wisdom, not coincidentally, has her home in the city (9:1-6). She is not ensconced in a secret garden or situated beyond human reach (cf. Job 28). To the contrary, she is found well established in the hustle and bustle of city life imparting her advice (Prov. 1:20-21; 8:1-3). If Wisdom is a "tree of life," as claimed in 3:18, she is a distinctly urban arbor.

Behind the scenes, however, we find a community in crisis. Racked by conflict between the returning exiles and those left behind in the wake of Babylonian invasion decades earlier, the emergent community is bereft of a native king. The Davidic dynasty had collapsed, and so the impetus of communal restoration had to be found elsewhere, apart from nationalistic aspirations of independence. On a local level, violence and theft seem to have run rampant in a community struggling to rebuild itself (Prov. 1:11-14; 3:31). Accumulation of debt was of serious concern, particularly involving loan agreements with strangers (6:1-5).[37] The father's dire warnings reflect something of the high-risk/high-reward monetary system put in place under Persian governance.[38] Some of the prophetic and historical works of the postexilic period, moreover, attest to crushing poverty and ethnic conflict. "For before those days there were no wages for people or for animals, nor was there any safety from the foe for those who went out or came in, and I set them all against one another" (Zech. 8:10). The prophet Haggai likens poverty to earning low wages and placing them in a bag full of holes (Hag. 1:6). Nehemiah cites a severe drought that has led the community to pledge their property and sell their own children into slavery (Neh. 5:1-5). In short, the economic situation in Palestine was "at times precarious."[39]

But perhaps the most fundamental crisis as perceived by the framers of the book of Proverbs is the crisis of "otherness." In Prov. 1–9 the threat of the other is cast in the image of the "foreign" or "strange" woman (2:16-19; 5:1-23; 6:20-35; 7:1-27).[40] The parent in Proverbs frequently warns the

---

37. For discussion of debt and debt relief in the Persian period, see Erhard Gerstenberger, *Israel in the Persian Period*, 114-15.

38. For more discussion on increased commercialization in the Second Temple period, see chapter 5 below.

39. Gerstenberger, *Israel in the Persian Period*, 113.

40. See most recently Tan, *"Foreignness" of Foreign Woman*, esp. 81-102, who determines in her lexical analysis of *zārâ* and *nokrîyâ* that ethnic foreignness is most central

son against succumbing to the wiles of the strange woman, who tempts the youth to engage in a sexual fling (e.g., 2:16-19; 5:3-14; 7:5). The parent's dire admonitions likely reflect something of the perceived problem of foreign assimilation in early Second Temple Judaism. One recalls the prophet Ezra denouncing mixed marriages to the point of espousing a policy of ethnic cleansing through divorce (Ezra 10:11). Nehemiah cites severe opposition from the Horonites, Ammonites, Moabites, and Arabs, as the Jewish community begins the arduous task of restoration (e.g., Neh. 4:7-8; 13:1). The problem of Jewish men marrying foreign women so vexed Nehemiah that he reports: "I contended with them and cursed them and beat some of them and pulled out their hair; and I made them take an oath" not to give their children in marriage to foreigners (Neh. 13:25). These were draconian measures for dissolute times. But the crisis (and promise) of otherness in Proverbs, as we shall see, extends beyond matters of ethnicity and sexual relations.

The sages place the crisis of social stress and suspicion right at the door of the patriarchal household, and so much of their attention is focused upon the family with the silent son listening at the feet of his parents. Why the family? Because it is the bastion of ideological innocence by virtue of the fact that everyone has or has had a family. Hence of all social domains, the family provides the strongest appeal and basis for preserving and shaping the community's praxis amid grave challenges and crises. And it is here in the familial setting that "instruction" finds its rhetorical home.

The Ethos of Instruction

Before exploring the ways in which the prologue's values and virtues are profiled in the prolegomena (Prov. 1:8–9:18), a few observations about the primary literary form of the subsequent chapters are in order. Following the introduction, a parental figure speaks to his son with these opening words: "Hear, my son, your father's instruction, and do not reject your mother's teaching" (1:8). It is no coincidence that parental discourse begins

---

in Prov. 1–9. Past and similar treatments include Camp, "What's So Strange?"; and Blenkinsopp, "Social Context of 'Outsider Woman.'" Tova Forti appropriately cautions against treating the figure as pure allegory (*"Isha Zara* in Proverbs 1–9"; see also Fox, *Proverbs 1–9*, 252-62). Yes, the "strange woman" is an adulteress. However, given the prominence of metaphorical language in Prov. 1–9, it is shortsighted to exclude any and all measure of symbolic import in association with this literary figure.

with reference to "instruction" *(mûsār)* and "teaching" *(tôrâ)*, the latter term having its home in ancient Israel's legal traditions.[41] Frequently paired with "commandment(s)" *(miṣwâ/miṣwôt)* in Proverbs (e.g., 3:1; 6:20, 23; 7:2), parental *tôrâ* exhibits rhetorical links with communal Mosaic legislation, particularly in Deuteronomy.[42] Parental "teaching" in proverbial wisdom echoes and extends, amplifies and supplements Mosaic "teaching" or "law" within the household and for the sake of the community. As noted above, "instruction" *(mûsār)* frequently exhibits a disciplinary nuance in Proverbs, as in 6:23, which refers to "the reproofs of instruction."[43] Furthermore, "instruction" is often used in the context of child rearing.[44] The pairing of *mûsār* and *tôrâ* in the opening line suggests that while wisdom is associated with *tôrâ,* it also extends beyond "law/teaching" as it becomes instrumental in forming character.

Parental "instruction" in chs. 1–9 is replete with admonitions, commands, warnings, and reproofs. The first speech is no exception (1:8-19). The father's instruction highlights the hierarchical relationship between him and his son, in stark contrast to the "sinners," who depict themselves as the son's peers (1:10-19).[45] With the frequent use of cohortatives ("let us" and "we shall"), the sinners' speech adopts an invitational style aimed at being irresistibly enticing. These words alone might suggest an egalitarian ethos of "all for one and one for all" (see v. 14), a tempting offer of gainful "employment" among youthful peers. But the offer is cast within the father's commanding discourse and thus becomes deconstructed. The father's strategy is effective: the son is compelled to step back from his peers' invitation so that he can witness the inevitable consequences of their actions. Their rallying cry is exposed as nothing more than a greedy scheme for profits that in the end will result in their own destruction (v. 19). The father exposes their entrepreneurial spirit for what it is, violence against the community (v. 12) and themselves:

---

41. E.g., Deut. 4:8, 44; 17:18-19; 27:3; 29:29. Elsewhere in Proverbs, *tôrâ* has much to do with communal codes of conduct (28:4, 7, 9; 29:18).

42. For an investigation of the use of *tôrâ* in Proverbs, see Brown, "Law and Sages."

43. Heb. *tôkĕḥôt mûsār.* See the frequent pairings of *mûsār* with *tôkaḥat* or *gĕʿ ârâ* (13:1; 15:10; 10:17; 12:1; 13:18).

44. E.g., 13:1, 24; 22:15; 19:27; 4:1. Two lamentable examples stand out: 23:13 and 22:15. It is evident, however, that the term for "discipline" or "instruction" is not used in a physically abusive way in Prov. 1–9. See Fox, "Pedagogy of Proverbs 2," 233, 241-43; Brown, "To Discipline without Destruction," 63-81.

45. Newsom, "Woman and Discourse," 144-45.

For in vain *(ḥinnām)* is the net spread
   in the eyes of every bird;
yet they lie in wait — for their own blood!
   They set an ambush — for their own lives! (vv. 17-18)

The father's instruction gives the son a bird's-eye view of the situation and in so doing exposes the peers' enticing offer as a deadly outcome of false desire. The fraught scenario depicted in these verses — the lure of quick profits through violence, the appeal of gang life, the conflict between youth and parents — is, of course, nothing new. It is framed as part and parcel of typical generational conflict, particularly between fathers and sons. Far from being a lecture on the intellectual virtue of prudence, the father's speech is urgently concerned about the preservation of his son's life and thus the preservation of the family and, more broadly, the community.

Formally opening the instructional material of Proverbs, the father's address is not unique. Disciplinary instruction, indeed, characterizes most of Prov. 1–9. Such discourse is ascribed even to YHWH: "My son, do not despise YHWH's instruction or be weary of his reproof, for YHWH reproves the one he loves, as a father [reproves] the son in whom he delights" (3:11-12). Instruction is the pedagogy of reproof; it signals parental compassion. For all its harshness, reproof is actually a sign of favor, even divine favor, and thus should be gladly borne.

The tenor of reproof is heightened to the nth degree in the speech that immediately follows the father's, a blistering address that does not so much express compassion as deliver condemnation and provoke fear. The sternest rebuke in chs. 1–9 comes not from the parent but from Wisdom herself (1:20-33). The term "reproof" is attested no less than three times in 1:22-33. Wisdom's discourse is part reproof (see vv. 22-23) but mostly indictment (vv. 25-32), the outcome of reproof rejected. Her opening lines:

²²How long, O simpletons, will you love being simple?
   How long will scoffers delight in their scoffing and fools hate
     knowledge?
²³Turn to my *reproof (tôkaḥtî);* I will pour out my thoughts to you;
   I will make my words known to you.
²⁴Because I have called and you refused,
   have stretched out my hand and no one heeded,
²⁵and because you have ignored all my counsel
   and would have none of my *reproof,*

> [26] I will even laugh at your calamity;
>   I will mock (you) when panic strikes you.

While the father warns his gullible son against potential waywardness, Wisdom indicts "simpletons,"[46] along with "scoffers"[47] and "fools," who have rejected her counsel (v. 25). At their own risk, her listeners have refused to heed her summons. Wisdom's approach is clearly strategic: the aim of her rhetoric is to ascribe a guilty conscience to her listeners. But more than instilling guilt, Wisdom also intends to inspire the dread of disaster. Her discourse resembles that of prophetic judgment, announcing certain doom (see vv. 26-27).

The position of Wisdom's rebuke following the father's warning is not coincidental; it has the effect of both extending parental instruction into the larger community, from "son" to "simpletons," and at the same time heightening it. Not confined within the cloistered walls of hearth and home, Wisdom's rhetoric invades the streets and central locales of public intercourse (1:20-21). Rather than mitigating the father's authoritative stance, Wisdom solidifies and intensifies the hierarchical relationship between parent and child, recast now as teacher and (failing) students. Whereas the father addresses the son exclusively, Wisdom casts her rhetorical net widely. With the tight juxtaposition of the father's discourse and Wisdom's, the targets of her rebuke, the "simpletons," "scoffers," and "fools" of 1:22, stand in rhetorical continuity with the son's wayward peers, against whom the father warned his son. But unlike the father, Wisdom is in a position to rebuke the scoffers and fools directly, who, inter alia, promote violence for quick gain. Wisdom's unrequited reproof echoes Amos's injunction against those who promulgate injustice against the poor:

> They hate the one who reproves in the gate,
>   and they abhor the one who speaks the truth. (Amos 5:10)

It is at the city gate that Wisdom reproves her detractors, speaking the plain truth of righteousness, justice, and equity. But her converts seem to be few.

---

46. Heb. *pĕtāyim* refers to those who are gullible and naïve. Although they are not as culpable as the "fools" and "scoffers" depicted in Proverbs, they nevertheless require reproof to save them from their naïveté. See Fox, *Proverbs 1–9*, 42-43.

47. Heb. *lēṣîm* refers to the arrogant who treat others with contempt (Fox, *Proverbs 1–9*, 42).

With the juxtaposition of the two addresses — the parental and the sapiential — the son overhears, as it were, Wisdom's shocking condemnation of those whose conduct is shared by his peers. What is cast as a harsh indictment against them serves as a stinging rebuke against the son.[48] But since "simpletons," on the one hand, and the "scoffers" and "fools," on the other, are lumped together in her address, all are roundly condemned, whether justified or not. Is there, one could ask, any chance for redemption, any chance of escape from the "calamity" that is to come (v. 27)? Seemingly no, until Wisdom's concluding words are pronounced:

> [32]For waywardness kills simpletons,
>   and the complacency of fools destroys them;
> [33]but the one who listens to me will be secure
>   and will live securely without dread of disaster.

The rhetorical shift is dramatic, from negative to positive, from plural to singular. It is as if Wisdom finally zeros in on the "son" addressed earlier by the father, with his fate remaining open, however slight.

Who is the "son"? As the object of parental address in these first nine chapters,[49] he is granted no agency. His discourse is nonexistent; he neither talks back nor utters a word of consent. He is neither round nor flat, character-wise. Rather, he is a "hole," a character void, at least at the outset. And yet, next to Wisdom, he may very well be the most central character throughout chs. 1–9, if not the entire book. He is at least the most necessary character, given the book's rhetorical framework. Without the son, neither the parent nor Wisdom would have anyone to address. Such is the nature of "instruction": it must be received in order to be heard, and it must be heard in order for it to be given. The figure of the "son" in Proverbs ensures that instruction is heard loud and clear. Consistently on the receiving end, the "son" is, in the words of Carol Newsom,

---

48. The way in which Wisdom addresses a double audience that includes both the son and the scoffers/fools confirms her as a consummate rhetorician (as one would expect). She appears to summon her audience for reproof (1:23) and at the same time indicts them for having rejected her reproof (vv. 25, 30). Note also the slide from second person address (1:22-27) into third person description (vv. 28-32). Such rhetorical features enjoin a change of heart on the part of the son while decisively condemning the recalcitrant who are doomed for disaster.

49. See "my son" 1:10, 15; 2:1; 3:1, 11, 21; 4:1 (plural minus first person possessive), 10, 20; 5:1, 7; 6:1, 3, 20; 7:1, 24 (plural); 8:32 (plural).

the "interpellated" subject.[50] Put less technically, the son is a literary hole waiting to be filled by the reader's own subjectivity. By (over)hearing instruction addressed to the "son," the reader is coerced or compelled, depending on the reader's attitude,[51] to assume the son's position in the ensuing discourse.

Now that both the parent and Wisdom have introduced themselves and the son's position is firmly established, the stage is set to explore the virtues set forth in the prolegomena.

The Profile of Virtue in Parental Discourse

The first cluster of virtues is found in the father's instruction in Prov. 2.[52] Here the virtue of wisdom assumes the first position amid a cluster of intellectual virtues that also includes knowledge, insight, and understanding (2:2-6). As in the prologue, there is progression from the intellectual to the instrumental to the distinctly moral, but now the various virtues are imbued with metaphorical power. The instrumental virtue of good sense or resourcefulness that ensures success *(tušîyâ)* acts as an effective shield for those who walk with integrity as well as guards the paths of justice.[53] Similarly, prudence and understanding play the role of protective guardians on behalf of those who walk on "every good path," preventing the sojourner from veering off into the crooked "ways of darkness" (2:13, 15). At the center stand the communal values: "Then you will understand righteousness, justice, and equity, every good path" (2:9; cf. 1:3b). Appropriating the virtues of right communal relations is the natural result of receiving wisdom. That these three virtues are community-oriented is confirmed by the way they are profiled in ch. 2. They comprise "every good path" (2:9), in direct contrast to "crooked" paths, which lead to death (2:15, 18). A dominant motif in proverbial discourse, a path can only be formed by the passage

---

50. Newsom, "Woman and Discourse," 143-44.

51. Or course, the reader can resist being placed in such a passive position.

52. For an analysis of the syntactical structure of Prov. 2, see Fox, "Pedagogy of Proverbs 2," 235-36.

53. Like most translations, NRSV mistakenly identifies the "shield" with YHWH ("He is a shield . . ."). However, the semantic similarity with vv. 11-12 suggests otherwise: the virtues of discretion and understanding also assume the role of protectors. The "shield" in v. 7b refers to "good sense" *(tušîyâ).*

of many feet.[54] As such, justice, righteousness, and equity constitute the guideposts for the community.

The metaphor of the path or way serves to set in topographic relief the relationship between many of the virtues first delineated in 1:2-7. As moral virtues constitute the path along which the community must follow, certain instrumental virtues serve as guardians along the way, preserving both the individual and the community from veering off into crooked ways. To welcome wisdom involves becoming a responsible citizen in a community shaped by justice and equity, formed by those who have gone before to lay a foundation for those to come. In stark contrast, the way of the wicked is one that threatens to collapse the established structures of the community, undermining its ethical foundations. This anticommunity ethos is most graphically represented by the personified form of the "strange" or "alien" woman, to whom the reader is first introduced in 2:16-19. From the very outset, this outsider is described as one who has severed and overturned the most basic of communal ties, the marriage covenant (v. 17), an act considered no less destructive to the community than the sinners' schemes to ambush the innocent in ch. 1. In both cases, at stake is the community's well-being, on behalf of which Wisdom and her arsenal of virtues wage their defense.

Elsewhere, the constellation of virtues echoes the profiles set forth in ch. 2. For example, the son is exhorted to "guard good sense *(tušîyâ)* and discretion *(mĕzimmâ),* for they will be life for your soul and adornment for your neck" (3:21-22). Such virtues ensure safe passage (v. 23). Like the prescribed phylacteries of Jewish tradition (cf. Deut. 6:6-9; 11:18-21), discretion and good sense are to be "worn" by the wayfarer. The son is enjoined to grasp and wear them; they in turn serve to protect him on his way. These instrumental virtues establish the individual's point of departure into the realm of communal responsibility. Discretion serves to safeguard the individual from undermining communal structures and relationships based on equity and fairness.

The communal orientation of such instrumental virtues is no better specified than in the list of five negative commands in 3:27-31, which define the form of the prudent lifestyle. How they hang together is readily clear. All deal with the maintenance of harmonious relationships. The importance of this list cannot be underestimated, since it indicates that even the instrumental virtues of discretion and good sense (3:21; cf. 1:4) are

---

54. See Newsom, "Woman and Discourse," 147.

intimately bound up with the community's welfare. The prudent lifestyle is profiled relationally, beyond the perspective of the efficient and successful attainment of individual goals.[55] The betterment of the individual per se is not the fundamental issue. Rather, instrumental virtues are nuanced in such a way as to highlight their salutary impact upon the community. It is in service to the community that these virtues find their moral legitimacy.[56]

Other admonitions given by the father confirm such a profile. Marital faithfulness is of utmost importance (5:15-20): fidelity preserves family structures and prevents violence aroused by jealousy (6:24-35). Credit surety and moneylending are discouraged, since such arrangements disturb the equilibrium of economic power within the community (6:1-3). Even the most practical virtues are given a communal twist. Diligent labor, illustrated by the wonder-provoking example of the ant, is profiled as the means to prevent the rapacious onslaught of poverty (6:6-11). Indeed, it is not simply in passing that mention is made of the ant being part of a community that maintains itself without chief, officer, or ruler (v. 7). A marvel! The colony somehow endures simply with each ant gathering for itself. Laziness, by contrast, invites poverty, likened to a military attack (v. 11). Even the graphic description of the scoundrel's speech and body language (e.g., crooked discourse, winking, shuffling, pointing) is rooted in the proclivity to provoke social conflict, perhaps in its most damaging form through unnecessary and false litigation (vv. 12-14). In short, instrumental or practical values are profiled in the father's discourse specifically within the context of the community and its well-being.

The Profile of Edifying Wonder: Woman Wisdom

Amid the father's "lectures," which offer advice and counsel to the son, Wisdom intrudes with "interludes" that evoke fear and wonder (esp. 1:20-33 and 8:1-36). Shared by both discourses — the parental and the sapiential — is the language of virtue. It is no surprise that the densest cluster of virtues to be found in Prov. 1–9, with the exception of the prologue, is in Wisdom's own discourse in ch. 8. As Wisdom again takes her stand at the crossroads of public discourse, the virtues come fast and furious beginning with v. 5. Similar to her opening address in 1:22, Wisdom targets the unintelligent

55. In contrast, e.g., to the way the instrumental virtue *tušîyâ* is used in Job 5:12; 6:13.
56. Cf. the list of seven vices in Prov. 6:17-19.

(pětāyim). But unlike her first address, what follows is not so much a stern rebuke as a character sketch that invites assent from her audience. The shift from prophetic imprecation to self-praise, from warning to wooing, is dramatic. She opens with a reflection on the nature of her discourse (8:6-9). Listed first are her words concerning matters of leadership[57] and equity in 8:6, values constitutive of a just order. The values of truth and righteousness follow (vv. 7-8). They, Wisdom affirms, are part and parcel of "straight talk," the defining mark of sagacious discourse (vv. 8-9). Such talk sustains the community, for whenever speech loses its integrity, so also does the network of relationships that uphold the community. Sagacious speech is the antonym of "doublespeak" (to borrow from George Orwell). In Wisdom's discourse form and content are mutually reflective: plain truth is correlated with equity; righteousness and straight talk are bound together.

The catalogue of virtues continues as Wisdom's discourse turns from the topic of speech to that of character in 8:12-21. Wisdom lives with prudence, discovers knowledge (v. 12), and walks in the paths of righteousness (v. 20). Such statements may sound strange as Wisdom's *self*-description, for the language seems more appropriate to the recipient of wisdom. But that is the point. Wisdom presents a character résumé specifically designed for the inquirer to embody. When Wisdom claims she possesses "wise counsel and good sense," she casts herself in the role of her ideal inquirer. By describing her own character, Wisdom invites appropriation via imitation so that the human self can be recast in the *imago sapientiae*. Wisdom walks the paths of righteousness and justice, and so also the individual in community (8:20). To do so is an act of "love," complete with unmatchable benefits (v. 21). Wisdom's self-appraisal, in other words, aims to awaken the reader's desire.

Wisdom's Wonder

Wisdom's self-description does not end simply with the profiling of normative character. After v. 21 Wisdom transcends the social level of sapiential embodiment and ascends to the cosmic and thus to the divine realm. What follows is her self-praise in cosmic wonderment, conveyed in one of the most exquisitely crafted poems in all of Scripture, a singularly evocative passage that has captivated readers for centuries, from ancient sages and church fathers (and heretics) to feminists and ecologists. Indeed, Prov.

---

57. Heb. *něgîdîm* is lit. "princely matters"; cf. 8:15-16.

8:22-31 has been fought over in the christological disputes of the past and theological controversies of the present. Through no fault of its own, the text bears a bruised legacy,[58] and before proceeding, the reader may do well to drop at least some of the interpretive baggage, weighty as it is, and wander about a little less encumbered in the text's world with eyes wide open, come what may.

The poem marks the pinnacle of Wisdom's discourse in Proverbs, and through it she establishes her preeminent place within the cosmic sweep of creation's genesis. Indeed, her account is not so much about creation per se as about the one who beholds and engages it. "It's all about me!" declares creation's "I"-witness. The poem is Wisdom's grand soliloquy, and it bears a distinctly rhetorical purpose within the larger scope of Proverbs' prolegomena: Wisdom lifts her voice above the fray of conflicting voices to persuade the reader of her inestimable worth and authority. She alone is the supreme object of wonder as she seeks to woo her audience into affiliation. Moreover, through her testimony Wisdom seeks to bond with the reader in a way that no parent (or deity) can, and she does so by identifying herself as a child frolicking with God and the world (vv. 30-31). By claiming an intimate, lively association with both the Creator and creation, Wisdom hopes to capture the imagination and, in so doing, claim once and for all the reader's allegiance to the God of Wisdom. It is here in Wisdom's wonder that character and creation find their consummation. Compared to the "foreign" woman, the detested "other" who threatens both family and community, Wisdom casts herself as the cosmic yet familial Other for the benefit of family and community alike.

The poem begins with Wisdom placing herself at (and as) the beginning of God's creative acts (vv. 22-23). Wisdom is "created" *(qnh)* by YHWH prior to the world,[59] she testifies, thus asserting her preeminent status in all creation. More specifically, Wisdom is conceived in v. 22, gestated in v. 23, birthed in vv. 24-25, present during creation in v. 27, and actively "playing" in vv. 30-31. The world's creation is told strictly from the standpoint of Wisdom's "genetic" primacy. While her origin is sharply distinguished from the origins of the cosmos, Wisdom nevertheless shares an intimate bond with the "inhabited world" (v. 31). Indeed, Wisdom needs

---

58. Particularly over v. 22 and the status of the verb *qnh*. See Fox, *Proverbs 1-9*, 279-80.

59. The verb *qnh* typically means "acquire" (Prov. 4:7a) but is used here in the context of giving birth, as in Gen. 4:1, perhaps best captured by translating the verse as "YHWH *had* me as the beginning of his way" (v. 22a), a case of acquisition through creation.

a world in order to be wise.[60] And what is it about the world that Wisdom needs? The opportunity to play. The world is her playhouse.[61]

The poem nowhere suggests that Wisdom collaborates with God in the task of cosmic construction. Wisdom is no child laborer, but neither is she a passive spectator. Every step of creation is graced by her playful presence.

> When [YHWH] inscribed the foundations of the earth,
>   I was beside him growing up.[62]
> I was his delight day by day,
>   playing before him every moment,
> playing in his inhabited world,
>   my delighting in the offspring of *'ādām.* (8:29b-31)

Wisdom's play serves double duty. Her activity engages both God and the world in the mutuality of play, holding Creator and creation together through the common bond of delight. She is God's delight, and she finds delight in creation, particularly in humankind. In short, Wisdom is "delight" of the world that enlightens the world.

The poem, in sum, is Wisdom's joy to the world. God has given her birth and nurtured her growth to take delight in her cosmic home. Here in Prov. 8, Wisdom is no mere instrument of God's creative abilities; she is more than an attribute, divine or otherwise (cf. 3:19). According to the sages, she is fully alive, interdependent, and interactive with God and the world. Wisdom is God's full partner in play, and all creation is hers to enjoy. The world was made for Wisdom.

---

60. See Fretheim, *God and World*, 206.

61. For more on creation as Wisdom's cosmic playhouse, see Brown, *Ethos of the Cosmos*, 271-80.

62. This much disputed line hangs on the meaning of one word *('āmôn)*. See, e.g., NRSV "master worker" and the footnote "little child." For an overview of the issues, see Scott, "Wisdom in Creation." Contrary to most translations, the grammatical form of the word appears to be verbal, specifically an infinitive absolute of *'mn,* "to support" or "to nourish" (see the same verb in Esth. 2:20b). The larger context, moreover, tips the scale semantically. Given the absence of any hint of creative activity on Wisdom's part in the poem, coupled with the theme of play immediately following, the image of Wisdom as a child fits the context best. See Fox, "*'Amon* Again"; idem, *Proverbs 1–9,* 285-87. Another option is to take the form as a nominal functioning as an adverbial accusative, meaning "faithfully" (so Weeks, "Context and Meaning"). In either case, the bond between Wisdom and God is marked by intimacy and delight.

What kind of a world? Wisdom revels in a world that is made both secure and enthralling by God, a world of delight and discovery, a world of wonder. As any child develops most fully by playfully exploring her environment, so Wisdom actively engages creation in her delight. Wisdom's world is more relational than referential: as God's partner in play she is "beside" the creator of all while beside herself in joy.

Though primordially established, Wisdom's joy stands ever available for human beings to partake of. It is no accident that Wisdom concludes her address in beatitudinal form: "Happy *('ašrê)* are those who keep my ways. . . . Happy is the one who listens to me" (8:32b, 34a; cf. 3:12-13). Wisdom's delight in the inhabited world gushes over into the happiness she desires her "children" to experience. Her discourse concludes with an invitation to her adherents to share in the exuberance she herself has experienced as a child. The language of admonition and instruction (1:20-33) has made way for the language of happiness. Harsh reproofs are no longer needed. Beyond the stern cadences of Wisdom's rebuke are the cosmic reverberations of her mirth.

In retrospect, Wisdom proves to be Proverbs' fullest character. She is filled with emotion, from anger to exuberance, and her audience in turn experiences emotion from shock and shame to awe and joy. Wisdom's first appearance explodes with wrathful words of threat and judgment (1:22-33). She inspires guilt and dread, the fear of disaster (1:26-28). The reader's shock stems, in part, from the awareness of having unwittingly rejected Wisdom and realizing the dire consequences that are in store. "You neglect Wisdom at your peril" is in part the lesson.

Yet wrath gives way to wonder, and dread fades into delight. Chapter 8 highlights Wisdom's power to edify rather than to afflict. Her discourse highlights her incomparable worth materially, ethically, and theologically, and all with a touch of the erotic: "I love those who love me, and those who seek me diligently find me" (v. 17). Earlier, she is to be called "sister" (7:4), a term of erotic endearment (see Song 4:9, 10, 12; 5:1, 2). Wisdom's wisdom far exceeds the worth of jewels and fine gold; her discourse is sound and righteous (Prov. 8:11, 19). What she offers is a potent combination of power and insight (v. 14b). "By me kings reign, and rulers decree justice" (v. 15). She is the unrivaled source of "honor" and "prosperity" (v. 18). And she has "love" to lavish on those who love her back (v. 17). Wisdom's aretalogy in ch. 8 serves to heighten her desirability, while her harsh discourse in ch. 1 highlights her power of accountability. Indeed, the movement from fear to desire and delight reflects something of the dynamic of wonder itself. As

Wisdom embodies the movement from shock to awe, she marks herself as the wondrous Other.

Wisdom's Hospitality

Wisdom's invitation to joy continues in her final discourse of ch. 9 in the form of open hospitality.[63] Her banquet abounds with food and wine, and the only qualification for admittance is the commitment to "lay aside immaturity *(pĕtā'yim)*, live and walk in the way of insight" (9:6), to let go and live. Wisdom's generosity is nothing short of gratuitous: "Come, eat of my bread / and drink of the wine I have mixed" (v. 5). But her invitation is only one of many that vie for the son's allegiance: "Come, let us lie in wait for blood," proclaim his peers (1:11); "come, let us take our fill of love" (7:18), says the strange woman (cf. 9:16). Wisdom's invitation to edifying joy and her gracious hospitality complete her profile, which began with the sternest of rebukes and now concludes with Wisdom receiving her disciples as welcomed guests, an approach that the patriarch could never take with his son.[64] The father can only exhort his son to love, embrace, and prize Wisdom, actions that suggest a relationship between marriage partners in a patriarchal household. Through Wisdom, the parental discourse of admonition is replaced by the discourse of affection between intimate companions (7:4).

Wisdom's role in the pedagogical discourse of Prov. 1–9 is multifaceted. Unlike the parent, she transcends the generational divide, serving as the pedagogical link between parent and child, family and community, God and creation. Wisdom is ageless and thus eternally youthful to the son (7:4); she is the cosmic child bonded to the instructed child. Wisdom is the primordial peer, ensuring that the values and virtues of the paterfamilias are extended into the larger community as the son ventures forth to make a successful and responsible transition from his family of origin to the larger community. Wisdom takes the voice of the parent outside the "house of the father" *(bêt 'āb)* and at the same time articulates the voice of the larger community that legitimates all those who exercise authority,

63. It is perhaps no coincidence that in Luke's "Road to Emmaus" story, Jesus' discourse to the two disciples moves through comparable pedagogical stages as Wisdom does in Prov. 1–9: rebuke (Luke 24:25), instruction (v. 27), and host (v. 30).

64. Cf. the father figure in the Parable of the Prodigal Son, who welcomes his lost son as a guest of highest honor, much to the dismay of the elder brother (Luke 15:11-32).

be they king or parent.[65] In the interplay between Wisdom and parent in Prov. 1–9, between "interlude" and instruction, the family is affirmed as the foundation and training ground for responsible communal life. The family is no isolated enclave; it is the beginning point and microcosm of the community. Like the father, Wisdom presupposes the virtues of self-restraint and fidelity, particularly in matters sexual. Prudence, straightforwardness, humility, discretion, hatred of evil, and "fear of the LORD" are all featured in Wisdom's discourse in ch. 8. But at the apex of the moral scale are the communal values of righteousness, justice, and equity. What the father can approach only indirectly, Wisdom attests directly as she takes her stand in the public squares and city gates.

The Profile of Seductive Terror: Woman Stranger

In addition to Wisdom, Proverbs profiles another woman, indeed, *the* other woman, graphically described in 7:5-27. While Wisdom and the "strange woman" represent rhetorical extremes in the prolegomena, they exhibit a measure of affinity, one might even say a strange symmetry.[66] For one, they share the same domain of agency: both are found in the street corners and public squares (1:20; 7:12). Both are powerfully feminine figures; both are full subjects of their own agency. Both are lovers. They even share some common language. If you were to meet both of them in passing, it would be difficult, at least at first, to distinguish them.

Nevertheless, whereas Wisdom distinguishes herself categorically by her genesis, the strange woman has no creation account and is thereby rendered cosmically, and thus socially, illegitimate, a purveyor of chaos. As the "foreign" other, she is an object of revulsion, while Wisdom is deemed the intimate yet transcendent Other, a source of edifying wonder. Their respective similarities and differences reflect a fundamental epistemological bond, namely the affinity between wonder and revulsion/terror. Both Wisdom and the strange woman are, to be sure, depicted as objects of desire, of potential affiliation.[67] But whereas Wisdom succeeds as an object

65. Newsom, "Woman and Discourse," 156.

66. This strange affinity between wonder and revulsion would lend rationale to why Murphy's favorite proverb in Prov. 30:18-19 features an addition in v. 20 on "the way of an adulteress."

67. See Yee's study of the strange woman's "smooth" discourse in "I Have Perfumed My Bed."

and source of wonder, the strange woman is depicted as a thing of horror, despite her *"seeming* beauty."[68] The strange woman's words are seductively "smooth" (5:3b; 7:5, 21; cf. vv. 14-20) and "drip honey" (5:3a).[69] They "enthrall and entrap,"[70] while Wisdom's words enthrall and edify. The strange woman's bedroom, despite its sensorial ambience of color and fragrance (7:16-17),[71] is exposed as fifty shades of darkness suffused with the stench of death. Her home, it turns out, is the facade of Sheol. Wisdom's seven-pillar abode, by contrast, is the fount of life, redolent perhaps of the temple or creation itself (cf. Ps. 36:8-10 [Eng. 7-9]).[72] With the strange woman, the young man loses himself entirely, marking the death of desire. In Wisdom the young man finds true fulfillment of desire and with it his life. In both cases, desire is satisfied. Such is the ambiguity of desire personified by these two larger-than-life figures: desire's destruction, on the one hand, and desire's fulfillment, on the other.[73]

So also the ambiguity of wonder: the figuration of the strange woman represents a fatal case of coerced affiliation. With Wisdom, however, affiliation is invitational and life-sustaining. As the "tree of life" whose knowledge is life-giving (3:18), Wisdom alone is deemed worthy of wonder and thus worthy of affiliation. The strange woman is depicted as a fatal attraction who must be resisted, an object ultimately of horror and revulsion: she is cast as a predator, lying in wait, like the son's peers, to ambush those who have no sense. Wisdom's approach, by contrast, is openly transparent, challenging, and hospitable. Whereas the strange woman pursues her victim to the death, Wisdom invites pursuit for life. For the one who affiliates with Wisdom, knowledge is freely shared, even if it is received as reproof. Nothing is held in secret. By wisdom YHWH founded the earth (Prov. 3:19); by Wisdom the contours of moral character are established. Wisdom has all to do with moral creation.

---

68. Van Leeuwen, "Liminality and Worldview," 116.

69. The ambiguity of discourse is reflected also in the way the image of honey is metaphorically deployed in Proverbs, associating it with wisdom, on the one hand, and yet warning of the dangers of engorging (16:24; 24:13-14; 25:16, 27; 27:7).

70. Yee, "I Have Perfumed My Bed," 53.

71. Cf. Song 3:6; 4:13-14; 5:1.

72. See discussion by McKane, *Proverbs,* 362-65; Washington, *Wealth and Poverty,* 124-25.

73. See Stewart, "Honeyed Cup," 189-238, where she discusses the paradox that desire's fulfillment also marks its cessation.

Instruction for the Wise: The Reciprocal Rebuke

Last but not least in the prolegomena is the constellation of virtues found in 9:7-12. Framed by the respective dinner invitations of woman Wisdom and woman Folly, this series consists of maxims that address the advanced student of wisdom, the wise. Sharing terminology with the last section of the prologue (1:5-7), the precepts that follow Wisdom's profile as host repeat the sage's need for further instruction.

> Instruct the wise,[74] and they will become wiser;
>   teach the righteous, and they will gain insight. (9:9)

In addition, the following verses invoke "the fear of the LORD" to state once again wisdom's epistemological starting point (v. 10). The themes of instructing the wise and divine reverence round out the first nine chapters in the same way they conclude the prologue in the first seven verses in ch. 1. But what is striking in these final words is that even the wise can warrant rebuke:

> Do not rebuke a scoffer, otherwise he will hate you;
>   rebuke the wise, and he will love you. (9:8)

Rebuke also applies to the wise, but in a different way from the kind that indicts one's peers as simpletons and scoffers, as in Wisdom's initial speech in ch. 1. Among the wise, the sharp rhetoric of rebuke is recognized as two-edged: rebuking the wise is an equal opportunity right, an exercise in reciprocity. To count oneself among the wise is to be able to give as well as to receive rebukes in gratitude ("love"). Here the defining character trait of the wise is the capacity to receive correction with a collegial sense of appreciation. An individual's willingness to accept correction gratefully is itself a mark of wisdom, and a wise community is thus a community of reciprocity, even cooperation.[75] Indeed, it is this spirit of collegial cooperation that distinguishes the "wise" from the "scoffer." Only the wise know most clearly that wisdom is their gain even at the cost of self-certainty and pride. Humility is key. This ethos of reciprocity among the sages mirrors something of the relationship between Wisdom and her disciples.

---

74. Lit. "give to the wise." The verbal object is absent from the Hebrew (cf. 1:4). However, given the alliterative repetition of *ḥkm* in the first colon and that it is Wisdom herself who is speaking, *ḥokmâ* is the understood object.

75. See Hall's illuminating discussion of "correction" as an indispensable quality of a cooperative, altruistic community (*Wisdom*, 162-65).

> I love those who love me,
>> and those who seek me find me. (8:17)

Such love is descriptive of and prescriptive for the wise, and the pedagogy of rebuke now finds its home in mutual edification, if not affection.

In conclusion, the prolegomena of Proverbs (chs. 1–9) profile the sapiential virtues listed in the prologue (1:2-7) with a touch of wonder. In the "lectures" and "interludes" that follow, wisdom becomes Wisdom, and the central place that the moral/communal values of righteousness, justice, and equity assume within the prologue is upheld, if not heightened.[76] Though tersely delineated in the prologue, this trinity of moral values represents the pinnacle of the moral life. Its inherently communal provenance readily corresponds to Wisdom's own arena of activity at the centers of public intercourse. Indeed, her presence at the city gates implies involvement in the administration of justice (1:21; 8:3).[77] But not only does she station herself within the arena of justice; she situates herself before God and all creation. In Wisdom such virtues are given transcendental weight; they are part of her cosmic play. Whereas disciplinary instruction is what characterizes parental discourse, Wisdom's discourse ultimately moves beyond rebuke and fear to revelation and invitation, to wonder and delight (chs. 8 and 9). In sum, the prologue's dense collage of virtues taken in combination with the prolegomena extends an invitation that compels readers regardless of experience, from novice to advanced, to appropriate Wisdom's instruction by cultivating wonder and arousing desire for Wisdom and for the virtues she upholds. But that is only the beginning, the "beginning of wisdom."

Pondering Proverbs

True to the book's title in 1:1 *(mĕšālîm)*, chs. 10–29 consist of a collection of collections of proverbs: terse and rhetorically compact poetic sayings that operate at various levels of interpretation. The prolegomena or first

---

76. Thus McKane's assessment that "the educational process was more occupied with developing mature intellectual attitudes than with morality" misses the mark (*Proverbs*, 265). To dichotomize intellectual and moral values would be farthest from the mind of the ancient sage.

77. See, e.g., Deut. 21:19; 25:7; 2 Sam. 15:1-6; Amos 5:10; Ruth 4:1, 11. For a discussion on the place of law at the city gate, see Boecker, *Law and Administration*, 31-33.

nine chapters of Proverbs have equipped the reader to forge through a seemingly impenetrable jungle of aphorisms and admonitions. Actually, *foraging* is more like it, for Wisdom's banquet scene in ch. 9 metaphorically sets the stage for all that follows. Wisdom offers a multicourse meal, a curricular cuisine, and it is precisely her rich fare that is featured in the following collections. More than simply food for thought, these terse sayings offer sustenance for the righteous as much as the woman of strength in Prov. 31 "provides food for her household" (31:15).[78] And what a smorgasbord it is! The following sayings address a wide range of topics, from just dealings to judicious speech, from table etiquette to child rearing, from wealth and poverty to good neighborly relations. As food is to be tasted, so proverbs are to be tested and critically appropriated.[79] Pondering proverbs is a matter of taste testing and digesting, not of the mouth but of the heart, the center of the will. And it all begins with a diet of discipline taken in discrete servings. Proverbs are meant not to be wolfed down and read in quick succession but rather to be savored and thoughtfully considered, each one pondered appreciatively and critically. Otherwise, they may cause indigestion (see below). Chapter 9, in effect, supplies the metaphorical setting and context for the collections that follow and, in so doing, gives the collected proverbs new life.[80] The metaphor of Wisdom's lavish banquet marks each proverb as a nugget of nourishment. Proverbs, varied as they are, provide the rich nutrients for developing and sustaining right character. What, then, is a proverb *in* the book of Proverbs? Edible words.

Proverb Power

The power of a good proverb lies in its ability to stimulate wonderment, often through the use of metaphor.[81] It is no coincidence, particularly in

---

78. That this industrious woman "brings her food from far away" figuratively acknowledges wisdom's international flavor (v. 14).

79. "Does not the ear test words as the palate tastes food?" Job asks rhetorically (Job 12:11; cf. 34:3).

80. According to Wolfgang Mieder, "The proverb in a collection is dead," since it is stripped of its oral, performative context (cited in Fontaine, *Traditional Sayings in the Old Testament,* 54). The editors of the book of Proverbs provide a new context.

81. This discussion is adapted from a section of my essay, "Didactic Power of Metaphor."

light of the previous discussion, that many proverbs in Proverbs employ the metaphor of edible fare:

> From the fruit of the mouth one's stomach[82] is satisfied;
> the yield of one's lips brings satisfaction. (18:20)

> The mouth of the righteous bears[83] wisdom,
> but the perverse tongue will be cut down. (10:31)

Both proverbs apply the metaphor of "fruit" to proper discourse. What do "fruit" and discourse ("mouth") share in common? Phonetically, they share alliteration and assonance: *pĕrî* ("fruit") and *pî* ("mouth").[84] Cognitively, they are linked in terms of their stated effect: they both satisfy. As delectable fruit is happily consumed, so a well-turned phrase renders pleasure to the speaker and listener.[85] Through its use of metaphor, the proverb discloses an inherent connection between the "edible" and the "edifying." The metaphorical schema generates other associations as well. The ear, the organ of auditory reception, is associated with the stomach; hearing (and understanding) is likened to digestion (see also 12:14; 13:2; Job 12:11). In addition, the mouth and the lips produce speech as the fruit tree yields its produce. Also, the imagery of the first line of Prov. 10:31 informs the second line by prompting the reader to imagine the "perverse tongue" not only as cut off but also as a barren tree to be felled.

The life-sustaining power of proper speech is made all the more explicit in the following proverb.

> The lips of the righteous feed[86] many,
> but fools die for lack of understanding. (10:21)

In this antithetical saying, the moral qualification of proper speech is given explicit reference: it is the discourse of the righteous that is nourishing *(rʿh)*, but fools, who refuse such "edible" fare, die in an abject deprivation,

---

82. See Prov. 13:25, which casts "appetite" *(nepeš)* and "stomach" *(beṭen)* as parallel items.

83. From *nwb*, to "bear fruit" (Ps. 92:15[14]; cf. 62:11[10]).

84. See also Prov. 12:14a and 13:2.

85. Owing to the use of the possessive, 18:20a gives primary attention to the one who utters the saying, not to the listener.

86. See also Prov. 15:14b. LXX exhibits a more conventional reading "know," perhaps the result of graphic confusion. The verb *rʿh* can also mean "protect, lead, rule" (e.g., 2 Sam. 5:2; 7:7; Jer. 3:15; 23:4; Ezek. 34:2-3, 8-10, 23; Ps. 78:71-72).

metaphorically of starvation. The deployment of the food metaphor among these various sayings, in sum, is designed to stimulate a certain kind of appetite, a hunger for edifying speech.

One saying in particular imbues the connection between discourse and food with even greater vividness.

> Pleasant[87] words are a honeycomb,
> sweet to the appetite and healing to the body. (16:24)[88]

The proverb deploys the particular image of honey to highlight the pleasing nature of eloquent speech, and evidently there is no danger of engorging on it, contrary to the following proverbs:

> The sated appetite despises[89] honey,
> but to a ravenous appetite anything bitter is sweet. (27:7)

> Got honey? Eat only enough for you,
> lest you be sated with it and vomit it.[90] (25:16)

> Eating (too) much honey is not good,
> so also searching for excessive honor.[91] (25:27)

Such sayings are clearly not limited to proper table etiquette whenever there is the occasion for honey to be served. "Honey" is so metaphorically potent that it includes anything that is "consumed," including wise discourse, in light of the precedent set in the Solomonic sayings for identifying discourse with fruit, including honey (16:24).[92] By (re)deploying the image of honey, the sages acknowledge the dangers and temptations of engorging on wisdom, particularly its trappings, such as esteem and honor. While promulgating wisdom's benefits, the sages were also wary

87. Or "kind words." See Prov. 15:26.

88. Cf. Prov. 24:13-14 and below.

89. Read *tābûz* instead of *tābûs* ("trample, tread"), which consistently targets enemies as its object (see LXX).

90. Cf. 26:11 and 23:8, which places in parallel fashion "vomit[ing]" food and "wast[ing] . . . pleasant words."

91. The second line is corrupt. The consonantal spelling could be the result of a misdivision of words, originally meaning "honor after honor." Otherwise, the final *mem* of the penultimate word may be enclitic.

92. Explicit connection between honey and wisdom is found in 24:13-14 ("My son, eat honey, for it is good. . . . Know that wisdom is such to your soul").

(or weary!) of overindulgence (cf. Eccl. 7:16). "Humility precedes honor" (Prov. 15:33b; cf. 16:18).

Certain proverbs revel in paradox, even irony, causing great wonderment. One proverb even adopts the language of violence in order to lift up the value of diplomacy.

> With patience[93] a ruler can be won over,[94]
> and a soft[95] tongue can shatter bones. (25:15)

The soft answer in this proverb does more than resist wrath, as in 15:1. The paradox of discursive power is heightened all the more: like a mace or sword, judicious speech serves as a weapon of attack. The paradox has come full circle: the metaphorical imagery (i.e., weaponry) most frequently signifies reckless, foolish, or duplicitous speech elsewhere in Proverbs.[96] But here the tongue, whose softness and healing powers are stressed both physically and metaphorically elsewhere,[97] constitutes the weapon. Mild, patient counsel can find its mark and break the intransigence of any king. The violent imagery in the second colon, moreover, suggests a more pointed and subversive rereading of the first: "With patience a ruler may be screwed,"[98] suggesting perhaps a further (and obscene) image of hardness. In any case, far from banal, this proverb owes its evocative power to its peculiarly tensive use of metaphor.

Such proverbs give pause for wondering. They stimulate reflection and occasionally even awe in the way metaphors perform, sometimes paradoxically so, within such compact lines. But then that is the power of a proverb at its most subtle. Other proverbs are not so; some of them prove to be banal, stale maxims rather than aphoristic prods for reflection. It is perhaps not coincidental that as one progresses through the various collections, from the "Proverbs of Solomon" (10:1–22:16) to the Hezekian collection (25:1–29:27) and the "Words of Agur son of Jakeh" (ch. 30), one finds increasing use of vivid metaphor and literary variety. Compare the following examples:

93. Lit. "length of nostrils."

94. Or "seduced." See Prov. 1:10; 16:29.

95. Cf. 15:1 (cited above). The adjective can even connote timidity and cowardice (Deut. 20:8; 2 Chron. 13:7).

96. See Prov. 12:18; 18:7; 25:18; 28:19.

97. See 12:8; 15:4; 16:24.

98. The verb *pth* can connote sexual seduction and rape (e.g., Exod. 22:15[16]; Deut. 11:16; Jer. 20:10).

A slack hand causes poverty,
>   but the hand of the diligent makes rich. (10:4)

Do not rob the poor because they are poor,
>   or crush the afflicted at the gate;
> for YHWH pleads their cause
>   and despoils of life those who despoil them. (22:22-23)

Better to be poor and walk in integrity
>   than to be crooked in one's ways even though rich. (28:6)

The rich is wise in self-esteem,
>   but an intelligent poor person sees through the pose. (28:11)

The poor and the oppressor share this in common:
>   YHWH gives light to the eyes of both. (29:13)

Speak out, judge righteously,
>   defend the rights of the poor and needy. (31:9)

The first aphorism identifies poverty as the outcome of indolence, and diligence as the bringer of wealth. Subsequent proverbs, however, make no such lazy equation: poverty can be the outcome of injustice; being poor may be preferable to being rich; the rich suffer from hubris. Ultimately, God gives life to both rich and poor and, moreover, advocates for the poor, even to the demise of the rich.[99] Finally, it is the king's solemn responsibility to defend the rights of the poor (31:9).

In short, the latter collections in Proverbs are frequently painted with splashes of gray that offset the strictly bifurcated worldview constructed by earlier proverbs. Some of the most vivid imagery is found clustered in chs. 25–26.[100] The forms of proverbs, moreover, become increasingly eclectic in the later collections, from simple antithetical sayings to more variegated and complex forms. It is as if a broad pedagogical movement

99. Though the sages of Proverbs did not espouse an ethic of societal transformation (e.g., Isa. 14:30; 26:6; 29:19; 32:7; Zeph. 3:12), the diverse perspectives on the poor featured in Proverbs imply a critical stance toward the community's responsibility to uphold justice and equity, particularly for the disenfranchised. See, e.g., Prov. 13:23; 14:31 (and 17:5); 15:25; 22:22-23; 30:14. See Washington *Wealth and Poverty,* 2-4, 179-85, 205-6. For a metaphorically oriented investigation of the ambiguity of wealth and poverty, see Sandoval, *Discourse of Wealth and Poverty.*

100. E.g., 25:11-14, 18-20, 25-26, 28; 26:1-3, 6-11.

is at work among these seemingly haphazard collections, from the basic and sometimes banal to the more advanced and challenging — literarily, ethically, and theologically.[101]

The Words of Agur

To top it all off, the opening "words of Agur" give searing testimony to the insurmountable limits of human knowledge in the face of the Divine. The speaker bitterly laments his ignorance before God with questions reminiscent of the whirlwind theophany featured in Job.

> Surely, I am too brutish to be human;
>> I have no human understanding.
> I have not learned wisdom;
>> I have not gained knowledge of the Holy One.
> Who has ascended to heaven and come down?
>> Who has gathered the wind in his cupped hands?
> Who has wrapped the waters with a garment?
>> Who has established all the ends of the earth?
> What is his name?
>> What is the name of his son?
>>> Surely you know! (30:2-4; cf. Job 38:5; 42:1-6).[102]

Agur's self-critical recognition of the limits of human understanding acknowledges more broadly the capacity for "wonder, reverence, and humility" in the sapiential enterprise (cf. 30:18-19, 24-31).[103] Is this, then, the ultimate destiny of the wise, coming up against the limits and inefficacy of human wisdom before the Divine?[104] With Agur's discourse, fearful wonder marks the end of wisdom — not wisdom's demise but its destination — as much as it signaled wisdom's generative beginning (1:7a). With Agur, the movement of wisdom's wonder in Proverbs comes full circle,

---

101. For more detail see Brown, "Pedagogy of Proverbs 10:1–31:9."

102. For similarities between Agur's words and God's words to Job, see Crenshaw, "Clanging Symbols," 55-57.

103. Yoder, "On the Threshold of Kingship," 263.

104. As Fox points out, Agur's ignorance has more to do with "erudition," specifically *theological* erudition, than with ethical knowledge per se (*Proverbs 10–31*, 861), a theme delineated further in Job 28 (see chapter 3 below).

with wonder trumping wisdom even as it sustains it. Such is wonder's *via negativa*.[105]

Wonder and the Journey of Character

While Proverbs acknowledges the intractable limits to sapiential erudition, a theme to be developed more stridently and rigorously in Job and Ecclesiastes, the journey of character does not reach a dead end. Rhetorically, Prov. 1–9, the book's prolegomena, provide an organizing framework designed to guide the reader in appropriating the rich material that follows beginning in ch. 10, including Agur's self-effacing words. With Wisdom personified in all her fearsome glory, childlike wonder, and edifying desirability, the prolegomena of Proverbs cultivate a sense of awe and delight, desire and wonder, even in the arduous process of adjudicating proverbs. The "fear of the LORD" (1:7) and Wisdom's delight in the world (8:30-31), the two sides of sapiential wonder in Proverbs, provide powerful, indeed transcendent, motivation for critically appropriating the vast array of "sayings," "proverbs," "figures," and "enigmas." Moreover, by maintaining the subject position of the silent adolescent beyond ch. 9, the reader discovers a host of various characters, a virtual cavalcade of heroes and scoundrels that expand and sharpen this young man's social horizon: kings and queens, the righteous and the foolish, the poor and the rich, God and dogs, the wise and the dumbfounded, all contribute to the youth's formation: "YHWH is the maker of them all" (22:2b).

Where then does that leave the implied, "interpellated" reader as represented by the silent son? The answer comes in taking a bird's-eye view of the book. Beginning with his parents' instruction followed by Wisdom's discourse, the youth moves out from the household to the Grand Central Stations of urban life. On the brink of adulthood, the silent son is ready to strike out on his own into the larger social arena. In this state of betwixt and between, the son must adjudicate the competing voices that vie for his allegiance. Underlying these various profiles lies a tension that is not only left unresolved but heightened by the fact that the final verses of Prov. 9 profile Folly and her alluring invitation (vv. 13-18). Will the son successfully appropriate the teachings of his parents and heed Wisdom's words, or like

---

105. This negative dimension of wonder will be played out further in Ecclesiastes. See chapter 5 below.

his peers meet his doom through violence or sexual promiscuity? The text does not say. The book of Proverbs is not, generically speaking, a narrative.

Nevertheless, there is a narrative-like resolution given in the last chapter of the book. There the profile of the "woman of strength" *('ēšet ḥayil)* features a matriarch who industriously provides for her household (31:10-31). She is, from a patriarchal perspective, the ideal mate, a visionary object of wonder,[106] yet one firmly rooted in the economy of Second Temple Yehud (as Israel was called at that time).[107] She is Wisdom incarnated in the household, and in her shadow sits a patriarch at the city gate, the very place where Wisdom regularly took her stand (v. 31). Because of her, the husband basks in the honor and esteem of his fellow elders, his peers (v. 23), and with an economy of words praises his marriage partner (v. 28). The book of Proverbs began with a silent son, instructed in the responsibilities of family fidelity and communal life, and it ends with an adult male who has successfully fulfilled these responsibilities by marrying well and finding his place among the elders.

But in the foreground of the beginning and ending of Proverbs stand two characters also linked by their common gender: Wisdom, whose stirring discourse rings throughout the first nine chapters, and the matriarch in the final chapter, whose actions speak louder than any words of praise. Together with the silent son and the patriarch, Wisdom and the silent matriarch provide a gendered, narratival symmetry to the book. And like the matured son and the patriarch, Wisdom and the matriarch encompass different social domains. Whereas Wisdom takes her stand in the centers of public discourse, the matriarch has her home at home. Yet her home serves as a base of operations for her activity in the community. Not only providing for her household, this woman conducts real estate and commercial ventures, even in remote lands and without her husband's permission (31:14). Indeed, she is described in ways that even borrow from traditionally masculine imagery: "She girds herself with strength, and makes her arms strong" (v. 17; cf. v. 25).[108] How is the triad of communal virtues

---

106. Emphasis on "patriarchal." Feminist and cultural critiques of this figure are well justified and illuminating. See, e.g., Masenya, "Proverbs 31:10-31," 56-68; Riess, "Woman of Worth," 141-51; Chitando, "Good Wife."

107. See Yoder, *Wisdom as Woman of Substance*; idem, "Woman of Substance."

108. The language is reminiscent of military rhetoric (e.g., Nah. 2:2 [Eng. 1]; Amos 2:14; Prov. 24:5). It is such language that prompts Al Wolters to translate *'ēšet ḥayil* as "Valiant Woman" or "woman of valor" and to classify the poem as a "heroic hymn" ("Proverbs XXXI 10-31").

embodied by this domestic warrior? They are fulfilled in v. 20: "She opens her hand to the poor, and reaches out her hands to the needy," the same hands that produce linens and plant vineyards. More than dispensing alms is implied. To "reach out" the hand establishes, first and foremost, a bond (cf. 1:24).[109] It is through this matriarchal act of hospitality that the community comes to be sustained. For this and everything else she is praised as one who "fears YHWH" (v. 30; cf. 1:7).

The book of Proverbs is more than a collection of lectures and aphorisms, more than a book of virtues, more than an intellectual pursuit. Proverbs is a "manual of desires"[110] and, relatedly, a work of wonder, of constructing, shaping, identifying the proper objects of wonder set in a rite of passage into moral maturity. Proverbs charts a liminal journey from the household to the larger community, a pathway that requires letting go of parental ties, resisting dangerous temptations, avoiding conflict, discerning right desires, pursuing Wisdom, and finding the right partner. The narratival shape of Proverbs fleshes out, socially and ethically, the primordial journey of the male from child to adult as he finds union with his mate: "Therefore a man leaves his father and his mother and clings to his wife, and they become one flesh" (Gen. 2:24). That union creates a new household and thus another anchor for the community.

If the destination of wisdom's path, according to Proverbs, is back to the household, it is never home again. All the virtues with which one is raised, from daily discipline to piety, from diligent work to exuberant delight, find their ultimate significance within the larger community and the values that sustain it. The network of virtues and values serves to open up new vistas of maturity and responsible living that, in turn, provide new avenues of engagement, including the opportunity for edifying intimacy, the fulfillment of deepest desire. As the parent urges the son to discover true intimacy with his future spouse (Prov. 5:15-20), so Wisdom reaches out to take her student by the hand, finding clear routes through the winding, confusing avenues of public intercourse. In wisdom, with Wisdom, wonder's wanderlust finds its direction and its destination. In Proverbs "fear seeking understanding" is ultimately "fear finding fulfillment," empowering moral agency.

---

109. The only parallel in Proverbs is found in 1:24, wherein Wisdom complains of being rejected: "Because I have called and you refused, have stretched out my hand and no one heeded. . . ."

110. Stewart, "Honeyed Cup," 197.

CHAPTER 3

The Wound of Wonder: Job 1–31

> Learning to dwell in wonder is a matter of . . . welcoming the most troubling of houseguests into the structure of identity.
>
> *Mary-Jane Rubenstein*[1]

For all its agonistic drama, Job is fundamentally a book of wonder. Job's response in ch. 42 to God's climactic speech puts him in good company with Agur of Proverbs:

> Therefore, I have declared what I did not discern,
> things too wonderful for me, which I did not understand. (42:3b)

The similarity to Prov. 30:18-19 is unmistakable (see chapter 1 above). But what exactly does Job discern that provokes his own confession of wonder? Clearly more than slithering snakes and soaring eagles. The way Job arrives at his state of wonder is strikingly different from the way taken in Proverbs. The same goes for Job's development of character. As the book of Job explores the more disorienting, indeterminate side of wonder,[2] it forges in

---

1. *Strange Wonder*, 190.
2. Much has been written recently about the subversive nature of Job in form and content, given the book's diversity of genres, perspectives, and language, all yielding a richly "polyphonic text" (Newsom, *Book of Job*, esp. 3-31). Dell, for example, considers the book of Job to be, generically speaking, a "parody" (*Book of Job*, esp. 109-57) and an example of skeptical literature ("Job").

turn a more radical, if not ambivalent, view of character. Job's journey is from wound to wonder, from the whirlpool of torment to creation's wild gravitas. If Proverbs is about the formation of character, then Job has all to do with its deformation and transformation.

Of all the books of the Bible, Job comes closest to being a thought experiment. As a non-Israelite, Job challenges traditional sapiential notions of God and the world. At the same time, Job's God is YHWH, Israel's God (e.g., 1:20-21; 12:9; 38:1), and Job the man is the paradigm of piety. Taking place in the land of Uz, a place nearly as elusive as Eden,[3] Job's story pushes the theological envelope in ways that no orthodox Israelite could have imagined. Given its penchant for raising questions and subverting texts and traditions, Job has even been called the one book of the Bible that is against the Bible.[4] In the face of rigidified forms of conventional, biblical norms, the book of Job hits the reset button on religious faith and piety, and it does so in the end by reaching back to the world of beginnings and venturing forward beyond the boundaries of human culture, Israelite or otherwise. Job shares much in common with Genesis; indeed, the book of Job has been called by one commentator "The Creation Story: Part Two."[5] Job the Gentile is the new Adam, and his story begins back in the well-cultivated land of Uz.

As a thought experiment, the book of Job revels in "What if?" questions about human integrity, divine intention, and the nature of the universe, all converging on (or more accurately crashing upon) the character of Job. What if the paragon of righteousness were to fall into unimaginable ruin and disgrace? What if piety were more than a matter of reward and blessing? What if righteousness invited vulnerability? What if God were no protector of the righteous? What if the world does not operate morally? What, then, is the shape of human integrity in such a world? What does it mean to "fear God" in a world devoid of retribution and filled with disaster? From the prologue to the climactic divine speeches and the epilogue, the book is filled with wonderings.

---

3. Both Uz and Eden are located vaguely in the east. There is disagreement among the biblical traditions as to whether Uz refers to a place south of Israel in Edom (Jer. 25:20; Lam. 4:21; Gen. 36:28) or to someplace northeast (Gen. 10:23; 22:21). See Balentine's suggestive comparison between Uz and Eden in *Job*, 41-44.

4. Oral communication with Matitiahu Tsevat at the SBL annual meeting, Kansas City, MO, November 1991.

5. Balentine, *Job*, 42.

The Crisis of Piety

Because Job lacks clear historical references, determining the book's background and dating is difficult.[6] The book's literary roots are found in "The Babylonian Theodicy,"[7] dated around 1000 BCE, and *Ludlul bēl nēmeqi* ("I Will Praise the Lord of Wisdom"), at least a couple of centuries earlier.[8] Although they serve to highlight Job's literary conventions and distinctions,[9] they do not shed much light on dating Job, at least in its final form. The figure of Job achieved legendary status by the sixth century BCE (Ezek. 14:14, 20), and the *book* of Job was likely codified sometime thereafter, when Israel's exile remained in full (re)view.[10]

Indeed, Job's misery on the ash heap could conceivably relate to Israel's misery as a result of Babylonian invasion and exile. His devastation could allude to Israel's desolation. Job is unmistakably deemed an outcast, suffering the trauma of displacement. Moreover, the drama of his displacement, from household head to ash heap squatter, leads to profound theological (and anthropological) dislocation. As Job regards himself as "a brother of jackals, and a companion of ostriches" (Job 30:29), so the book situates itself in a landscape devoid of ethical closure, or put positively, a land filled with demoralization.[11] But as will be discovered by Job and the reader in the final chapters, this landscape of exile is no lifeless terrain.

However, despite such imagined connections, Job is no representative of exiled Israel, symbolic or otherwise. His story is too individualized to be collectively interpreted and too universal to be restricted to Israel's plight.[12] As traditionally viewed, Job addresses the crisis of theodicy, of unmerited suffering in relation to God's supposed goodness and providence (see, e.g., 4:17; 10:15; 9:24; 10:1-22; 21:7-34). Relatedly and perhaps fundamentally, the book wrestles with the crisis of piety.[13] In the face of

---

6. See Schifferdecker, *Out of the Whirlwind,* 13-21.

7. For translations see *ANET,* 601-4; *BWL,* 63-91; *COS* 1.154.

8. For translations see *ANET,* 596-600; *BWL,* 21-56; *COS* 1.153.

9. "The Babylonian Theodicy" is particularly helpful from a genre-studies standpoint, given its dialogical form.

10. See Seow's arguments for dating Job in the late sixth to mid-fifth century based on literary parallels with Second Isaiah and Zech. 3:1-2, as well as the historical reference to the Chaldeans in Job 1:17 (*Commentary on Job 1–21,* 40-44).

11. See chapter 4 below and Tsevat, "Meaning of Job," esp. 102.

12. See the discussion in Morrow, *Protest against God,* 134-35.

13. Morrow casts the crisis broadly, both socially and intellectually, as part of a transcultural "Axial Age," in which the tension between the transcendent and mundane orders of

undeserved suffering and divine neglect, amid the moral breakdown of the world, what is the point of piety? The book of Job offers no explanation for suffering, even as it provocatively sets up the problem. But it does provide a new framework for reconsidering moral integrity, one that begins with posing a radical scenario and ends with a radical worldview that complexifies the notion of character, of piety. To borrow from the language of science and intellectual history, the book of Job marks a "paradigm shift,"[14] a shift that is facilitated, as we shall see, by the movement of wonder.

The Prologue: Testing Integrity

Job's story begins where Proverbs ends. The silent son of Proverbs has successfully secured his life within the community as head of a prosperous household in part because he has married well (Prov. 31:10-31). Job's story begins with the character profile of a successful patriarch whose household is abundantly prosperous. But, of course, there is one stark difference. The focus shifts from the supermatriarch of Proverbs to Job, the superpatriarch. Job's wife remains ever in the background except for the mere six words she pronounces (in Hebrew, Job 2:9) and becomes the object of Job's rebuke.[15]

At the very outset, Job's character is identified with four key traits: he is "blameless," is "upright," "fears God," and "avoids evil" (Job 1:1). Each trait is integrally related to the other, together forming a comprehensive, if superficial, profile of normative character. Nevertheless, the first and third descriptors, "blameless" *(tām)* and "fear" *(yr')* of God, take center stage throughout the narrative. "Blameless" denotes moral completeness or integrity. Integrity is more than a virtue; it is the operating system, one could say, in which all the virtues are nested and find their consonance, not unlike the way "prudence" functions in Aristotelian thought (see chapter

---

reality is heightened by the rise of "new social elites" (*Protest against God*, 135-36). In such a light, Job might represent the extreme of social elitism. In any case, Job is not representative of Everyman, "one of the great feats of eisegetical legerdemain in the history of biblical interpretation" (Cooper, "Sense of the Book," 231).

14. See Kuhn, *Structure of Scientific Revolutions*. Kuhn defines "paradigm" as "the entire constellation of beliefs, values, techniques, and so on shared by the members of a given community" (175). A paradigm is more than a conceptual system; it is a fundamental pattern of perception, explanation, and practice.

15. By comparison, the husband of the "woman of strength" pronounces eight words (Prov. 31:29).

1 above). Taken together, these virtues profile Job's character as above reproach; they present a thesis about Job that will soon be tested. But for the time being, everything around Job provides ostensible confirmation of his piety. His vast wealth and status as the "greatest of all the people of the east" provide material demonstration of his character (1:3). Job is the preeminent patriarch and paragon of piety,[16] both YHWH and the narrator agree. "There is no one like him on the earth . . . ," YHWH declares twice (1:8; 2:3a), echoing the narrator's initial assessment. In the honorable (and lucrative) business of righteousness, Job is a serious man.

With Job's character and conduct firmly established in the narrative, coupled with effusive divine approbation, the stage is clearly set for catastrophe. In the course of the prologue, two central questions are raised; their strategic placement highlights their critical importance to the narrative.

Question 1: "Fear of God"?

In response to YHWH's boast about Job, the satan or adversary,[17] whose job is to cast suspicion on the upright, introduces a test by which to assess Job's integrity: "Does Job fear God for nothing *(ḥinnām)?*" By raising the issue of disinterested piety or unconditional fidelity to God,[18] the satan cuts to the very heart of piety and in so doing accuses YHWH of having made it worth Job's while to behave in such an ethically credible manner. If the satan is right, then Job's character is less credible than it appears. Is Job's righteousness simply a means to divine blessing? Does Job have an ulterior motive behind his upright behavior? Perhaps his riches were gained by extortion. Perhaps Job's regular morning sacrifices are aimed to protect his honor as head of the household. Though the question posed in 1:9 could lead one to suspect Job's behavior, Job's accuser does not press the matter. Instead, the satan drags God into the picture by acknowledging that Job's character is intertwined with YHWH's. Suspicion ultimately falls upon God.

16. See Newsom, "Job," 133-34.

17. I avoid the common translation "Satan" here, since the Hebrew term *(haśśāṭān)* is not a proper name but rather a title and hence should not be identified with the archenemy of God found in apocalyptic and NT literature. In the prologue, this character functions as a roving, semi-independent prosecutor within the heavenly council under YHWH's charge. For a full discussion of the satan's place in Hebrew Scripture, see Day, *Adversary in Heaven*.

18. For a full discussion of the issue of "disinterested piety" in the book of Job, see Tsevat, "Meaning of Job."

The satan's accusation operates on two levels. On the one hand, if Job "fears God" *for something,* then his integrity is a facade. The question turns on whether Job's reverence has a telic twist, a taint of self-interest, and if so, then the uttered curse will surely displace the deference that has so far characterized Job's discourse, so the satan reasons. On the other hand, the satan's questioning of Job's integrity points an accusing finger at YHWH, Job's benefactor. Ironically, the satan accuses God of acting in a way that echoes Job's own behavior toward his children: an overprotection that shields them from all possible harm, preempting any degree of personal accountability. YHWH stands accused of two interrelated "crimes," according to this "inciter"[19] and bona fide member of the divine council: affording Job and his family special protection and effecting their prosperity. YHWH does not refute these charges. The question is whether YHWH's blessings have had a decisive hand in shaping Job's integrity, in motivating Job's fear of God. So YHWH consents to the satan's challenge. Let the tests begin.

Perhaps with a touch of voyeuristic guilt, the reader gets drawn into the narrative to see whether Job, when pressed beyond the limits of his endurance in the face of horrific suffering, will step out of character as the world around him seems precisely to have done. Job has unwittingly become the focus of an experiment of the most egregious kind, an experiment in suffering that holds an irresistible grip upon the reader, who, like God, guiltily wants to know the outcome. Will Job curse God now that his own world has become accursed? Will he disparage the God who tests him?[20] No way, claims the narrator. By enduring a progressively worsening series of divinely permitted disasters, Job succeeds in maintaining his "integrity" (*tummâ,* 2:9). As famously known in the New Testament and in pseudepigraphical literature,[21] Job proves himself enduring under the worst of circumstances by accepting his misfortunes with complete deference. Such is the way of integrity as profiled in the prologue. One who is *tām* or who has *tummâ* is one whose life is coherent and consistent in the ways he or she makes ethical choices within the life of the community.[22] While Proverbs focuses primarily on specific virtues, the book of Job begins with the issue of their internal coherence, specifically in light of Job's world now turned topsy-turvy.

19. See the wordplay in 2:3 with *śāṭān* and *wattĕsîtēnî* ("you incited me"). See Cooper, "Sense of the Book," 230.

20. See the definition of curse *(qll)* in Fox, "Job the Pious," 360-61 (including n. 18).

21. See Jas. 5:11 and the *Testament of Job* (*OTP* 1:829-58).

22. See Davis, "Job and Jacob," 205; cf. Newsom, "Job," 131.

In the prologue, Job keeps his integrity and therefore refuses to step out of character when he responds with uncompromising acceptance of his fate (1:21). Such acceptance also characterizes Job's response to his wife: one cannot receive the good without the bad and remain ethically competent (2:10). The narrator makes explicit the connection between Job's integrity and his discourse: "In all this Job did not sin or give offense[23] to God" (1:22); "In all this Job did not sin with his lips" (2:10). Thus the outcome of the test will be determined by what Job has to say about and to God.

As in proverbial wisdom, speech is revelatory of character. In Job's case, accusing/cursing God would irrevocably compromise Job's integrity. It is precisely this issue that dramatically contrasts the characters of the satan and Job. Job, the blameless one, would forsake his integrity if he were to assume the role of the satan by giving offense to God, by accusing God of wrongdoing. Perhaps that is the sole prerogative of this heavenly prosecutor. It is, however, clear that the satan is a foil for Job: Job adamantly refuses to do what the satan has done, namely accuse YHWH of moral indiscretion, specifically of partiality or playing favorites with humanity. On the one hand, the satan accuses God of granting Job *special privileges,* making it worth Job's while to act piously. On the other hand, if Job were to accuse God of anything, it would be for having singled him out for *special afflictions,* as he does in the poetic discharges that follow the prologue. Does God punish humans *for nothing?* Job could certainly ask with all justification (see 9:17). And to add insult to injury, Job suffers without knowledge, without any inkling that his suffering is the product of a divinely ordained test. Perhaps it is best that he does not know, so God may reason.[24] In any case, no complaint is heard from Job's lips, not even a mumbling word. Instead, his grip on integrity remains as firm as his character remains flat in the prologue.

Question 2: "Integrity"?

The question that Job's wife poses identifies another central concern of the prologue and, as it turns out, the book as a whole, namely Job's integrity. In

---

23. Heb. *nātan tiplâ* (for the latter term, see Jer. 23:13; Job 24:12). For the range of possibilities, see Seow, *Commentary on Job 1–21*, 282-83. I suspect that, along with Seow, the ambiguous phrase can refer to both "ascribing an offense to God" and "offending God."

24. As Geeraerts argues, God is too embarrassed to tell Job ("Caught in a Web").

the history of tradition, Job's wife is given short shrift.[25] Within the book, she has no name, and no mention is made of her in the epilogue. Nevertheless, what she says to the biblical Job strikes at the very heart of the matter. In 1:21 Job has anticipated death and blessed YHWH's name. Job's wife now asks the question, "Are you still holding fast to your integrity?" followed immediately by her infamous advice: "bless God and die" (2:9).[26] Her words echo both the satan's prediction in 2:5 and God's confidence in 2:3.[27] Both blessing and cursing, moreover, find common ground in the prospect of death. The blessing in 1:21 indicates Job's full acceptance of what he expects to be an imminent death; the curse is meant to quicken and ensure death's realization. The way in which Job's wife casts the issue is significant. Does she exhort Job to step out of character, to let go of (i.e., compromise) his integrity by cursing God? Or does she plead for Job to curse God in consonance with his integrity? Her observation[28] that Job still retains his integrity is taken verbatim from the divine proclamation in 2:3b. To put it another way, the question is whether her observation is meant to be an approval or an indictment. If the latter, then Job's wife is clearly admonishing Job to give up his integrity and curse God to ensure a quick death. If the former, then she highlights aspects of integrity that can in fact provide warrant for Job to curse God, namely his courage and uncompromising honesty.[29] Is she saying to Job, "Your integrity be damned!"

25. See, e.g., the *Testament of Job* (*OTP* 1:829-58) and Garrett, "Weaker Sex." For both negative and alternative traditions in literature and art, see Seow, "Job's Wife."

26. "Bless" is likely used euphemistically here for "curse," as in the satan's discourse, although the reason remains unclear. The language of curse is evidently barred from the tale of Job's travail, perhaps in part to emphasize Job's "hyperscrupulous character" (Newsom, *Book of Job*, 55). Although this does not explain the wife's use of the euphemism, Job clearly takes the wife's advice as a euphemism for "curse." For an alternative view, see Cooper, "Sense of the Book ," 133, who takes "bless" literally as a petition for the "blessing of death." See also Seow, "Job's Wife," 371-73.

27. Seow, "Job's Wife," 372.

28. It is not clear whether she is asking a question or stating a simple fact, since the interrogative particle is absent from the Hebrew.

29. See Moore's discussion of Job's integrity in the poetry ("Integrity of Job"). Newsom has sharpened the issue by locating the ambiguity in the wife's question ("Job," 132). My reading suggests that the prologue by itself claims the wife's statement as an admonishment and not an exhortation for Job to muster his integrity. However, the dialogues that follow reconstrue the wife's advice in favor of the latter interpretation. Here is a case among many cases in Job whereby the prologue and the epilogue take on a different nuance through their juxtaposition to the poetry (see Newsom, *Book of Job*, 37).

or "Be true to your integrity!"? Ambiguity reigns, and the reader is left to ponder and negotiate.[30]

Job, however, has no need to negotiate: he immediately regards his wife's advice as an admonishment to compromise his integrity, warranting immediate rejection. Job again claims that unconditional acceptance of his fate, be it death or suffering subsistence, must be the crowning mark of his integrity. Overcome by grief, Job stands ready to accept his death, even welcome it, but not at the expense of his integrity. Death must come while his integrity remains intact. Yet the narrator has made it all too clear that such a scenario will not work. On the heavenly plane, the divine stipulation limiting the satan's commission is a restraining order against outright murder. On the earthly plane, Job's reliance on his integrity also precludes death. But survival may be more bane than blessing in such a time as this. Thanks to Job's wife, the relationship between integrity, curse, and death remains moot.

So Job lingers on. Either by sanction from above or by integrity from below, death does not come to release Job from his misery. What does come, however, are three friends, whose mission is to "console and comfort him" (*lānûd lô ûlĕnaḥămô*, 2:11). Beginning with silence, this trio sets the stage for the rest of the discourse that follows. Their very presence raises an interesting question: If Job is so accepting of his fate, regardless of the outcome, and remains ever willing to bless YHWH, does he actually need consolation? Job has just rebuked his wife, and in so doing, rejected death as the final solution. But reliance upon his integrity cannot nullify his sense of loss and agony. If release from life is not the resolution for Job, then what is the shape of consolation? Enter Job's friends.

In summary, the prologue masterfully sets the stage for all that follows by way of high drama and probing questions.[31] It presents Job as a flat, one-note wonder of embodied wisdom in the face of horrific circumstances. It powerfully conveys traditional values and their broad appeal in extremis, values that will, however, become a source of contention once the reader ventures into the tension-filled discourse that begins in ch. 3. The prologue raises two questions of utmost importance to the book of Job: "Does Job fear

---

30. Newsom, "Book of Job," 346.

31. In a now classic essay, Clines appropriately claims that the prologue is "a well wrought narrative that plunges directly into issues of substance that reach as deep as the fraught dialogues themselves" ("False Naivety," 127). I disagree, however, that the prologue's "naivety" is a guise meant to subvert the prologue and provoke a misreading (see pp. 127-28). Rather, the prologue is a "surprisingly philosophical tale," guise or no guise (Newsom, *Book of Job,* 56).

God for nothing?" and "Do you still hold fast to your integrity?" In these two questions lie the book's two central, interrelated foci: "fear" and "integrity," both of which become reoriented in the poetic discourse that follows.

The Character of God in the Prologue

One troubling element that has provoked concern among readers, and rightfully so, is the way God is depicted in the prologue. How could God allow Job to suffer so? Norman Habel describes this God as a "jealous king, who is apparently willing to violate human life to gratify personal ends."[32] The prologue's characterization of God is, however, more nuanced. YHWH is introduced at the outset as the head of the divine council in typical ancient Near Eastern style.[33] The image of the council indicates a distribution of power to heavenly subordinates, including the satan. In both conversations with the accuser, YHWH hands Job and all that he has over to the satan's power with certain restrictions. The royal image Habel uses to describe God is appropriate, but the charge of petty jealousy not so quite.

YHWH initiates the conversation with the satan by boasting of Job, God's beloved servant. Like a patriarch boasting of his children, God takes pride in Job. By repeating the narrator's description in 1:1, YHWH is appropriately effusive. The sharp response from the satan, however, throws the Deity's praise into question, casting doubt on Job's credibility. When YHWH accepts the satan's challenge, expressed in the form of an oath or self-curse,[34] it is out of neither jealousy nor doubt but confidence that Job is worthy of divine admiration and praise.[35]

---

32. Habel, "In Defense of God," 26.

33. For the rich Canaanite background of the divine assembly as family, see Smith, "Divine Family."

34. The use of the oath formula 'im-lōʾ in 1:11b, as well as in 2:5b, indicates that the satan has put his reputation on the line in the form of a self-imprecation. Perhaps the best translation of the satan's statement is the one offered by Clines: "I'll be damned if he doesn't curse you to your face" (*Job 1–20*, 26). That the satan appears nowhere in the epilogue suggests that the self-curse has been fulfilled. See Good, "Job and the Literary Task," 475; and Day, *Adversary in Heaven*, 81 n. 30.

35. The other possibility is that YHWH simply does not know whether Job's reverence toward God can hold up under such suffering, and so is interested in the outcome as much as the satan is (so Fox, "Job the Pious," 361-62). I take YHWH's boast to be rooted in unwavering confidence, even in the face of the satan's "incitement." YHWH's rationale for such a test is not to seek knowledge about Job but to find objective demonstration and hence vindication.

The description of God as tester is common throughout the Hebrew Scriptures. God, for example, tests Abraham's obedience in the *Akedah* story of Gen. 22.[36] Particularly relevant is Ps. 26, a lament in which the speaker petitions God to test his "heart and mind" in order to vindicate him (26:2). The speaker testifies to his integrity at the outset as well as at the conclusion of the psalm (v. 11): "Vindicate me, YHWH, for I have walked in my integrity" (26:1). For the psalmist, integrity involves unwavering trust (26:1b), truth (v. 3b), dissociation from the wicked (vv. 4, 5), innocence (v. 6), and praise (vv. 7, 8, 12), all behaviors and traits that constitute estimable character. Relying upon God's benevolence (*ḥesed*, v. 3), the psalmist is confident that God will vindicate him. In the case of Job, however, it is not out of Job's need that the test is given but out of YHWH's. Job has no need for vindication,[37] but YHWH apparently does in response to the satan's suspicions concerning Job's (and YHWH's) integrity.

In the second conversation, YHWH expresses confidence in Job, now seemingly confirmed in his integrity, as well as regret for having allowed the satan to "swallow" Job (2:3). The language smacks of sarcasm, for YHWH turns the satan's words against him: "You have incited me against him, to destroy him *for nothing*" (cf. 1:9). While boasting that the test has proved Job, YHWH laments that it has done irreparable damage to Job. YHWH's meager protest gives voice to the theological dilemma of divine testing. The test's rationale is pushed to an absurd extreme in the acknowledgment that the means has outweighed the end. This act of vindication has backfired, nearly destroying the defendant in the process.

More than a flat, petty deity, YHWH exhibits a degree of inner turmoil no less poignant than the regret described in the Deity's decision to flood the earth in Genesis: "YHWH was sorry that he had made humankind on the earth, and it grieved him to his heart" (Gen. 6:6). These two regrets mirror each other. Owing to pervasive wickedness among human beings, YHWH regrets having created life and painfully arrives at the decision to destroy it. The God of the Joban prologue, on the other hand,

---

36. God tests Israel's obedience in Exod. 15:25b-26; 16:4. In Exod. 20:20 Moses assures the people that the fearsome theophany at Mt. Sinai serves only to test rather than to destroy. Deuteronomy locates the time of testing in the wilderness period: God tests to discern Israel's heart and whether the commandments will be followed, in short, to determine whether Israel truly loves YHWH (Deut. 8:2; 13:4 [Eng. 3]). Similarly, Hezekiah is tested so that God can determine "all that was in his heart" (2 Chron. 32:31).

37. It is only after the test that Job finds the need for vindication, which leads him to call God to court (see below).

regrets the destruction wrought upon his servant Job, owing to Job's unassailable righteousness. Both accounts depict a remorseful God. Unfortunately for Job, however, the story does not end there. The purveyor of suspicion is not satisfied and thus raises the stakes. Once again, YHWH's desire for vindication silences the voice of compassion. YHWH's very ability to judge character is at stake, thus also YHWH's impartiality. The irony runs deep: in order for God to remain impartial regarding Job's integrity, Job must be selected for *special* suffering. Such is the dilemma of testing.

YHWH's consent results in further suffering for Job, which in turn drives the remainder of the plot, beginning with the wife's leading question and the friends' mission of consolation. Had the narrator intended to portray the Deity as one who acted willy-nilly or callously, there would have been no need to bring in this second conversation between YHWH and the satan. Rather, permission would simply have been granted to the satan to tighten the circle of disaster up to Job's very life at the outset. Consequently, it is this second conversation that is the most revealing of YHWH's character in the prologue: a God who, although confident in Job's integrity, struggles with the business of testing, who bears the tension between compassion and the desire for vindication even at Job's expense. It is both God's boast and protest that betray a glimpse of the divine character as the struggling Tester, but a glimpse is all it is. In the consuming desire for vindication, YHWH's character has become callous, serving as a foil for Job, as will become clear in the dialogues that follow.[38] At the end of this didactic tale, the reader is left to struggle with this flawed character of a Deity until the concluding theophany, whereby YHWH is revealed to be of a different character altogether. But in the meantime, much more remains to be said about Job.

The Poetic Discourse: Integrity Reprofiled

Job's character unites the prose and poetry of his story as well as provides for the story's primary tension.[39] From ch. 3 onward, the reader encounters a drastically different Job from the one profiled in the prologue. Job is

---

38. But, as will be seen, an ironic bond is formed between the God of the prologue and Job of the poetry, because Job too will be consumed by the need for personal vindication, seemingly at God's expense.

39. As Moore points out, the center of the tension between the prose and poetry is Job ("Integrity of Job," 21). See also Westermann, "Two Faces of Job," 15-22; Sternberg, *Poetics of Biblical Narrative,* 345-46. The same could also be said of God.

no longer the object of an experiment to satisfy the reader's curiosity and YHWH's vindication, no longer a stock character who stoically accepts what God has allotted him. From here on out, Job becomes enfleshed with pathos and complexity. Here the reader gains something of Job's subjectivity: his words from the heart, his pathos starkly revealed, his inner life exposed by adversity. As Job's character develops, culminating in his final testimony and oath (chs. 29–31), so sympathy for Job is cultivated. The reader becomes drawn into him, even while knowing what Job does not. In the dialogues, the reader's center of gravity shifts from outside to inside, brought in part by the shift from prose to poetry.

What holds Job's prose and poetic characterizations together, contrastive as they are, is Job's consistent appeal to his integrity (27:6). In the poetry, Job's integrity is never jettisoned; it is reformulated as the patient endurance that so characterized him in the prologue becomes overturned.[40] Job the silent has become Job the verbose, full of bitter complaints. Indeed, the verbal excess with which Job complains gives expression to what is essentially unspeakable in the prose. It is no coincidence, then, that the *Testament of Job,* a rewriting of the biblical story, largely passes over Job's outbursts against God and the friends, preferring rather the unambiguous portrait of Job presented in the prologue.[41] Yet enmeshed in the unorthodox words of his poetic discourse, the biblical Job is somehow able to lay claim to his integrity, an integrity that is defamed by his friends, deconstructed by the poet, and ultimately transformed by YHWH.

Job's Birthday Curse

> Job did not sin with his lips, but he did sin in his heart.
>
> *Babylonian Talmud, Baba Batra 16a*

> In all of this he did not sin with his lips, but in his thoughts he was readying a protest.
>
> *Aramaic Targum of Job*[42]

---

40. Moore, "Integrity of Job," 31.
41. Baskin, "Rabbinic Interpretations of Job," 104.
42. At the end of Job 2:10, quoted in Cooper, "Sense of the Book," 233.

The first red flag regarding Job's character is raised even before Job utters his first word in ch. 3. The narrator marks the following discourse as Job's birthday "curse" (*qll*, 3:1). No euphemism here. While Job had rejected the curse as an appropriate response to his suffering, now his lips are filled with it.

Since Job's initial speech lays the groundwork for almost forty chapters' worth of talk, it is helpful to treat Job's curse in ch. 3 in some detail. The thick network of metaphors sets in relief the two themes of life and death. With death are associated the cosmological images of impenetrable darkness, gloom, cloud, sea, night, and the underworld. Together they represent the powers of chaos invoked by Job to overcome the light of his life. By calling for a reversal of creation, Job curses not only a particular day on the calendar, his birthday, but by extension all creation, signified by light, the first act of creation in Genesis. Job cannot but help perceive the world through the prism of his tormented life. His curse begins with a structural and theological antithesis to Genesis.[43] "Let that day be darkness!" (Job 3:4a), as opposed to "Let there be light" (Gen. 1:3). Moreover, the reference to the seven days during which Job's friends remain silent (Job 2:13) may also be a counterecho to the Priestly creation account, in which creation is brought about by divine speech (Gen. 1:1-31).

Job's lament is a veritable assault on creation.[44] He curses his birth and, by extension, all the world. As the inception of Job's life functions *pars pro toto* for the moment of cosmic creation, so his desired death becomes a metonym for creation's demise. Although Job has not cursed God directly, his self-curse is only a technical distinction, for God is invoked by Job in his curse. Job commands God not to seek the day, since it is to be overcome by darkness (3:4). Such darkness stands at odds with God's creative purposes. Furthermore, Job accuses God of having "fenced" him in (v. 23). The identical expression is found in 1:10, in which the satan accuses YHWH of protecting Job at the expense of his character. From Job's mouth, however, a much different accusation is leveled. God has not only hidden Job's "way"; the Deity has made it inaccessible to him. Job is kept in the dark. The "way" *(derek)*, as noted in Proverbs, is a root metaphor for wise conduct and character. Job complains that God has blocked all access to wisdom, and thus all means of sustaining integrity. All in all, by cursing his life and creation, Job's character teeters on the edge of collapse, and God seems ready to give it a final push.

---

43. E.g., Habel, *Book of Job*, 104; Perdue, *Wisdom in Revolt*, 97-98.
44. Perdue, "Job's Assault on Creation."

In Job's curse, death is cloaked in positive images, highlighting Job's desire to find permanent rest even at the expense of creation. Job desires the womb as his tomb (3:10-11, 16; cf. Gen. 3:19b). The rest that Job seeks through death is cast in terms of communion with the dead, both great and small (Job 3:18-19). Job sees himself in solidarity with those who long for death (3:21-22). Death offers a radical reconfiguration of social relations for Job. Bereft of family, Job now looks through the threshold of death toward a new, all-inclusive community.

Job is ready to join the democracy of the dead, where the "agitation" *(rōgez)*[45] of the wicked ceases (3:17). But right now "agitation" has come to disturb Job's longed-for peace:

> I am not at ease, and I am not quiet;
> I cannot find rest, for "agitation" has arrived. (3:26)

Job dreads *rōgez*. The term has been taken to refer either to Job's personal agony[46] or to divine wrath.[47] Its scope is wide-ranging. As Newsom aptly states, "*Rōgez* is to the order of lived experience as chaos is to cosmic order."[48] *Rōgez* comes in many forms, but its effects include a quivering collapse of order, a shaking of the foundations, whether personal or cosmic. Job's personal "agitation" mirrors the world's turmoil, viewed through the prism of his calamity. Rest is now mere wishful thinking, an impossible possibility. The immediate context includes an added focus. In 3:17 *rōgez* is connected with the disquieting behavior of the wicked. In the prologue, what "has arrived" are Job's three friends (2:11b), who are now poised to offer their "condolences" after seven days of mournful silence that would have acknowledged Job as already dead.[49] Job's final words in his lament anticipate the verbal onslaught he is about to suffer from his friends. Whereas Job fervently seeks the solitude necessary for him to die and thereby find rest, Job's friends rudely stand (or more accurately "sit") in the way. The peaceful communion

---

45. The nominal (participial) form *rōgez* in 3:17 finds its antithesis in the parallel colon in the verb "to rest" *(nwḥ)* and likely includes the rantings of the wicked (cf. Gen. 45:24), a common stereotype of the wicked in biblical and Egyptian wisdom literature (cf. Job 37:2). In death the wicked are quieted.

46. So Habel, *Book of Job*, 112; Pope, *Job*, 33.

47. So Perdue, *Wisdom in Revolt*, 94.

48. Newsom, *Book of Job*, 94.

49. Clines, *Job 1–20*, 64.

for which Job yearns among the dead is about to be displaced by strife among the living.

Job is the lament made flesh. His words undermine the confident assessment of his stoic character profiled in the prologue. Instead of the patriarch of patient endurance, Job is filled with angst and is determined to make a quick end of it by cursing his life — a variant of his wife's advice! — and in so doing drag all creation down with him. With a masterful control of rhetoric, Job reverses the images of life and death as he rejects what little is left of his own life. Unconditional acceptance is replaced by bitter complaint. Job's lament begins to give credence to the satan's charges. Indeed, the next step for Job would be to curse God and end it all. But, for better or worse, his friends interrupt Job's inexorable slide into oblivion, the comfort he seeks, by offering their own "consolations."

Clash of the Sages

In the dialogues that follow, Job is among peers in a debate first and foremost over his character, and by extension over the moral coherence of the world. Any formal hierarchy typical of the pedagogy of proverbial wisdom is lacking. Gone are the categories of teacher and pupil, parent and child. Now only the teachers, the sages, have their say among themselves. Job is a peer among peers; his friends come to a level playing field. Nevertheless, the rebukes reciprocated between Job and his friends do not elicit much collegial appreciation (cf. Prov. 9:8-9). Unlike the silent son, Job is not reluctant to talk back. Despite the *apparent* collegial relationship between Job and his friends, much of the mounting tension is rooted in the friends' strained attempts to press the dynamics of collegial discourse back into the hierarchical mode of wisdom teaching, which Job regards as a pedagogy for the oppressed. At one point Job taunts his friends in their attempts to force him into the role of student: "Teach me, and I will be silent; make me understand how I have gone wrong" (Job 6:24).

So Job's friends, ignoring the sarcasm, attempt to teach him. Praise of proverbial wisdom is most pronounced in Bildad's speeches. His appeal to the unbroken chain of inherited tradition presents the classic testimony to the veracity of sapiential tradition:

> Inquire now of former generations,
>   and consider what their ancestors have discerned. . . .

> Will they not teach you and tell you
> and utter words out of their understanding? (8:8, 10)

Bildad urges Job to hearken to the univocal voice of the past, the vehicle of traditional wisdom.[50] As the parental figure in Proverbs imparts the wisdom of his own father (Prov. 4), the past generations — the *'ābôt* — are given unanimous voice demanding assent from the inquiring heart.

Intermixed with such appeals to tradition is the language of character. In Job 4:6 Eliphaz appeals to an essential incompatibility between integrity and the impatience exhibited by Job in his lament. Impatience, according to Eliphaz, constitutes a character flaw for a master teacher and comforter like Job. You have instructed and supported others in the past, so reasons Eliphaz, but now your situation has forced you to reverse character. Eliphaz presses further by raising up for the first time the issue of guilt and innocence (4:7), setting the direction for the remainder of the dialogue.

Eliphaz's "comfort" is both a subtle indictment and an attempt to diffuse the issue of just desert. The upright and the innocent are not cut off (4:7), but all mortals are unrighteous before God (4:14-21; 5:7), an insight Eliphaz received by nocturnal revelation. His argument then turns to an appeal for Job to seek God, who saves the needy and the poor as well as thwarts the wise in their craftiness (5:8-16). Which category of character has been reserved for Job is left open or is altogether evaded by Eliphaz, particularly given his brief treatise on the necessity of divine discipline in vv. 17-18. The demarcation between victim and wrongdoer with respect to Job is deliberately blurred by Eliphaz. Yet any insinuation against Job's character is in Eliphaz's mind outweighed by the prospect of Job's restoration (vv. 19-27). Job needs only to accept his condition as a matter of divine discipline. Eliphaz's "collegial" rebuke, meant to evoke from Job a response of grateful consideration, is an exemplar of sagacious discourse.

The dialogic exchanges between Job and his friends, however, degenerate from there. Job is forced to defend his integrity as his "friends" resort to accusations. From the friends' perspective, recourse to blaming is a legitimate mode of instruction. Job's defense is that such blame is egregiously miscast. The most strident example of the slippery relation between instruction and blame is found in Eliphaz's second speech in ch.

---

50. See Crenshaw's discussion of the three major rhetorical strategies present in wisdom literature: ethos, pathos, and logos ("Wisdom and Authority").

15. Eliphaz denounces Job's "windy knowledge" (15:2) and accuses him of undermining the "fear of God" in v. 4, attributing Job's subversive speech to moral failure (v. 5). Rather than a student of wisdom, Job has become a disciple of iniquity.

The friends find Job's defense a matter of arrogant pretension and condescension. Bildad is particularly offended: "Why are we counted as cattle [by you]? Why are we stupid in your sight?" (18:3). In addition, Eliphaz sarcastically asks Job: "Are you the firstborn of the human race? Were you brought forth before the hills? . . . Do you limit wisdom to yourself?" (15:7-8). The implication is that Job has identified himself with ageless Wisdom, the height of arrogance and tantamount to sapiential blasphemy. The severity of Eliphaz's charge responds to Job's refusal to assume a subordinate position in the sapiential hierarchy (13:2).

And so the "dialogue" is anything but collegial. The friends condescendingly try to force Job back into the role of the silent son, the unquestioning recipient of wisdom. Job needs to be reeducated, and the first step is for him to acknowledge his inferior status before his "consoling" colleagues. By invoking wisdom's pedagogy of the simpleton, Eliphaz compels Job to regress back to his childhood to relearn the values of traditional wisdom. In his state of *rōgez,* Job needs to hit the "reset" button on his character, Eliphaz insists, or in Newsom's words, return to a "sense of narrative."[51]

Job refuses: "No doubt you are the people, / and wisdom will perish with you. / But I have understanding as well as you; I am not inferior to you" (12:2-3; see also 13:2). Job questions their pedagogical foundation: "Is wisdom with the aged, / and understanding in length of days?" (12:12). Age and wisdom need not intersect. Moreover, long life and prosperity, wisdom's by-products, seem equally available to the wicked as to the wise: "Why do the wicked live on, reach old age, and grow mighty in power?" (21:7). The distinctions so firmly established in proverbial wisdom between the righteous and the wicked can either reverse themselves, a case of moral inversion, or merge indistinguishably (9:22).

Eliphaz presents the most blistering attack on Job's integrity in ch. 22. He accuses Job of inhumane treatment of his family and of those marginalized by society (vv. 6-11). But more grievous are the theological offenses: Eliphaz blasts Job for claiming that God is limited in knowledge (vv. 13-14) and, in a masterful twist of words, accuses Job of mimicking the discourse of the wicked: "They said to God, 'Leave us alone,' / and 'What can the

---

51. Newsom, *Book of Job,* 101.

Almighty do to us?'" (v. 17a).[52] Eliphaz's portrayal of the wicked is characterized by an attitude of confident defiance against God. The irony lies in that Job has uttered similar words (7:16a, 19b; 10:20b). Whereas Eliphaz reads the demand of the wicked to be "left alone" by God as a mark of defiance and a move toward impunity, Job's own words are nothing more than desperate pleas for respite from suffering.[53]

From Job's perspective, the friends have sorely failed in their responsibility to comfort him in his pain. He accuses them of treachery (6:15), of withholding kindness (v. 14a), of forsaking the "fear of Shadday" (v. 14b), and of abandoning him in his moment of need (vv. 17-18). Such accusations smack of betrayal, motivated by greed: "You would even cast lots over the orphan, / and bargain over your friend" (6:27). Equally damning is Job's charge that his condition has put his friends to shame and even inspired fear (6:20-21). Job perceives cowardliness behind his friends' vehemence. Job's observation in effect answers the question he poses in 16:3b: "What afflicts you to argue (as such)?" The answer is fear of the anomaly, of the moral dissonance Job's case provokes before their eyes. Job had hoped to receive encouragement and consolation (16:5). Instead, he is received by his friends as a hideous incongruity, a veritable monster in their midst. Job must be tamed, reshackled to sapiential tradition.

The anomaly that is Job requires a fundamental change in the cultural framework in which wisdom has customarily had its home. In defending his character, Job refuses to be the listening heart, refuses to accept reproof, despite the urgings and protestations of his friends. Job accuses his friends of betrayal while his friends see themselves as instructive (15:11). In their eyes, both Job's situation and his character are horrendously out of sync; they do not fit any schema of moral or theological coherence the friends know. Job's protestations of innocence cannot be tolerated in light of his suffering condition. Hence the friends' language becomes increasingly strident: Job is accused of blasphemy and of seeking the collapse of the cosmic order (e.g., 15:4, 13; 22:13-14, 17). As Bildad pointedly asks: "You who tear yourself in your anger — / shall the earth be forsaken because of you, / or the rock be removed out of its place?" (18:4). While echoing Job's lament

---

52. Reading with the LXX and Syriac. The MT casts the object in the third person (*lāmô*).

53. Any common ground between Job and the wicked is, however, erased in the second colon of Eliphaz's accusation (22:17b). Nowhere does Job entertain the possibility that God is *not* in control over his livelihood. Quite the opposite: Job accuses God of having singled him out for unwarranted abuse (see below).

in ch. 3, Bildad's reference to cosmic disruption is rooted in the moral inversion Job himself represents. Job is a threat to both himself and the world order. To the friends, it is Job who is the source of *rōgez*. To Job, it is God.[54]

The friends' assessment of Job as a monstrous threat to moral coherence is also shared by his family and closest friends. With his patriarchal position undermined (19:13-17), young children despise him (v. 18) and youth "make sport" *(śḥq)* of him (30:1). In surely one of his most poignant protests, Job laments:

> [God] has alienated[55] my family from me,
>   and my acquaintances are wholly *estranged (zārû)* from me.
> My relatives and close friends have ceased to be (for me);
>   the guests in my house have forgotten me;
> my serving girls have reckoned me a *stranger (zār);*
>   I have become an *alien (nokrî)* in their eyes. . . .
> My own breath is *strange (zārâ)* to my wife;
>   I am loathsome to the children of my belly. (19:13-15, 17)

It is significant that the words for "alien" and "strange," found also in Prov. 1–9 with reference to the "strange woman" (2:16; 5:20; 7:5), are employed here to refer to Job himself in relation to his household. Abhorred as a "stranger" and "alien" by his own family and closest friends, Job is the subject of social stigmatization of a magnitude matched only by the harsh rhetoric that targets the feminine outsider profiled in Prov. 1–9.[56] Even his breath has become "strange" *(zārâ)*. Job has become an object of fear and revulsion. Thus it is perhaps with whispers of agreement or the slight of nodding heads from his friends that Job plaintively cries out to God: "Am I the Sea, or the Dragon, / that you set a guard over me?" (Job 7:12). Is Job a moral monster before God and his community? Like the God who prescribes bounds for the sea, Job's friends feel compelled to contain his damaging discourse at all cost. To them, Job's words, uttered from his disease-stricken body, threaten to shatter their sense of moral and cosmic coherence. Job is the purveyor of chaos.[57]

---

54. See, e.g., chs. 12, 16, and 19, in which God is depicted as an indiscriminately destructive force in the world.

55. Lit. "distanced, separated" *(hirḥîq)*.

56. See chapter 2 above.

57. Indeed, the chaos invoked by Job in ch. 3 resonates with the chaos Job's friends perceive vis-à-vis his character.

Under three things the earth convulses;
   under four it cannot bear up:
a slave becoming king,
   a fool glutted with food;
an unloved woman getting a husband,
   a female slave succeeding her mistress. (Prov. 30:21-23)

To which Job's friends would add a fifth: "and a suffering sinner protesting his innocence."

Wisdom's Inaccessibility?

As the dialogue runs itself into the ground, another voice intervenes, intoning the evocative wisdom poem in ch. 28.[58] Following Job's jumbled discourse,[59] this intricately crafted poem conveys an entirely different tone by suspending itself above the fray of heated debate. The poem begins with a pronouncement concerning the existence of a "source" *(môṣāʾ)*[60] or "place" *(māqôm)* for precious metals and then proceeds to describe the daring enterprise of exploration in the guise of mining (vv. 2-11).[61] Such activity is appropriately described with verbs denoting perception (vv. 3, 7, 10b, 11), construction (vv. 4a, 9, 10a), and extraction (v. 2). The imagery in vv. 7-8 takes a detour with reference to the unknown path, suggesting that something more than mining activity is meant. Indeed, there is something

---

58. Its closest parallels can be found in Prov. 8; Sir. 1; 24; and Bar. 3:9–4:4. For discussion see Newsom, *Book of Job*, 172-74, who identifies the genre as a "speculative wisdom poem."

59. The lack of a heading for ch. 28 suggests that the chapter either belongs to Job or is simply left unattributed. I opt for the latter, given the markedly different tone and perspective it offers. Jones contends that the poem belongs to Job and serves as a critique of his friends (*Rumors of Wisdom*, 103). However, the poem can just as well serve as a critique of Job's own claim to possess wisdom over and against his friends (see, e.g., 12:3, 11-12; 13:2; cf. 15:7-8). Greenstein argues that Job 28 is a dislocated section of Elihu's discourse in 32:6–37:24 ("Poem on Wisdom"). See also Clines, who independently argues the same thesis, in "Fear of the Lord," esp. 78-85. That may very well be; nevertheless, I would argue that its (dis)location was by no means accidental.

60. Lit. "a place to go out." For detailed linguistic analysis and discussion of the worth of the precious metals listed in this poem, see van Wolde, "Wisdom, Who Can Find It?" 3-22.

61. Jones argues that the theme of exploration in the poem is akin to the exploits of Mesopotamian kings, particularly Gilgamesh, rather than to mining specifically (*Rumors of Wisdom*, 31-62).

more, for the poem abruptly redirects its focus in v. 12 by posing the question of wisdom's location. The rugged geological landscape of precious metals gives way to the hidden topography of wisdom's domain. Human beings, even the most diligent and daring of inquirers, indeed all living things (vv. 7-8, 13, 21), know not the place of priceless wisdom.[62] Only God knows (vv. 23-27).

As a "parabolic subversion of the trope of the search for wisdom,"[63] Job 28 serves as a "veiled judgment" on the preceding dialogues.[64] The cycles of discourse that seem to go nowhere between Job and his friends illustrate well the poet's point that despite its inestimable worth wisdom remains unreachable. Wisdom in Job 28 is as hidden as proverbial wisdom is openly accessible. The poet arouses the reader's desire for wisdom by casting wisdom as invaluable (28:15-19; cf. Prov. 3:13-15) and as the object of heroic and arduous exploration (Job 28:3-11; cf. Prov. 25:2), only to frustrate such desire by placing wisdom utterly out of reach.[65] Compare Prov. 2:4-5:

> If you seek [wisdom] like silver,
>   and search for it as for hidden treasures,
> then you will discern the fear of YHWH
>   and find the knowledge of God.

However, the point of Job 28 thus far is that wisdom can *not* be sought like "silver" and "hidden treasures." In the eyes of the Joban poet, wisdom is of a different order; it is transcendentalized to the point of being made unattainable to human probing and possession. Wisdom, it turns out, is not an object of human extraction but the object and subject of divine ordering at creation (28:23-27).

In light of its strategic placement in the larger narrative, the poem highlights the failed attempts on the part of both Job and his friends to make sense of his suffering. On the one hand, the friends espouse ad nauseam an inadequate model of wisdom that obfuscates rather than illuminates Job's situation. "See, we have investigated this; it is true. Hear and

---

62. Greenstein argues that God is the subject of vv. 3-11 ("Poem on Wisdom," 267-69), and indeed that is possible with the verbs featured in this section. However, what God has to do with finding precious metals is left unexplained. See the balanced discussion in Crenshaw, *Reading Job*, 122-25.

63. Jones, *Rumors of Wisdom*, 242 (drawing from Newsom's work).

64. So Habel, *Book of Job*, 392. See also Sawyer, "Authorship and Structure," 255.

65. See also Newsom, "Dialogue and Allegorical Hermeneutics," 303; idem, *Book of Job*, 179-80.

know it for yourself," declares Eliphaz (5:27). As a result, Job complains that they "seek out . . . and search" for his iniquity but to no avail (10:6-7). Job, on the other hand, is incapable of giving account of his predicament, theologically or otherwise. Any admission of failure on his part is precluded by his caustic attacks against his friends and God — certainly not the model of sagacity. As Alan Cooper aptly states: "If Job represents virtue without wisdom, then surely his friends represent 'wisdom' — in quotation marks — without virtue."[66] And that may very well be the point of v. 28.

The last line of the poem is a surprising conclusion in light of the previous material. It is as if wisdom, deemed inaccessible to human reach, now returns through the back door in the form of embodied piety. But so be it. Job 28:28 identifies the one point of "access" to available wisdom as a posture of awe before God and dissociation from evil. Such a motto-like statement both echoes the proverbial sense of fear as the epistemological beginning point of wisdom (e.g., Prov. 1:7; 9:10) and recalls more immediately the "fear" embodied by Job in the prologue (Job 1:1, 8; 2:3). In Job 28, however, such virtuous "fear" is deemed the inevitable outcome of discovering wisdom's inaccessibility to probing and possession. The Joban poet thus tweaks Prov. 2:4-5, quoted above, to read: when you *fail* to "seek wisdom like silver and search for it as hidden treasures, then you will understand the fear of YHWH." Without wisdom as an object of search and extraction, what is left for human beings is reverential "fear" — that is true wisdom. "The fear of the Lord" is thus the alpha *and* omega of wisdom, a posture of awe and the embodiment of virtue *coram Deo*.[67] In the end (and at the end of the poem), appropriating wisdom is not about excising knowledge and insight but about exercising piety and virtue, a matter of "moral creation."[68]

The divine proclamation in v. 28 introduces a new dimension to the model of wisdom. Wisdom, unfathomable intellectually, becomes embodied in humility, in "fear." Unreachable wisdom thus does not sever its ties from conduct and character. To the contrary, appropriating wisdom involves acknowledging, fully and freely, human limitation and ignorance,

---

66. Cooper, "Sense of the Book," 237.

67. Jones likens such "fear" to "numinous dread" (*Rumors of Wisdom,* 104, 209-10). Although there is surely a hint of this, the association of "fear" with "understanding" *(bînâ)* at the end of the verse tips the scales toward the proverbial sense of piety. To adopt Clines's semantic terminology, the connotation expands without entirely eliminating the denotation (cf. Clines, "Fear of the Lord," 64).

68. Newsom, "Dialogue and Allegorical Hermeneutics," 304.

thereby highlighting wisdom's moral import all the more profoundly. In the quest for wisdom, according to Job 28, it all comes down to virtuous "fear." Carole Fontaine notes that this final verse captures the heart of the book of Job in its final form.[69] It is certainly a major artery. Cut off from ultimate knowledge or revealed wisdom, Job can still lay claim to virtue, as he continues to hold fast to his integrity (27:5-6; cf. 1:8). "Virtue without Wisdom" is itself wisdom.[70]

Job's Fear(s)

The prevalent theme of fear has its own plot in the book of Job. It remains a moving target that is difficult to pin down until perhaps the end (see chapter 4 below). "Fear" begins in the prologue with the opening description of Job's character (1:1), which comes into question in the satan's challenge to God, "Does Job fear God for nothing?" (v. 9). In the prologue, "fear" exhibits a proverbial sense of piety and reverence mixed with a certain amount of anxiety, as evidenced in Job's sacrificial concern for his children's well-being (v. 5).[71] Such fear motivates, as Job vividly demonstrates in the prologue, unquestioning acceptance of one's fate in the hands of God. To "fear God" is to surrender the self to whatever God has in store, without resistance, without lament. Such "fear" is piety without protest.

Once in the thick of dialogue, however, "fear" takes a more dreadful turn. Instead of the godly fear to which one aspires, fear turns darkly afflictive:

> For the arrows of Shadday are in me;
>   my spirit drinks their poison;
>   the terrors of God are arrayed against me. (6:4)

God has set Job up for target practice. Elsewhere, God gnashes him with sharpened incisors (16:9). To Job, God has turned monstrous, and fear, consequently, has become filled with terror.

---

69. Fontaine, "Wounded Hero," 79.

70. For an alternative interpretation that also distinguishes wisdom and Wisdom, see Hankins, "Job and Limits of Wisdom," 337-78. Hankins's take on v. 28a is that it features an "apposite metaphor," which can generate a host of new meanings (pp. 370-71).

71. Job's diligent offering of sacrifice on behalf of his children derives from "a subjective position of uncertainty" (Hankins, "Job and Limits of Wisdom," 100).

If he would only take his rod away from me,
  and not let dread of him *terrify* me,
  then I would speak without *fear* of him. (9:34-35)

The "fear" that motivated obedience and inspired his discourse of acceptance in the prologue now robs Job of speech. Tortured by terror, Job is beset with paralyzing fear or anxiety, the one thing that prevents him from addressing God. Piety devolves into phobia — *theo*phobia.

[God] stands alone and who can dissuade him?
  Whatever he desires, he does.
For he will complete what he appoints for me,
  and many such things he has in store.
Therefore I am terrified at his presence;
  when I consider [God], I am in dread of him.
God has made my heart faint;
  Shadday has terrified me.
If only I could vanish into darkness,
  and thick darkness would cover my face! (23:13-17)

The root of Job's fear lies in the inefficacy of his integrity before a God who cannot be thwarted from torturing him (vv. 11-13), a God who cannot be reasoned with (vv. 14-15).

Throughout the book of Job, "fear" traverses freely between sapiential piety and debilitating dread. Paradoxically, it is the latter that motivates Job's laments and fuels his protests. And in the course of the dialogues, lament leads to lawsuit and grief gives way to grievance as Job's discourse builds momentum, culminating in powerful testimony.

If only I knew where I might find [God],
  and how I could go to his dwelling!
I would set out my case before him,
  and fill my mouth with arguments. . . .
He would give heed to me. . . .
  and I would be acquitted forever by my judge. (23:3-7)

If only I had someone to hear me!
  (Here is my signature! Let Shadday answer me!)
  (If only) I had the indictment written by my adversary!
  Surely I would carry it on my shoulder;

> I would bind it on me like a crown;
>> I would give him an account of my steps;
>>> like a prince I would approach him. (31:35-37)

As Job develops his case against God, his speech-robbing dread is overcome, replaced by an all-consuming desire for vindication. So Job comes to speak "without fear" of divine intimidation (9:35), unrestrained, much to his friends' dismay (see also 13:20-21). As Eliphaz aptly complains, "You are subverting fear *(tāpēr yir'â)* and restraining meditation *(tigra' śîḥâ)* before God" (15:4; cf. 6:14). By maintaining the link between sapiential fear and theological discourse ("meditation"), Eliphaz contends that subverting the former only undermines the latter. But Job has severed the two, for he speaks of God without fear. Contrary to the satan's suspicion, the issue is no longer whether Job "fears God for nothing" but whether Job fears God at all! In Job's final defense, fear itself is deconstructed, replaced by the audacity of blasphemy (from the friends' perspective). In Job, integrity has subverted fear.

The wisdom poem, in light of the failed dialogues, attempts to retrieve something of fear's proverbial and prosaic roots (28:28). However, if such an operation is to have any credibility in the face of Job's blistering deconstructions, it must also point forward to the book's climax, in Job's encounter with God. There fear takes on a new form, as we shall see.

Integrity in Transition

It is Job's fearless integrity that motivates his iconoclastic words,[72] vindicating, in effect, his wife's advice. For Job to concede to his friends' arguments would not reinstate but surrender his integrity. In defiance, Job protests (27:5-6):

> Far be it from me to declare that you are right;
>> until I die, I will not put away my integrity from me.
> I hold firm to my righteousness and will not let it go;
>> my heart does not reproach me as long as I live.

Such a statement marks a culmination in the unfolding of Job's character, which began in bitter lament and ends in resolute self-assurance.

---

72. See Newsom, "Job," 132.

Job's self-characterization is initially that of a victim who yearns for death, his only consolation (6:3-10). Yet interrelated to Job's death wish is an emerging posture of self-defense. Job musters enough stamina to accuse his friends of betrayal and defend his righteousness (*ṣedeq;* v. 29). Here the issue of honesty moves front and center. Job drives a wedge between his honest words and the reproving words of his friends (vv. 25-26). Honest words, particularly of a desperate person, are not inconsequential, contrary to the friends' perspective (v. 26b). An uncompromising honesty comes to possess Job, snapping the muzzle that had restrained all previous discourse (7:11). Contrary to the traditional ideal of the sage, Job's integrity loosens rather than restrains his tongue.

As Job's integrity comes to be redefined, so Job's relationship with God is recast. Job dramatically portrays God as his oppressor in a scathing parody of Ps. 8:5-7 (Eng. 4-6) in Job 7:17-18. God is mindful of humanity only as tester and tormentor rather than as benefactor (cf. Ps. 8:5 [Eng. 4]).[73] Whereas the prologue suggests that God's testing is prompted by a confident conviction in Job's character, Job himself attributes divine testing to God's merciless desire to torture human beings. Ruthless in pursuit, God is constantly targeting human beings. Hence Job's initial appeals to God consist of pleas for respite (e.g., 7:16b; 10:20). Notably lacking is any reference to God's absence. Quite the opposite: God is omnipresent in abusing Job, but for what reason Job cannot comprehend (9:11). Though elusive in character, God is ever present in torture, a terrorist without a cause. Job would rather be left alone (see 10:20-22).

Parallel to the satan's probing question, the question for Job is whether God punishes "for nothing," without rhyme or reason (see 9:17). How can Job, the innocent victim, justify himself before God in court, before the God who is both judge and accuser? Job's answer is resignation: it makes no difference, Job thinks, whether he is innocent or guilty, for God's wrath undermines all rational adjudication (9:22). Job discovers there is no basis to which he can appeal in order to call God to account, since justice lacks all compelling force before an arbitrary deity (9:19). The perceived contradiction between the character of God and the nature of justice is internalized by Job to the point that he himself suffers an epistemological split:[74]

---

73. See Fishbane's discussion in "Book of Job."

74. Attempts to explain away this epistemological contradiction are unconvincing, such as the translation "I do not care about myself" (Clines, *Job 1–20*, 237) or reference to loss of consciousness in an Akkadian medical text (Paul, "Unrecognized Medical Idiom").

> Though I am innocent, my mouth would condemn me;
> though I am blameless *(tām)*, he would prove me guilty.
> I am blameless *(tām)*; I do not know myself;
> I loathe my life. (9:20-21)

Job knows, yet senses doubt about his innocence, given the apparent certitude of God's intention to declare him guilty (cf. 9:35b). By questioning God's character, Job casts his own character into question, and so drives himself deeper into despair. The verb that describes Job's self-loathing or self-rejection *(m's)* in v. 21 indicates a decisive rejection of his own life. Not only do Job's physical afflictions, the castigations of his friends, and abuse by God provide more than sufficient reason for Job to yearn for death. Now self-doubt appears to be the final straw to break Job's will.

Yet against all odds, Job does not give up his life but boldly presses on with his case. In the end Job is able to identify and overcome what prevents him from presenting his case, namely his fear of divine intimidation (9:33-35). For the first time Job refers to an outside party, an "arbitrator" *(môkîah).*[75] This third party is invoked twice more (16:19; 19:25) as Job's discourse gains momentum and sharpens in focus. Job appeals to this enigmatic figure in order to guarantee a hearing before a God who by all appearances has thrown Job's case out of court. Tentatively at first, Job allows himself to speak without "fear of [God]" (9:35a). Again, as Eliphaz notes, Job has in his new-found courage undermined the very fear of God that is foundational to all wisdom (15:4). But from Job's perspective, the requisite reverence of God, stripped of its sapiential trappings, is nothing more than divinely inspired terror.

Job's speech in ch. 10 marks a decisive turning point, for Job now freely gives voice to his complaint without fear of recrimination. (What does he have to lose?) The charges against God are prefaced in v. 1 by the revulsion Job feels toward his life. But self-loathing turns into courage as Job begins to prepare and articulate his case against God. The enormity of his suffering has overcome both his concern for self-preservation and his sense of terror before God. Counterintuitively, Job's suffering has empowered him.

Job, once among the powerful, now among the disenfranchised, publicly declares his desire to engage God directly, regardless of the consequences (13:13). Such courage is expressed in the formulaic saying of "putting one's life in one's hands" (v. 14; see Judg. 12:3; 1 Sam. 19:5). However, unlike the English cliché, Job's declaration operates in a profoundly ironic way. Job

---

75. See Habel's discussion of *môkîah* in *Book of Job,* 196-97.

assumes control of his life with the full knowledge that God will kill him (Job 13:15). Life, specifically survival, is no longer a concern for Job; his quest for vindication has become all-consuming, and Job is ready to risk all (v. 18). Two obstacles, however, remain before Job can engage God. He petitions that God's hand be removed from him so that terror will not incapacitate him and that God provide the proper forum for a hearing (13:21-22; cf. 14:15). The latter, however, is not fulfilled: God refuses to be arraigned, and Job is thereby forced to contend with God's "hidden face" (13:24a). The theme of God's absence, which only now begins to emerge, allows Job to freely pursue his quest for vindication. Nevertheless, as Job will ultimately find out, "the crisis of abandonment is, if anything, more grave than the crisis of justice."[76]

Job makes a more daring petition in ch. 14. He requests temporary asylum in Sheol until God's anger subsides so that a proper appointment can be established for a juridical accounting (vv. 13-17). With such hope, Job could patiently wait, even indefinitely (v. 14).[77] His willingness to wait out God's transient emotions in hope, in the safety of Sheol, ironically confirms Zophar's prediction in 11:18-19a:

> You will be secure, because there is hope;
> you will look around and take your rest in safety.
> You will lie down, and no one will terrify you.

The crucial difference, however, between Zophar's remedy and Job's hope is that Job seeks vindication, not repentance. Job's public declaration is worlds apart from his initial plea for mercy from his divine accuser (9:15).

Job's character has changed remarkably from the one presented in his initial discourse. The rhetoric of victimization has become the basis of his impervious defense. Job repeatedly points out that he has done nothing to provoke such unwarranted action by God. Indeed, in concluding perhaps the most graphically violent description of the Divine Warrior in all of biblical literature, Job offers a telling statement about his integrity in contrast to God's: "There is no violence in my hands" (16:17a). Job's characterization of God as a divine terrorist marks his dissociation from God. Job, the "pacifist," will have nothing to do with this violent tyrant. Job's defense is as much a personal vindication of his character as it is a scathing condemnation of God's integrity. Contrary to the prologue's claim in 1:22,

---

76. Janzen, *At the Scent of Water,* 82. See chapter 4 below.

77. Such a statement marks a stark contrast to Job's earlier statements regarding his inability to wait.

the poetic Job accuses God of deliberately undermining justice (9:24). Without an appeal to a just God, Job realizes that there is no option except to appeal to a third party who can guarantee due process (16:19-21). Job is through with pleading to God;[78] his only avenue of redress now is to bypass God by appealing to another member of the divine council, his arbitrator/vindicator/redeemer (9:33; 16:19; 19:25).[79]

In developing his case, Job takes another remarkable step in mustering self-support for his cause: Job renounces death, which he formerly had been so eager to embrace. He comes to the realization that there is no hope in death (17:13-16). After death, vindication is a non sequitur. From this point on, Job becomes unflinching in his pursuit and wholehearted in his commitment to prove himself innocent in the face of divinely inflicted punishment. Job charges God with having put him in the wrong with violence (19:6-12), much in the same way his friends have done with their defamatory words (vv. 2-3). In a protestation of faith, Job bears witness one final time to his vindicator (v. 25). He has come full circle in mustering support for the exclusive aim of holding God accountable. With no lack of courage, Job confidently contends that God would give heed to him rather than overwhelm him, if God could only be found (23:6, 8-9; cf. 9:19). But God appears missing within the governance of human affairs as the wicked run roughshod over the poor of the earth (24:2-12).[80] For Job, a preferential option for the poor simply does not exist.

So out of his defenselessness, Job constructs a powerful defense. Before God and his friends, Job defiantly wages a battle for the sake of his integrity. His arsenal consists of words of weakness and vulnerability, powerless words that overcome the authoritative, sapiential words of his friends. His friends see only misdirected anger bent on self-destruction (18:4). Within the arena of human intercourse, words can either assuage and empower (16:5) or afflict and oppress. Discourse can be consoling or destructive. Job plaintively asks:

> How long will you torment me,
> and crush me with words?

---

78. Patrick notes the marked decrease in Job's appeals to God after ch. 14 ("Job's Address of God").

79. See Habel's discussion of 16:20 in *Book of Job*, 265-66, 275.

80. Given the theological tension, I take 24:1-17 as representing Job's own position, whereas vv. 18-25 seem to mimic Job's friends, all cast as Job's discourse. See also 27:13-23. For the interpretive possibilities, see Newsom, *Book of Job*, 165-66.

> Ten times now you have cast reproach upon me,
> and abused[81] me without shame. (19:2-3)

Stripped of its initially guarded protocol, such "sagacious" discourse has degenerated into a crossfire of contention. It is in such a context that Job can speak with the heaviest of sarcasm in exhorting his friends to attend carefully to *his* words of consolation (21:2). Whereas a credible debate aims at articulating arguments and marshaling evidence for support, here the rhetoric of sapiential discourse stoops to the level of ad hominem attacks and outright defamation (e.g., 22:5-6). But then it is Job's character, his integrity, after all, that is the topic of discussion.

What initially was meant to be a pastorally sagacious conversation among friends devolves into mudslinging, words of insight and compassion replaced with slings and arrows, words of accusation and betrayal. The language of comfort has become riddled with the rhetoric of adversity. The dialogues are not only a parody of consolation; they serve as an indictment of the sapiential collegium as a whole. Job, too, is complicit. He does not say, "Father, forgive them, for they know not what they do," but rather, "God, damn them, for they know very well what they are doing!"

Job 27:1-12 represents a high-water mark in Job's self-defense so far. With vitriolic flair, Job utters an oath meant to guarantee, at his own risk, the credibility of his discourse, while at the same time indicting God for having violated his right to redress (v. 2). Job's oath lifts the level of discourse to new heights. No longer is he locked in rhetorical combat with his friends; rather, Job attempts to elicit a response from God, but not in the form of a prayer or plea. In swearing by God, Job aims to compel God.[82] As Habel points out, Job's oath provides a counterbalance to the curse that Job's wife had proposed for the purpose of provoking God to end his life.[83] Yet the oath also echoes the satan's self-imprecation (1:11; 2:5), which had "incited" God to act in the first place.

With Job's declaration of his integrity in 27:6, an overarching inclusio is established with the prologue (2:3), a literary envelope that also closes the cycle of discourse with Job's friends. From here on out, Job's discourse will be directed primarily to God,[84] but in a manner quite different from

---

81. The verb *hkr* is uncertain; read *ḥkr*. See *HALOT*, 1:315; Habel, *Book of Job*, 291.
82. Habel, *Book of Job*, 380.
83. Habel, *Book of Job*, 380.
84. If one assumes that 27:7-12 was originally part of the Joban discourse (vv. 13-23

that of the bitter prayers, supplications, and grievances Job had uttered earlier. In his final oath Job's hope for vindication begins to give way to a more fundamental desire.

Job's Final Defense

Following the wisdom poem of ch. 28, Job's discourse dramatically changes course. His final defense in chs. 29–31 is not a heated disputation but a compelling testimony, the crowning mark of his discursive power. In it Job is no longer springing rhetorical traps against his friends and God. Now sincerity and vulnerability take center stage.[85] Here, finally, Job finds his own narrative, constructing it without the "help" of his friends.

The first part (ch. 29) consists of a series of recollections in which Job was considered the paragon of righteousness. But it begins with Job's personal relationship with God, which extends to his family and ultimately to his community. Faintly echoing the satan's charges against God's selective benevolence toward him, Job discerns that God used to watch over him, guiding and protecting him amid the darkness. What the satan identifies as a point of contention concerning the nexus between Job's character and God's beneficence, Job recasts as a seamless connection. For Job, blessing and righteousness coexist naturally. The transition from divine benevolence to human conduct is both gradual and subtle:

I.	Divine benevolence	29:2-5a
	A. Protection	29:2b
	B. Guidance	29:3
	C. Companionship	29:4-5a
II.	Consequences for Job	29:5b-6
	A. Familial companionship	29:5b
	B. Material provision	29:6
III.	Job's conduct	29:7-20
	A. Social esteem	29:7-11
	B. Social service	29:12-17
	C. Social security	29:18-20

are more doubtful), then Job's discourse in chs. 29–31 is meant not only to compel God to act but also to serve as the final demonstration of Job's integrity to his friends (and readers).

85. Newsom, *Book of Job*, 196.

Job was once a leader of his community, commanding respect from young and old. As his circle of influence widens to include even the fringes of society,[86] Job's self-declared status rises figuratively to that of royalty as he himself declares in conclusion: "I lived like a king among his troops, / like one who comforts mourners" (29:25). Job boasts of his beneficence to the disenfranchised (vv. 12-16), of vanquishing the power of the wicked (v. 17), of being clothed with justice (v. 14), and of dispensing advice like spring rain (vv. 22-23). As the final jewel in his crown, Job refers to the light of his countenance in encouraging the downcast (v. 24). All in all, ch. 29 describes the apotheosis of Job's character in consonance with God's.

Job's final defense is also important from the satan's perspective. The natural movement from divine blessing to right conduct and high esteem is unapologetically expressed in ch. 29. Thus the satan's charge that God has made it worth Job's while to act with integrity seems to be conceded: blessing does indeed have a role in the life of piety. Nevertheless, in his defense Job contends that his righteous acts are free of ulterior motives. It begins with the simple testimony that God has graciously provided for Job, without mention made of warrant or desert. The natural movement from divine provision to righteous behavior suggests that God consistently remains in the background, guaranteeing the proper conditions for Job's conduct. Ultimately it is God who provides the basis for Job to "break the fangs of the unrighteous" (v. 17), to become eyes to the blind (v. 15), and to put on justice like a robe (v. 14b). Job's defense suggests that righteousness is the fruit of, not the means for, divine blessing. Implied is that gratitude has directed Job to act in these ways. Explicit is the denial that self-interest has been a driving force behind Job's integrity. In short, Job's rehearsal of the past acknowledges God's role in the formation of character, yielding a life of gratitude and opportunity for service, but free of manipulation. Thus the *telic* twist with which the satan questioned Job's conduct (1:9) is in Job's defense consigned to a *causal* one: Job explains his conduct as a response to rather than as motivation for divine beneficence. Regardless of whether this would clear Job of the satan's accusation, the relationship between divine blessing and human conduct is sufficiently nuanced so as to release Job from first-degree condemnation.

All the evidence that Job has marshaled in ch. 29 to affirm his integrity is, however, overthrown in ch. 30. All the blessing, honor, and prosperity, the by-products of wisdom that had for so long confirmed his

---

86. E.g., the poor, orphan, and the widow in 29:12-13.

character, have now been taken away. Social disconfirmation has forced Job into the position of victim, analogous to those whom he once helped (30:24-26). As one whose bitter mourning has alienated him from his community, Job regards himself exiled among the jackals and ostriches (30:29), "the denizens of the landscape of desolation."[87] In the light of proverbial wisdom, which claims an inextricable link between inward character and outward success (cf. Prov. 31:10-31), Job's once estimable character appears to have betrayed itself.

Consequently, the chain of oaths presented in the last chapter of Job's defense follows upon the heels of his poignant description of present misery in order to lay to rest any doubt regarding his integrity. The series marks the grand finale of Job's defense and summation of his character. Together the oaths offer a personal confession of innocence designed to inflict divine punishment if Job is found to have violated any one of them. These self-imprecations are fundamentally intended to compel God to come and assess Job's integrity: "Let me be weighed in a just balance, / and let God know my integrity!" (31:6).

The oaths cover a wide-ranging catalogue of vices and violations that Job denies outright.

1.	General ethical violation (false way)	31:5-7
2.	Adultery	31:9
3.	Violation of slave rights	31:13
4.	Inhumanity toward the needy	31:16-21
5.	Avarice	31:24-25
6.	Idolatry	31:26-27
7.	Vindictiveness	31:29-30
8.	Inhospitality	31:32
9.	Hypocrisy	31:33-34
10.	Land violation	31:38-39

The list is not structured in any particular way, except in that the first oath is cast in the most general of terms, hence an appropriate formal introduction to the series. In addition, appropriately near the end of the list is the sin of hypocrisy, of withholding confession of any moral indiscretions (vv. 33-34). Job's final oath denies any violation of the land, which begins with the conditional clause: "If my land has cried out against me, / and its

---

87. Newsom, *Book of Job,* 240.

furrows have wept together . . ." (v. 38). In antiquity the land's integrity, or lack thereof, reflected the community's conduct, moral or otherwise. When Israel sinned, the land mourned or reacted adversely.[88] As Job had appealed to his own actions throughout the series of oaths, he now appeals to the reaction of the land as witness to his integrity. Also of note is the oath on maintaining the right of the slave (v. 13). On the surface, Job maintains his innocence against the charge of negligence in preserving the legal rights of his slaves. Job claims that he has never dismissed any just complaint submitted by his slaves. Yet, ironically, this is precisely Job's charge against God: God has dismissed the case of Job, servant of the Lord, by refusing to appear in court.

Job's negative confession is typical of ancient Near Eastern legal or oath lists, particularly Egyptian and Babylonian,[89] yet it is far more comprehensive and specific than any comparable piece of Hebrew Scripture, such as the psalmic protestations of innocence (e.g., Pss. 17:3-5; 26:4-7).[90] Given the predominant theme of Job's integrity throughout the book, such an extensive list is by no means surprising. That the confession is cast as a series of oaths invites comparison with the two oaths uttered by the satan in the prologue (Job 1:11b; 2:5b). Both Job's and the satan's self-curses serve to challenge, indeed compel, God to act. The satan incites God to wreak havoc upon Job with the hope of exposing Job's integrity as a facade. Job challenges God to examine his character so that he might be vindicated and his relationship with God be restored. In the prologue Job did not need to be tested for the sake of his own vindication. Now Job pleads for such a test; his negative confession is meant to provoke a written indictment from God (31:35), his ticket of admission to come before God with confidence "like a prince" (31:37).

As the climax of Job's discourse, Job's bold words in chs. 29–31 are unequaled in their persuasive power: they silence friends and ultimately provoke God. Far from pleading for a quick death to relieve himself from unbearable pain (ch. 3), Job has turned full circle, renouncing death and seeking at all costs a hearing with God. As the direction of Job's rhetoric has shifted, so has Job's character. The cycles of discourse that seemed to go in circles, progressing nowhere, in actuality trace the journey of Job's developing character, reshaping the contours of his integrity. Committing

---

88. See Hos. 4:3; Jer. 12:4; 14:1-8; cf. Gen. 3:18; 4:10-12.
89. See Fohrer, "Righteous Man in Job 31," 9-10.
90. Habel, *Book of Job,* 429.

himself to the pursuit of redress, Job has found the courage to call God to account, regardless of the consequences, perhaps "for nothing." Ostracized with the "jackals" and "ostriches," Job has found strength in his character far surpassing the passive patience featured by the Job of the prologue. The final series of oaths in ch. 31 reaffirms Job's own sense of integrity and equips him for the impending confrontation with the Divine.

Job's final defense returns, ironically, to the world of the prologue. The hallmark qualities of Job's character set forth in 1:1 appear again in different language in ch. 29. The debate between Job and his friends that culminates in Job's final defense is a battle over Job's past, including the story world of the prologue. In Job's final defense, the poet "rounds out," or better fleshes out, the flat characterization of the Job of the prologue.[91] The poet reprofiles Job's character without undermining the basic thesis that Job retains his integrity throughout, even as he seeks to challenge God face-to-face.

Nevertheless, Job's integrity does break the traditional mold cast in the prologue. The more Job is challenged by his friends, the more he gives expression to his moral outrage, the more he widens the gulf between his integrity and the kind of righteousness that requires unquestioning submission and didactic humility. The words that scandalize the theological sensibilities of his friends reflect a Job whose integrity is anchored not so much in the traditional categories of moral virtue as in his newfound freedom and courage, founded upon his vulnerability.[92] Job embraces an ethos of grievance necessary for his transformation. The road to "moral perfection no longer subsumes but opposes unquestioning acceptance."[93] But the work of ethical "perfection" is far from over. In his final defense, Job commends himself to God more for the sake of restoring relationship than for the sake of vindicating himself. And in the final answer (Job 38–41), God commends all creation to Job for the sake of his transformation.

91. I disagree with Newsom's claim that Job remains a flat character throughout the dialogues, specifically an "equally static character type of the complaining skeptic" (*Book of Job*, 26). Job is a skeptic, yes, but much more, given his character development thus far, culminating in his final oath.

92. Gilkey is correct in noting the striking shift in the dialogues from Job's "innocence or virtue" to his courage and autonomy ("Power, Order, Justice, and Redemption," 164). However, the basis of Job's reconstructed integrity is to be found precisely in his innocence (rather than at its expense), without which Job's unorthodox discourse would lack all credibility.

93. Sternberg, *Poetics of Biblical Narrative*, 346.

CHAPTER 4

Wonder Gone Wild: Job 32–42

A well-timed flash of sublimity scatters everything before it like a
bolt of lightning.

Cassius Longinus[1]

OH WOW. OH WOW. OH WOW.

Steve Jobs[2]

Job rests his case, but on a softer note. In his quest for vindication, Job
commends himself to YHWH instead of leveling another protest: "Let
God know my integrity" (31:6b). His pursuit of vindication *at the expense*
of God's integrity has been redirected. Job's bold cause is no longer defined
as a zero-sum game between him and his God. He does not say, "May God
be proved wrong!" (cf. 16:19; 19:25). Rather, he puts himself on trial: "May
I be proved wrong."[3] By encapsulating his life in the form of a testimony,
Job comes to identify a deeper longing, one of reestablishing intimacy with
God, as anticipated in the opening words of his defense:

> Would that I were as in the months of old,
>   as in the days when God preserved me;

---

1. Longinus, *On the Sublime,* 125.
2. Quoted in Mona Simpson, "Sister's Eulogy for Steve Jobs."
3. Newsom, *Book of Job,* 196.

when his lamp shone over my head,
  and I walked by its light through darkness;
when I was in the days of my prime,
  when God's intimate counsel *(běsôd)*[4] was upon my tent;
when Shadday was still with me,
  when my children were all around me. (29:2-5)

What Job lost most was his intimacy with God, intimacy like that shared between Moses and God at the "tent of meeting" (Exod. 33:11; Job 29:4b), intimacy like that shared between him and his children (v. 5b). In such a light, Job's plea that "God know my integrity" is uttered not so much out of self-righteous grievance as out of the yearning for restored relationship. To be sure, Job's desire for self-vindication is alive and well, but it is now coupled with a deeper longing to reestablish ties with the God who was once "with" him (v. 5a).[5] Through, and perhaps underlying, the stridency of his litigation, his legalized longing for self-vindication, Job has heightened his personal desire for God.

It is at this point of greatest self-disclosure on the part of Job that YHWH is set to enter, stage right. But another figure suddenly commands the scene, stage left.

Elihu: Renegade Sage, Wonder's Herald

An unannounced figure interrupts the movement of the drama, effectively postponing the expected theophany. The appearance of this new character marks a last-ditch effort to save Job from himself. It is no accident that his name is Elihu, which means "He is my God." He comes not as a friend but as an arbiter, someone Job himself had requested (see 31:35).[6] Elihu's character is disparaged by some scholars with remarkable vehemence. He is variously described as a "fool, albeit a brilliant young fool,"[7] "an insufferable bore,"[8] and unintelligible.[9] Such judgments, however, teeter on the

---

4. See also Ps. 25:14; Prov. 3:22.

5. For similar and poignant discussion of Job's oath see Janzen, *At the Scent of Water,* 87-94.

6. Habel, *Book of Job,* 36-37.

7. Habel, "Role of Elihu," 88.

8. Crenshaw, *Reading Job,* 134.

9. Good, "Job," 429.

edge of character assassination. The figure of Elihu in all likelihood was intended to speak to a generation of readers who would have regarded him as offering a credible response to Job's damning protestations.[10] Elihu was written into the book of Job in order to critique and salvage the friends' arguments in full view of YHWH's imminent appearance in chs. 38–41.

Regardless of how one reads the literary history of the book of Job and Elihu's place therein, it is significant that Elihu's character is depicted as a starkly different figure from Job's friends. He is their literary nemesis: Elihu is youthful yet learned in the ways of wisdom, but of a wisdom granted solely by God (32:6-14). Elihu critiques the friends by overturning the long-held tenet that associates wisdom with age: "It is not the old[11] who are wise, / nor the aged who understand what is right" (v. 9). Although humility does not befit this brash speaker, Elihu's sweeping statement is not without warrant, for the young sage had once given deference to his elders: "I thought, 'Let days speak, / and many years teach wisdom'" (v. 7). But no more. Age and experience have proved to be sapientially bankrupt. Rather, "it is . . . the breath of Shadday that makes for understanding" (v. 8b).

Elihu rejects the traditional picture of the sage, whose head is hoary and back is bent, and arrives at a more prophetic-like understanding of wisdom, whose source is unmediated revelation.[12] As a result, Elihu turns the conventional model of sapiential appropriation on its head.[13] It is telling that no reference is made in his discourse to the proverbial "fear of the LORD/God," which implies a developmental paradigm. Elihu casts himself as God's veritable mouthpiece, as God's virtual surrogate, and his youthfulness undergirds, rather than undermines, his self-declared status. Age corrupts. Unlike Proverbs, the Elihu speeches do not define the ideal of youth in terms of receptivity of the past within a hierarchical human

---

10. It is important to note, e.g., that Elihu's verbose style is evident only against the relatively succinct speeches of Job's three friends, in contrast to Job, whose verbosity is matched by Elihu's. Redactionally, Elihu's character was inserted at a later stage in the literary development of the book. For the literary placement of the speeches, see Freedman, "Elihu Speeches"; Zuckerman, *Job the Silent*, 88, 238 n. 230; Newsom, *Book of Job*, 200-202. Although often assumed that Elihu serves as a foil for God, much of what Elihu says coheres with the divine speeches of YHWH that follow. Indeed, Elihu concludes with a fitting introduction to the theophany in ch. 37. If Elihu is a foil, he is more a foil for Job's friends. He fills a hole in the friends' argumentation brought about by their unwillingness to address Job in the legal language that Job himself employs (Zuckerman, *Job the Silent*, 147, 150-55).

11. Reading with the LXX, Peshitta, and Vulgate. The MT is haplographic.

12. Perdue, *Wisdom in Revolt*, 249.

13. E.g., Prov. 1:7; 2:1-5; 9:10; see chapter 2 above.

framework. True wisdom is not a hand-me-down from preceding generations. It is received, rather, as inspiration. Youth is the sturdy vessel of divine wisdom.

As a self-declared prodigy of sagacity, Elihu develops the youthful ideal in his discourse on the human condition in 33:15-28. God chastens with fear and pain in order to compel mortals to repent (vv. 15-22). For one who is righteous, there is deliverance (vv. 23-24), and it comes in the form of rejuvenation: "Let his flesh become fresh with youth; / let him return to the days of his youthful vigor" (v. 25). Elihu calls Job back to his youth and at the same time calls Job to place himself in the subject position of Elihu, the ideal youth,[14] in order to relearn from God's mouthpiece what age has evidently corrupted (33:31, 33). Such is the new vision of sapiential authority that Elihu offers.

The Character of Wisdom in Elihu's Discourse

At best, wisdom as traditionally conceived assumes secondary status in Elihu's discourse. Indeed, there is a dearth of references to wisdom in his speeches, the majority of which are either sarcastic (34:1-2) or directed polemically against Job and his friends (32:7, 9, 13; 34:35). Elihu declares that he is full of words of wisdom, but his wisdom is not gained through age and experience. Wisdom, rather, is identified with the "spirit/wind" *(rûaḥ)* and "breath" *(něšāmâ)* "of Shadday" (32:8). Elihu spiritualizes, or more accurately "theo-centrizes," wisdom. Consequently, his discourse attests to God's direct, unmediated role in human affairs. It is not wisdom that reminds "one what is right" but a divine "messenger" *(mal'āk)* or "interpreter" *(mēlîṣ;* 33:23).

How then is it possible to teach wisdom? Given Elihu's perspective, it seems absurdly ironic that the young disciple casts himself as a teacher (33:33), particularly when he emphasizes repeatedly that he is not divine but a figure of clay just like Job (v. 6). Such talk reveals the challenge inherent in casting wisdom in strictly revelatory terms without abandoning the sapiential enterprise altogether. In Elihu's eyes, wisdom cannot be imparted laterally from human to human. Only God is the true teacher (36:22). Nevertheless, the human capacity to appropriate wisdom is inher-

---

14. Elihu, in effect, summons Job to "interpellate" himself in Elihu's character, i.e., to identify with his sapiential ideology (see chapter 2 above).

ent in the creation of life: "The spirit of God has made me, / and the breath of Shadday gives me life" (33:4; see 32:8). Elihu sees himself as one called to clear the cobwebs of age so that wisdom can be apprehended directly from the divine source. Elihu's job, in other words, is to fine-tune the reception.

The Character of Elihu's God

Elihu's discourse empties wisdom of all self-sustaining content and, in turn, refills it with revelation. The motifs of journey and pursuit, of development and accumulation, are replaced with the dynamics of reception and discharge (32:19-20; cf. Jer. 20:9), in effect a prophetic paradigm. Since the element of human initiative has been all but eliminated, wisdom is completely subsumed by the Divine. Any examination concerning wisdom's character (or lack thereof) must point directly to the character of the Divine. God is depicted as an immediately perceivable, vigorous force directly in charge of earthly affairs. The cosmos is transparent of divine presence, hence Elihu's frequent use of theophanic language. Much like Elihu himself, God shows no partiality to those who are on top of the cultural hierarchy, including the nobles and the rich (Job 34:19), Job not excluded. Indeed, earthly royal figures are frequently the object of Elihu's scorn (34:17-20). Conversely, God is depicted as a mighty sovereign and divine warrior (vv. 20-30). The theology of retributive justice is replaced by a theology of retributive terror (v. 20).[15] All creation hangs precariously by the thread of divine favor.[16]

Elihu's brand of wisdom depends entirely upon divine inspiration, as opposed to accumulated appropriation. His style is not so much pompous as it is audacious. His willingness to step on the toes of his elders is by no means a character flaw meant to undermine the young sage's credibility. To the contrary, Elihu's unabashed demeanor is more an indication of what he is up against: the lumbering inertia of traditional wisdom and the corruption of divine instruction. Elihu aims to make his voice heard among a group of elders rendered silent by Job's bitter complaints. By championing the voice of youth and wisdom's inspiration, Elihu is a renegade among the sages. He is a rebel *with* a cause; no silent son is he.

As for Elihu's character, his unabashed confidence, defiant asser-

15. Perdue, *Wisdom in Revolt*, 252.
16. Perdue, *Wisdom in Revolt*, 251.

tiveness, and passionate zeal are traits paradoxically shared by Job. Such qualities Job comes to embody as his character progresses from stoic resignation and surrender to defiance against God and humanity. But Elihu's character traits are mustered for a different aim: to put Job in the wrong by defending God. One could say that Elihu is Job's alter ego.

Elihu's character is one that reflects the sentiments of certain early readers of Job who espouse a more prophetic understanding of wisdom over against the traditional model of human observation and accumulated insight. Elihu's insertion into the dialogic fray injects a new dimension into the Joban conflict. He introduces a level of contention between the aged and the young over the issue of who truly possesses the lion's share of wisdom. Elihu reflects a rebellious, new model of the sage who not only talks back to his elders, but has the audacity to expose their folly. Indeed, this gifted, rhetorically adept youth provides a prototype of the young Daniel depicted in the story of Susanna and the elders in the Septuagint, who successfully undermines the alibis of the two lascivious elders in a trial of sexual misconduct.[17] Before Elihu, the elder Job stands accused of theological misconduct.

Elihu vanishes as quickly as he appears, but not without an appropriate exit strategy, one that effectively sets the stage for YHWH's appearance:

> Listen, listen to the thunder of his voice
>   and the rumbling that comes from his mouth. . . .
> Hear this, Job;
>   pause and consider God's wondrous works. . . .
> Shadday — we cannot find him;
>   he is great in power and justice. (37:2, 14, 23a)

Elihu reveals as much as he conceals regarding what is about to transpire.[18] In his own rebellious way, he is a herald of wonder. He has come to ensure that wisdom has not withered on the vine in the course of sagacious discourse, now exhausted to the point of silence. For Elihu, wonder — the

17. The tale is usually dated near the end of the second century BCE. See Engel, *Susanna-Erzählung*, 180. As Engel points out, Daniel is the "spiritually gifted youth," the paradigmatic opponent of the religious authorities represented by the two elders. Daniel's charge that the elders have grown old in wickedness counters the ethos of conventional wisdom found in Proverbs. The Theodotion text of the story, on the other hand, softens the contrast between the aged and youth.

18. The placement of Elihu's speeches between Job's defense and YHWH's response is also theologically strategic, for it softens the aim of Job's defense to compel YHWH to act, thereby safeguarding YHWH's freedom to show up at will.

wonder of God — is the key to wisdom's renewal. Though rhetorically misguided, Elihu's discourse serves as the warm-up for YHWH's onstage appearance, the theophany of the God of "wondrous works."

Wonder Gone Wild: YHWH's Discourse

As Elihu takes his exit bow, YHWH bursts upon the scene in the form of a whirlwind *(sĕʿārâ),* an image that conjures unmitigated terror (38:1). It was by a "great wind" *(rûaḥ gĕdôlâ)* that Job's children were killed (1:19). In the third cycle, Job describes a storm wind *(sûpâ),* paralleled with the "east wind," scattering the wicked (27:20-22). Jeremiah refers to God's "whirlwind" *(sĕʿārâ)* "whirling about the head of the wicked" (Jer. 23:19; 30:23). Now Job is faced with the same destructive wind. Indeed, he anticipated it in 9:16-17:

> Even if I summoned him to court and he answered me,
>   I do not believe he would hear my voice.
> He would wipe me off with a whirlwind *(sĕʿārâ),*
>   and multiply my wounds for no reason *(ḥinnām).*

Is Job destined to be blown away like chaff, along with the wicked, or crushed like his children? No. The whirlwind, it turns out, is no display of raw destructive power. It is, instead, overwhelmingly discursive in nature. YHWH talks nonstop of cosmic structures, wild animals, and mythological beasts through a rapid series of rhetorical questions and challenging pronouncements that scarcely allow Job a chance to respond. Is this merely an evasive tactic or blustery snow job on the part of the Divine? On the surface, YHWH intimidates Job into submission through a dazzling display of discourse that seems to diffuse rather than resolve Job's case. But there is much more going on than meets the ear.

YHWH's discourse is filled with probing questions about matters of identity,[19] knowledge,[20] and ability.[21] As Job defended the veracity of

---

19. E.g., 38:2, 8, 25, 29, 36, 37, 41; 39:5; 41:2b, 3, 5, 6 (Eng. 10b, 11, 13, 14).

20. E.g., 38:4, 5, 18, 19, 21, 24, 33a; 39:1.

21. E.g., 38:12, 16, 17, 22, 31, 32, 33b, 34, 35, 39; 39:2, 10, 19, 20, 26 (wisdom); 40:9, 10-14 (imperatives), 25 (Eng. 41:1), 26, 27-28, 29, 31, 32 (Eng. 41:2, 3-4, 5, 7, 8). YHWH's questions are essentially moral questions that deal with Job's role and identity (Janzen, *Job,* 225-28; Newsom, "Moral Sense of Nature," 16).

his perception before his friends, so YHWH reveals the limitations of his experience before creation. But in doing so, YHWH by no means defends the ethos of traditional wisdom as represented by Job's friends. Far from it. What YHWH has to say to Job breaks with long-held principles and boundaries set by traditional wisdom in order to reframe wisdom. YHWH's questions are not the kind intended simply to pique intellectual curiosity.[22] The questions thrown at Job are profoundly existential, having all to do with the nature of human identity and role vis-à-vis creation. They are meant to challenge Job in his creaturely status as well as broaden the perceptual horizons of his worldview. To be sure, God aims to compel Job to recant his charge that a travesty of justice has been committed: "Shall a reprover *(yissôr)* contend *(rōb)* with Shadday?" God presses Job (40:2; cf. vv. 8-9). This question lies at the heart of God's rebuttal. Like Job's friends YHWH "answers" Job harshly, but unlike them the Deity responds with authentic rebuke rather than vitriolic blame (see chapter 2 above). YHWH's rebuke aims to edify Job, not to demoralize him. Such is the way of wisdom. Elihu was right: a Teacher stands behind the tempest.

Job's Cosmic Tour

The Teacher begins with a taunt. Introducing both divine speeches, the opening command that Job "gird up" his "loins like a combatant *(geber)*" (38:3a; 40:7) seems more like a challenge to a duel than an act of intimidation. Pedagogically, YHWH's opening line dares Job to teach the Deity a thing or two, challenging him into taking on the position of teacher.[23] But Job is in no position to serve as either YHWH's pedagogue or combatant. The teaching remains squarely on God's end, and the learning falls entirely on Job's end of the pedagogical spectrum, and no doubt by design. Job barely gets a word in edgewise. (For God's 123 verses of discourse Job has only 9.) YHWH's answer discharges one question after another, waves pounding relentlessly at the shorelines of Job's worldview. Call it the pedagogy of the oppressor, for the first and most basic lesson learned is that Job's power and judgment are no match for God's. God is God, and Job is not. And for many interpreters that seems to be the only lesson.

But there is so much more to divine discourse in these penultimate

---

22. See Habel, "In Defense of God," 33.
23. A more elaborate dare is found in 40:9-14.

chapters. The poetic content is far too rich to be reduced to a single affirmation of divine omnipotence. YHWH's opening line in 38:2 plays on
Job's own rhetoric in 3:4-10. There Job had invoked darkness to invade
the day of his birth, indeed, the day of creation itself. YHWH now accuses Job of "darkening counsel." "Counsel" *('ēṣâ)* generally refers to a
well-conceived plan. Here it designates YHWH's design of the cosmos.[24]
Implied in the charge is that Job has obfuscated that design. YHWH's
response in ch. 38, not coincidentally, treats the same cosmic domains of
earth, sea, heavens, and underworld as found in Job's curse.[25] YHWH re-
constructs these domains to counter Job's cosmic devaluation. And it does
not end there. Not satisfied with broad cosmic categories, YHWH pushes
the language of reconstructive cosmology into other realms, to which Job
is utterly oblivious. With increasing specificity, the divine speeches even
touch upon the realms of animal and myth, worlds filled with terrifying
yet fascinating creatures. Through the power of divine poetry, Job is taken
into the unknown, into realms only hinted at in Job 28 (see, e.g., 28:11,
14, 22; 38:8-11, 17).

Rhetorically, YHWH's discourse is filled with challenging questions
and admonitions. Poetically, YHWH's answer evokes new realms of perception. The Teacher behind the tempest is a poet through and through.
The fabric of divine discourse interweaves harsh questioning and edifying
content, both rebuke and revelation. For Job, they serve to crack open the
cosmic expanse of creation, affording him new eyes to see. Through these
questions, YHWH imparts knowledge and experience, and plenty of it. As
Job had appealed to his own experience to counter his friends' attacks, so
now God shares with Job something of divine experience and perception,
giving him a god's-eye view of creation. In YHWH's elaborate rebuke, Job
is granted nothing short of a revelation of creation, a vision of the ency-
clopedia of life, a world of wonders. While YHWH chastens Job for not
having "walked the recesses of the deep" or having "seen the gates of deep
darkness" (38:16-17), the poetry takes him there to imagine. The world
that Job had deconstructed in his curse is poetically re-created by YHWH
in Job's ears and, through his imagination, before his eyes. Whereas Job
invoked the amorphous domains of gloom and darkness in his birthday
curse, YHWH speaks of solid pedestals and the colorful dawn. Job spoke

24. See also Job 12:13; Prov. 8:14; Isa. 5:19; 46:10; Perdue, *Wisdom in Revolt*, 203;
Habel, "In Defense of God," 34.
25. For a structural outline of these domains, see Perdue, *Wisdom in Revolt*, 204-5.

of the darkening and silencing of the morning stars (3:7, 9); YHWH defers to their joyous accolades (38:7).

Through the power of poetry, Job is taken on a cosmic tour, a roller coaster through the vast expanse of the universe in all its dimensions, beginning with the earth's foundations (38:4-7): measurements are determined, lines are drawn, bases are sunk, and a capstone is laid. The celestial joy that erupts in response suggests that the earth is no ordinary edifice but a cosmic temple. Meticulously planned and executed, the earth is given a sanctuary structure. In biblical tradition, as well as in ancient Near Eastern literature,[26] the temple was commonly regarded as a microcosmos. Conversely, the world described here is a cosmic temple that elicits worshipful praise from the celestial creatures.[27] References to measurements, lines, pillar bases,[28] and the cornerstone[29] depict a world characterized by order and stability, and God as its supreme and celebrated artisan. Strikingly absent, however, is any "image of God," human or otherwise, to inhabit (much less rule) the earth.

Creation, however, does not end with the erection of this earth-temple. Next comes the sea, metonymic of chaos, introducing a dissonant note into the univocal symphony of the cosmos (38:8-11). In contrast to the immovable bedrock of earthly creation, the sea *(yām)* is alive and livid with rage. Its destructive waves are stopped only at the bolted doors of the cosmic temple. The sea is a tempestuous newborn whose birth is facilitated by God in the role of midwife.[30] Chaos is contained, and the boundaries of its "proud waves" are prescribed.[31] Yet containment is not the only divine action. YHWH wraps chaos with a cumulus swaddling band (38:9b). Perdue

---

26. E.g., *Enuma elish,* in which Marduk constructs the Esharra over the Apsu in the same way the earth is constructed (*ANET,* 67). For a perceptive discussion of both the inner- and extrabiblical parallels, see Levenson, *Creation and Persistence,* 78-130.

27. The completion of the temple's foundation is occasioned by festive praise (Ezra 3:10-12; Zech. 4:7). Praise is also given at the time of Marduk's completion of the cosmos and the temple (*ANET,* 68-72), as well as upon completion of Baal's temple (*ANET,* 134).

28. The architectural term *'eden* is found frequently with reference to the tabernacle in Exod. 26–27 and 35–40. The word refers to the base or pedestal upon which the pillars of the tabernacle or earth are supported.

29. The well-known cornerstone references are found in Ps. 118:22 *(pinnâ)* and Isa. 28:16 *(pinnat yiqrat),* both of which draw from temple language to describe restoration and salvation.

30. See Schifferdecker, *Out of the Whirlwind,* 77. Cf. comparable language in Prov. 30:4.

31. The motif of containment is paralleled in Ps. 104:9; Prov. 8:29; Jer. 5:22.

correctly notes the stunning language of individual creation.[32] But more stunning is its specific purpose: to provide a counterpart to Job's account of his own birth in ch. 3. Job lamented that the doors of his mother's womb had opened to allow his birth (3:10). Ironically, *yām* also has its birth from the womb and is nurtured. The dark clouds for which Job had yearned (3:4-10, 20-21) provide the seas' protective wrap. Chaos is controlled neither by brute force nor by destruction, but by playful parody. Chaos has its own rightful, albeit confined, place in the cosmic schema. The sea's destructive power is likened to an infant with an attitude.

Next comes the sun, whose restorative powers are vividly highlighted (38:12-15). Divine help in the morning is a powerful motif that runs deeply throughout ancient Near Eastern tradition, including the biblical tradition.[33] The action of the morning sun is particularly vivid: it seizes the corners of the earth, shaking the wicked out, molds and gives color to the earth, and withholds light from the wicked. Indeed, nowhere else in biblical tradition does the dawn assume such a vividly active role in the restorative maintenance of the cosmos (cf. Gen. 1:16). Newsom likens the dawn to turning on the kitchen light early in the morning, sending the cockroaches scurrying into the dark corners and cracks.[34] While the dazzling rays of the morning sun clear the world of its nocturnal chaos, divine agency is relegated to assigning the dawn its function. A celestial being has assumed the role of divine intervention in the art of cosmic maintenance.[35] The preservation of the cosmos is a delegated task.

The following two sections (38:16-18 and 19-21) explore creation's cosmic depth and breadth: the watery depths, the gates of death, the dwelling places of light and darkness, and the ends of the earth. Darkness, death, sea, and light all dwell in remote areas. God assigns and leads them along their respective paths. From Job's perspective, the deep darkness for which he had longed reemerges (vv. 16-17). YHWH asks Job whether he has been to the gates of death and deep darkness. Job, of course, must say no. His own experience has thus far not touched upon such realms, since his impassioned plea for death remains unfulfilled.

Following the paired constituents of the cosmos (earth and sea, dawn

32. Perdue, *Wisdom in Revolt*, 207.

33. E.g., Isa. 17:14; Ps. 46:6 (Eng. 5); 88:14 (Eng. 13); 90:14; 143:8. See Ziegler, "Hilfe Gottes am Morgen"; Janowski, *Rettungsgewissheit und Epiphanie des Heils.*

34. Newsom, "Moral Sense of Nature," 20.

35. As has been often noted, the dawn here is reminiscent of the sun-god Shamash, who traverses the heavens discovering and judging evil (e.g., Perdue, *Wisdom in Revolt*, 208).

and darkness, life and death), more cosmic elements are introduced to Job, namely meteorological phenomena (38:22-28). Although more familiar to Job than the extremities of creation, they are described in such a way that they too retain a sense of the mysterious. With the focus upon their source and creation, "the ordinary is made sublime."[36] Snow and hail, for example, are stored for "the day of battle." Torrents are channeled "to satisfy the waste and desolate land" (vv. 25-27). Gushing wadis are considered God's "channels." Creation at its seemingly most desolate bears life and beauty. Each element of creation has its own role to play in the grand pageant of creation, each having its assigned task and vector path, but each pointing to the mysteries of origin. Through the power of poetic discourse, Job comes to view the world "through a lens of wondrous estrangement."[37]

YHWH's world is overwhelmingly larger and more complex and wondrous than Job's. Job's own world is provincially anthropocentric: a world full of interventions, dependencies, and hierarchies. God is depicted as directly intervening in human affairs, wreaking, for the most part, irreparable havoc (e.g., ch. 12). In Job 38, however, God is one step removed, allowing the cosmic elements to run their course without ruining creation. The language of intervention is diminished in this cosmological schema, contrary to Job's own accounting, in which everything rests directly upon God's shoulders. From God's perspective, however, the lively balance of cosmic powers is what sustains the world's dynamic structure.

The Animal "Kingdom"

Following Job's remedial course on the cosmos, the animal realm processes two by two into Job's purview: lion and raven, mountain goat and deer, onager and aurochs, ostrich and war-horse, hawk and vulture. They are, with one mild exception, quintessentially wild animals characterized by their special strengths and needs. The lion and the raven testify to YHWH's role as provider. The mountain goats revel in their independence. The same goes for the onager or wild ass, who scorns the burdensome life of the city. Like the mountain goat, the aurochs or wild ox will never serve a master. These animals are affirmed in their wildness and independence. Not one is subject to another; all have equal standing in God's wild kingdom. Indeed,

---

36. Newsom, *Book of Job*, 242.
37. Newsom, *Book of Job*, 242.

the animal kingdom is more an ordered anarchy. Each with its habitat, every animal is a world unto itself in God's pluralistic, polycentric universe.[38]

These animals are fraught with background. With the exception of the raven and the war-horse, all the animals listed constituted wild game for Egyptian and Mesopotamian kings.[39] The royal hunts were not conducted for entertainment purposes, thrilling as they may have been. They were staging grounds for the king's prowess on the battlefield, a symbolic exertion of royal power. By slaying wild animals, the king was "fulfilling his coronation requirement to extend the kingdom beyond the city to include the wilderness."[40] In the lion hunt, specifically, the king identified himself as both the hunter and the lion; hence, the leonine carcass was never mutilated.[41]

In Job, however, these denizens of the wild are not trotted out for him to kill and thereby prove himself. To the contrary, these animals are deemed untouchable. In a remarkably ironic turn, God begins with the iconic lion (38:39), the quintessential predator and the most prized game of kings, and asks, "Can you hunt prey for the lion?" The question is more than rhetorical. God challenges Job not to kill the lion, like any king eager to prove his prowess on the battlefield, but to provide for it. Can Job hunt *on behalf of* the lion? Such an invitation turns human identity, as royally conceived, on its head. Job is not to gird up his loins against lions.

Nor are these animals to be named or defined in some way by Job — far from it. Job is transported poetically into the wild to behold their dens and nests, their mountain lairs and vast plateaus, their native habitats and habits, their lives in situ. Unlike Adam, to whom the animals of the garden were brought for him to name (Gen 2:19-20), Job is displaced from his own surroundings to learn something of their native habitats and habits. On this tour, Job is driven out to where the wild things are, driven into the wilderness to encounter these denizens within their native surroundings, not to give them names but to learn about them. YHWH's answer is Job's "Earth Trek." To Job, the wild is the quintessential Other, a place of hostility and desolation, an object of fear and loathing, an unknown land. He is a stranger in a strange land. But this strange land is God's wild Eden. In his forced mi-

---

38. For further discussion on the polycentric nature of the world as conveyed by YHWH's answer to Job, see Brown, *Seven Pillars of Creation*, 133-34.

39. For fuller discussion, see Brown, *Ethos of the Cosmos,* 351-60; Keel, *Jahwes Entgegnung an Ijob,* 65-81.

40. Dick, "Neo-Assyrian Royal Lion Hunt," 255.

41. Dick, "Neo-Assyrian Royal Lion Hunt," 244-45. For an exhaustive survey of leonine imagery in the Hebrew Bible, see Strawn, *What Is Stronger?*

gration, as it were, Job discovers the wild to be rife with life, alien life with inalienable value, creatures endowed with strength, dignity, and freedom. They are God's treasured exotica. The mountain goat kids "go forth and do not return" (39:4); the onager freely roams beyond human reach (v. 5); the aurochs resists domestication (vv. 9-12); the ostrich fiercely flaps its wings (vv. 16-18); the stallion exults in its thunderous strength (v. 22); and the raptors survey the land to spy out their prey (vv. 26-30).

To borrow a noun-turned-verb from Christopher Southgate, these animals are wholly "selved": each expresses its identity unhindered.[42] They live and move and have their being as God intended them. And for all these fierce and fully "selved" animals, God provides, hunting the lion's prey (38:39), satisfying the raven's cry (v. 41), and directing the raptor's flight (39:26). God admires each in loving detail, and with such detail Job is afforded new eyes to see, a perspective that is distinctly God's yet includes that of the animals. Job is invited to see the looming battle through the eyes of the war-horse, to spy out corpses on the battlefield through the eyes of the vulture, to roar for prey as the lion, to cry for food like the raven's brood, to roam free across the vast plains, to laugh at fear, and to play in the mountains. Job's "Earth Trek" is no descent but an "ascent to Nature."[43]

Job's cosmic tour renders him speechless, so he says (!). But YHWH is not satisfied. And so the tour resumes, forging a path into the realm of myth and monster, an ascent to terror. YHWH's second speech profiles two horrifically magnificent animals that loom mythically large: Behemoth and Leviathan, perhaps drawn in part from the water buffalo (or hippopotamus) and the crocodile, respectively, both formidable creatures in their own right.[44] Whatever they are, these larger-than-life beasts are the quintessential embodiments of the wild; they are highly esteemed rather than deeply loathed by God.[45] Nothing is said of God's *intent* to subjugate either of them; freedom reigns for both these fearsome creatures. Behemoth is claimed as the "first [*rē'šît* or 'chief'] of God's great acts" (40:19), assuming

42. Southgate, *Groaning of Creation*, 63.

43. The phrase is borrowed from Edward Wilson, *Creation*, 13, 163.

44. Hippos do not, as a rule, dwell in the mountains, nor are they to be found in the Jordan River, and crocodiles do not breathe fire. For the difficulties of pinpointing their natural counterparts, see Newsom, "Book of Job," 618.

45. Behemoth as a proper name is attested only in Job; otherwise, Heb. *běhēmôt* is a generic term for cattle or domestic animals. The plural form designates intensity or majesty: Behemoth is a "superbeast" (Balentine, *Job*, 83). In Egyptian religion, moreover, the hippopotamus is associated with the god of chaos, Seth, the enemy of Horus.

the preeminent status of Wisdom in Prov. 8 and cosmic light in Gen. 1. The tour concludes in Job 41, the only chapter in the Bible devoted entirely to an animal.[46] With Leviathan, Job takes the plunge into the watery depths of chaos. This creature of the deep marks the culmination of creation's otherness before Job. The description of Leviathan's strength and corpus, all the way down to its impenetrable scales, evokes such sublime terror and splendor that the creature's appearance verges on the theophanic.[47] Leviathan is the one animal in YHWH's litany of creation that comes closest to evoking the "numinous, wholly otherness of God."[48]

Job's tour began with the cosmic temple, the crown of creation, as it were, and concludes with monstrous Leviathan dwelling in the heart of the watery abyss. As a whole, YHWH's answer to Job moves in an anticreational direction, a de-evolution, as it were, from creation to chaos.

Character of Creation

Whereas the overall movement of divine discourse is anticreational, there is nothing anticreational about creation's character in YHWH's answer. The world revealed to Job is no cozy cosmos, no peaceable kingdom. Rather, it is terrifyingly vast and alien, brutal as much as it is beautiful. In many respects, creation is shown by God to be an "arbitrary world,"[49] lacking harmonious coherence. Unlike in Prov. 8, creation in Job is not childproofed by God. But it is far from being utter chaos or desolate: creation teems with life characterized by fierce strength, inalienable freedom, and wild beauty.[50] Certain limits, moreover, are set in place: the earth rests on stable foundations, the tempestuous sea is contained like a swaddled infant, and the dawn renews the face of the earth (38:4-15). In perhaps the ultimate exercise of irony, Leviathan, the king of chaos, serves to maintain order by limiting pride, human and otherwise (41:26 [Eng. 34]). Nevertheless, the world is no object of micromanagement.[51] Land, sea, and sky

---

46. In the Hebrew Bible, Leviathan looms even larger than a chapter.

47. See particularly 41:2-3, 11-13, 16 (Eng. 10-11, 19-22, 25). See also Newsom's perceptive description of Leviathan, complete with a plausible emendation of the MT, in *Book of Job*, 250-52.

48. Newsom, *Book of Job*, 252.

49. Crenshaw, *Reading Job*, 154.

50. For an exploration of this last theme, see O'Connor, "Wild, Raging Creativity."

51. See Fretheim, *God and World*, 235, 239.

are host to myriad life-forms, all alien to the human eye and untamable to the human hand,[52] but all admired by God. YHWH's world is filled with scavengers and predators, even monsters (cf. Gen. 1:21), all coexisting, though not necessarily peacefully. The lions have their prey; the vultures feast on the slain. Creation pulses with "pizzazz,"[53] vibrantly and tragically.

YHWH revels in the wildness of creation. Boldness, courage (stubbornness in one case), conflict, and laughter characterize God's world. This is no orderly world of Gen. 1, which unfolds methodically and hierarchically, culminating with the establishment of human authority over creation. To the contrary, YHWH's world is irredeemably and wondrously messy, populated with individual characters fiercely passionate about their existence, from procreating and eating to roaming and playing . . . and killing. It is a "disordered" kingdom oblivious to human authority and hierarchy. It is a world devoid of dominance. YHWH, in effect, *denaturalizes* the world in which human beings consider themselves the pinnacle of creation and lords of the world.[54] It is the nonhuman forms of life, particularly the wild animals, that roam and play on the margins of civilization, that receive YHWH's special attention. Their worth is not grounded in service to a higher order, human or divine; they are the objects of God's gratuitous attention. YHWH does not refrain from sending rain on the uninhabitable wastelands (38:25-27). It is not a waste of resources but a labor of love. Humanly perceived, the Creator creates "for nothing"!

Character of YHWH

What kind of a God is behind this vibrant, alien creation? The God who stands beside even the creatures of chaos is a God who embodies alien otherness, a "whirlwind" of terrifying wonder. If Behemoth and Leviathan are made in the image of God, then God's very self verges on the monstrous. Yet the God who finds a rightful place for the beasts of chaos is not

---

52. With the possible exception of the war-horse in 39:19-25, whose strength cannot be entirely tamed.

53. Davis, *Getting Involved with God,* 139.

54. The term "denaturalize" is preferable to Tsevat's claim that YHWH "de-moralizes" the world, which misrepresents YHWH's positive valuation of the cosmos ("Meaning of the Book of Job," 102). YHWH presents a world that exhibits moral coherence, but a coherence much different from the one presupposed by Job and his friends, one that values and finds intrinsic worth in every form of life.

a force for chaos. YHWH remains king, whose sovereignty is a different beast altogether. It is a kingship of care and freedom. YHWH expresses an unbounded admiration for the lowly onager as much as for the regal Leviathan. God, in short, is awestruck: all the denizens of creation are found by YHWH to be "unbearably beautiful,"[55] even if Job finds them utterly terrifying. The God who harshly answers Job lingers lovingly over every entry in the zoological catalogue of the wild. YHWH chooses to approach the beasts of the wild not with a sword, as Job is dared to do (40:19b), but with a word of admiration and an open hand.

In Job the conquering spirit of Marduk is effectively replaced by the sustaining care of Israel's God. All the more, YHWH exhibits a sense of "abiding astonishment" toward creation.[56] This marks perhaps the greatest theological transformation documented in the book of Job. Whereas the Deity of the prologue boasted singularly of Job, with tragic results, YHWH of the cosmos boasts of every alien, even monstrous creature of the wild, and with a great deal more (com)passion. "Have you considered my servant Job? There is no one like him on earth," YHWH addresses the satan (1:8; 2:3). In YHWH's final address, the Deity demands that Job consider the creatures of the wild, each one unique, each one inalienable. Like a proud mother, YHWH displays creation as if every element and animal were her child, Leviathan notwithstanding. Rare it is that we find in the Bible God rendering praise to creation. But so it is in Job. YHWH is captivated by nature's wonder and vitality, so much so that YHWH even takes on the creatures' point of view, their instincts and their joys, their adaptive strengths and their failures. God the sovereign is God the parental provider.

Far different from a divine tyrant who subjugates to eliminate conflict and chaos, YHWH is characterized by creativity, self-restraint, and gratuitous pride. YHWH allows the host of creaturely characters not only to exist but also to develop and exercise their endowed qualities, both positive and negative. Unlike the Egyptian and Mesopotamian kings, who hunted the wild animals in order to assert their sovereign authority, YHWH cares for them, allowing them to develop true to their nature. To use an analogy from Dorothy Sayers and Iris Murdoch, good dramatic literature contains characters whose defining traits and personalities are neither extensions of the author nor foils. Rather, they are allowed to develop their own, in-

---

55. McKibben, *Comforting Whirlwind*, 43.
56. The expression is coined by Brueggemann, *Abiding Astonishment*.

dependent characteristics. In the art of writing, the author must exercise restraint and care in creating authentic characters.[57] Such an act involves stepping back.[58] It is out of gratuitous delight that YHWH steps back and lets creation thrive, allowing the citizens of the cosmos the freedom to maneuver and negotiate their respective domains and lives. YHWH's providential care embraces each creature's individuality and unique role within the brutally complex network of life.

What, then, about the Deity profiled in the prologue? Like the Job of the dialogue, the God of the (lopsided) dialogue is remarkably different from the corresponding figure featured in the first two chapters. The great and powerful God, YHWH of the whirlwind, consummate creator, parental provider, and master orator, contrasts with the chief deity of the heavenly assembly who allows a member to have his way with a human individual and half regrets it. Nevertheless, there are some remarkable similarities or at least parallels. As noted above, the God who boasted of Job to the satan now boasts of wild animals to Job. The God who consented to let the satan implement the test delights in letting myriad creatures "selve" fully and freely, even if that entails conflict and violence. It is as if the wild creatures have all but replaced the heavenly realm, populated by the "sons of God" *(bĕnê hā'ĕlōhîm)*, as well as by the "civilized" children of *'ādām*. The divine assembly in the prosaic prologue is now the wild kingdom in YHWH's poetic discourse, as much as Job's own community now consists of ostriches and lions. God among the animals, God of the wilderness, God of the outcasts is the God who meets Job on the ash heap and shows him a wholly new world. As Job's full character shines through in the dialogues, supplanting the Job of the prologue, so the God of the final answer surpasses once and for all the Deity of the prologue.[59]

Character of Job Transformed

YHWH's re-creation of the world reinscribes Job's perception and, in turn, his character. Before his encounter with the God of the whirlwind, Job

---

57. Allen, *Traces of God*, 35.

58. See Gilkey, "Power, Order, Justice, and Redemption," 166-67.

59. For an ethical critique of the character of God in Job, as well as the book as a whole, see Clines, "Job's Fifth Friend."

viewed YHWH's wild kingdom in less than wondrous terms. Case in point: Job likened the outcasts of society to wild scavengers:

> Like onagers in the desert they go forth in their toil,
>   scavenging the wasteland for food for their young. . . .
> They pass the night naked, without clothing,
>   and without covering in the cold.
> They are drenched with mountain rains,
>   as they cling to the rock for lack of shelter.
>
> (24:5, 7-8; see also 30:3-8)

Job viewed life in the wild as impoverished and fragile, a wasteland of subsistence. But whereas Job disparaged such marginal existence, YHWH invests it with strength and nobility. Fragility is replaced by resilience, impotence with power, enslavement with fierce independence. To be a "brother of jackals" and a "companion of ostriches" is to keep honorable company indeed (30:29). Job has landed in a place where humans fear to tread, a place where the trappings of patriarchy and human control are stripped away. Job is in a no-man's-land. This is no anthropocentric world that God so loves. The world is a hodgepodge of life in all its wondrous and repulsive variety. As these animals become fully "selved" before Job's own eyes, Job enters into a process of becoming "unselved." Job, as with all humanity, is decentered in God's strange and alien world. By all appearances, it would seem that Job has been rendered irrelevant in God's wild kingdom.[60]

But does Job really have no place in such a world? To be sure, the animals that populate the landscape of divine discourse exist and thrive without the kind of social bonding that characterizes humans and domestic animals.[61] But in one place Job is given the benefit of a direct reference:

> Look at Behemoth,
>   which I made along with you *('immāk).* (40:15a)

For all the alien otherness of creation, Job is afforded a connection, a strange familiarity. The clue lies in the preposition. Behemoth is created

---

60. See Hankins's discussion of beauty and the sublime in "Job and Limits of Wisdom," 392-407. Although he is ultimately not satisfied with either notion, they do remain important heuristic categories for understanding creation presented in YHWH's answer to Job.

61. Newsom, *Book of Job,* 241.

with Job. This preposition is as key here as it was in Gen. 3. In the garden, the man was "with" the woman (3:6); the woman was given to the man "to be with" him (v. 12). Call it the preposition of companionship. God has given Job a strange bedfellow. As the woman and the man share a common identity, so Job shares a special bond with this monstrous creature of the wild. Job knows a thing or two about monsters, for he himself was tantamount to one in the eyes of his friends and family, and no less of God from his perspective (cf. 7:12). In this revelation of revelations, Job is shown to be created along with his monstrous twin, who receives the credit of being born "first" or "best" (*rē'šît*, 40:19). But unlike the biblical Jacob, Job has no recourse to steal his elder twin's birthright. Job finds himself to be a monster's companion, and by extension, a companion to all the denizens of the margins.

This, then, is the crux of the Joban "thought experiment." Imagine, if you will, that you are kin to a monster — not an evil twin, but a monstrosity nonetheless. What, then, could Job possibly share in common with Behemoth? Habel suggests a common destiny, that of subjugation.[62] However, subjugation is not at all the issue here. Where one might expect reference to humanity's place and role in the order of creation, one instead finds effusive descriptions of two monstrously magnificent beasts. They have displaced humanity's elevated position at the "top" of the created order.

Behold Behemoth, whose loins are girded with strength and whose confidence does not waver before the surge of chaos (40:23). Can Behemoth be a model for Job? What does that say about Job and his relationship to the world of the wild as a whole? In a neglected but highly suggestive essay, John Gammie discerned certain connections between Job and the two monstrous beasts. Gammie claimed that Behemoth and Leviathan are "intended by the author as caricatures of Job himself, images put forth not only to put him down, but also to instruct and console."[63] Behemoth, for example, "neither fled in fear nor abandoned trust" when oppressed (40:23). Gammie, in other words, discovered certain *character* links between Job and the monsters, and even more are evident when one looks beyond those limited to linguistic correspondence.

Indeed, such a comparison between Job and Behemoth is established much earlier in Job's dialogue with his friends. In 6:12 Job ironically refers

62. Habel, *Book of Job*, 565.
63. Gammie, "Behemoth and Leviathan," 218, 222.

to his lack of strength: "Is my strength the strength of stones? / or is my flesh bronze?" Such language is not alien to Behemoth.

> Its strength is in its loins. . . .
>> Its bones are tubes of bronze,
>>> its limbs like bars of iron. (40:16a, 18)

The connection is ironic: Job finds himself bereft of strength (see 16:15b), quite the opposite of Behemoth. Yet Job claims that God is treating him as if he were a mythological beast that must be tamed or destroyed (e.g., 3:8; 7:12). As noted above, Job's continual lament over his vulnerable state eventually turns in his favor in his quest to engage God in disputation. His laments become powerful weapons of protest. His words become weapons in his battle for recognition. By the time Job presents his final defense, he has developed a hide as tough as bronze.

Similarly, the last words concerning Behemoth's indomitable strength focus on the beast's confidence.

> Even if the river is turbulent, it is not frightened;
>> it is confident though Jordan rushes against its mouth. (40:23)

The curious reference to Behemoth's mouth provides another allusion to Job's verbal battle with his friends. Despite the onslaught he must suffer at the insults of his friends, Job emerges victorious in the end, rendering his three friends silent by his own mouth. But is Job, at the height of his confidence and discursive power, to be subjugated, taken "with hooks" and "pierced" through the nose? Nowhere is Behemoth given such an ignominious fate. Rather, its strength is praised by God, and vicariously so is Job's.

As for Leviathan, the allusions to Job's character are even more plentiful. It is not fortuitous that in his first discourse, his birthday curse, Job likens himself at birth to Leviathan (3:8).[64] As Gammie points out, the extensive references to what comes out of the monster's mouth resonate with Job's "verbal defenses."[65] This is clear from the very start of YHWH's description of Leviathan, in which speech comes immediately into the foreground: "Will it make many supplications to you? / Will it speak soft words to you?" (40:27 [Eng. 41:3]). Certainly to his friends, Job was not known for gentle speech. What comes out of Leviathan's mouth are flam-

---

64. Gammie, "Behemoth and Leviathan," 224.
65. Gammie, "Behemoth and Leviathan," 225.

ing torches, sparks of fire, smoke, and flames (41:11-13 [Eng. 19-21]). Leviathan's "speech" incinerates everything in its path. Likewise, Job's discourse has reduced his friends' deliberations to ashes: "Your maxims are proverbs of ashes, / your defenses are defenses of clay" (13:12).

In his inflammatory deliberations, Job the verbose relentlessly pursues his vindication against the onrush and torrents of unfounded claims. Job defends his "tongue" as honest, a sure defense and weapon against the baseless reproof of his friends (6:25-27). Yet it is precisely his tongue that gets him into trouble.

> Therefore I will not hold back my mouth;
> > I will speak in the anguish of my spirit;
> > > I will complain in the bitterness of my soul.
> Am I the Sea, or the Dragon,
> > that you place a muzzle[66] over me? (7:11-12)

The pairing of the theme of bitter speech with the image of the sea monster is deliberate. Who is that sea monster? None other than Leviathan, whose speech spares no one. Both Job and Leviathan are linked together by their overpowering discourse. Before Job's masterful display of rhetoric, all the friends' counterarguments are exposed for what they are, emptied of all rhetorical force. Indeed, more than bad breath is implied when Job laments, "My breath (*rûaḥ*) is strange to my wife, / loathsome to the sons of my own mother" (19:17). The statement is charged with irony in the light of Leviathan's searing exhalation (41:12-13 [Eng. 20-21]).

As Job gains confidence through his discourse, he arrives at the point where he is able to speak without fear. Job has reached, in his eyes, a status of invincibility. Similarly, what makes Leviathan unique among all the creatures is its lack of fear and invincible presence (41:25 [Eng. 33]). Job's connection with Behemoth and Leviathan extends to the other creatures that populate YHWH's discourse. Through an unwelcomed solidarity with these denizens of the margins, Job is compelled to acknowledge their estimable qualities by recognizing a bit of himself in each. Like the animals, Job remains undefeated and untamed within the arena of human disputation. In every case, from lion to Leviathan, Job is presented with a glimmer of himself that reflects his new-found tenacity, fearlessness, courage, and stubbornness (cf. the ostrich, 39:13-18), as well as vulnerability (cf. the

---

66. See Dahood's analysis of *mišmār* ("*Mišmār* 'Muzzle' in Job 7:12"); and Habel, *Book of Job*, 153.

raven, 38:41) and tragedy (see, e.g., 39:14-15, 30). Though Job complains that he is treated like the sea, confined and muzzled, in the battle over his integrity, he comes to realize that, like the sea, he also receives his life and legitimacy from YHWH. God does indeed know Job's integrity (cf. 31:6) and demonstrates it by displaying Job's linkage with all of creation. Even as Job finds himself a stranger in a strange land, he also finds himself strangely mirrored in the alien otherness of creation. The *Unheimlichkeit* of creation, it turns out, is not entirely *unheimlich,* for Job finds his place among God's gloriously alien world. Job's tour of terror, in the end, becomes an excursion into wonder, as epistemological barriers break down and an awareness of deep connectedness emerges. I link, therefore I am.

Through YHWH's final answer Job has come to a greater knowledge of the world and, in turn, a deeper knowledge of himself in the world, as one who sits in dust and ashes yet also, as modeled by Leviathan, "surveys all that is lofty" (41:26 [Eng. 34]).[67] YHWH's revelation of creation does nothing less than transform Job's perception and thus his very identity. He is to find in himself Behemoth's strength and Leviathan's fearlessness when confronting human presumption, theological distortion, and rampant injustice. But he is also to see himself among the brood of ravens that "cry out to God" for food (38:41) and the ostrich that stubbornly stands its ground against all odds and laughs at fear (39:13-18). Rather than partaking from a "tree of knowledge" in a secret, pristine garden, Job has been force-fed the wisdom of the wilderness. His eyes are opened, and he begins to see as God sees, while at the same time becoming more acutely aware of his own vulnerability (cf. Gen. 3:7). Job discovers himself as a child of the wild. The frail and the fierce are both his kin. Although Job's transformation is not yet complete, now is the time for him to "gird up his loins" and respond.

Job's Response: 42:1-6

Job's response presents a major crux for understanding his transformed character and hence for interpreting the book as a whole. Job begins by acknowledging YHWH's supreme strength, conceding that nothing can stand in the way of divine purpose, and in 42:3a, 4 he utters two approximate quotations of YHWH's challenge to him in 38:2, 3b (see also 40:7b).

---

67. For example, Job exposes his friends' false confidence and pride (13:2-12; cf. 4:11-13 [Eng. 19-21]).

Together, Job's final words mirror YHWH's opening words. His ostensible failure to meet YHWH's challenge is indicated in the way in which Job responds not by pressing the case he had prepared but by imitating divine speech, internalizing it, thereby taking on YHWH's own perspective of the cosmic design and fully acknowledging wonder (v. 3b).[68] Job has gained a new foundation for his knowledge of God, a vibrant, visual, direct knowledge couched in sublime wonder (42:3b).[69]

Job's final words are found in 42:6, in which he declares his own position in response to all that he has witnessed. But what appears to be decisively conclusive is actually rife with ambiguity, as indicated by the wealth of interpretations the verse has generated among interpreters.[70] To the large pool of interpretations, I offer what I believe to be the best rendering of this contested verse given the context.[71]

> Therefore I waste away,
> > yet am comforted over dust and ashes.

The verb of the first clause (from m's) occurs seven times in Job with an object, meaning "despise," "loathe," or "reject."[72] However, in 42:6 the verb lacks an object, in which case the verb can mean "become weak" or "waste away" (see 7:16; 36:5).[73] In 7:16 the verb is set in parallel with an expression of the transient nature of Job's life.[74] Likewise in 42:6, hence

---

68. See van Wolde's linguistic study in "Job 42,1-6," esp. 240-42.

69. The notion of wonder here includes Newsom's notion of the "sublime" as, in the words of Lap-chuen Tsang, the experience of "being . . . at the threshold from the human to that which transcends the human; which borders on the possible and the impossible; the knowable and the unknowable; the meaningful and the fortuitous; the finite and the infinite" (quoted in Newsom, *Book of Job,* 236).

70. One cannot begin to cover the variety of suggestions offered. See Habel, *Book of Job,* 576, for the suggestions from commentators; Pope, *Job,* 348-50, for the textual versions, particularly 11QtgJob; Curtis, "On Job's Response to Yahweh"; Patrick, "Translation of Job XLII 6," 369-70; Kaplan, "Maimonides"; Alonso Schöckel and Sicre Díaz, *Job,* 592-93. Others are mentioned below.

71. My translation draws primarily from that of Krüger, "Did Job Repent?" See also the similar conclusion reached in Janzen, *At the Scent of Water,* 108-9. For various options and accompanying bibliography, see Newsom, "Job," 628-29; van Wolde, "Job 42:1-6," 242-50; Morrow, "Consolation, Rejection, and Repentance."

72. 5:17; 8:20; 9:21; 10:3; 19:18; 30:1; 31:13.

73. For details see Krüger, "Did Job Repent?" 224-25.

74. NRSV supplies "my life," which is not in the Hebrew; cf. also Clines, *Job 1–20,* 157, 165-66, 191.

the translation given above. Job is dying. Indeed, he has acknowledged seeing God with his own eyes, thus anticipating his death (cf. Exod. 33:20).

The first clause of Job's "confession" suggests that the whole scene of YHWH's final answer (38:1–41:26 [Eng. 34]) is intimately associated with Job's dying. It is in his advent of death that Job is taken by God on a tour of the cosmos and granted new eyes. But instead of simply being taken down into the depths of Sheol (38:16-17; cf. 3:13-22), Job is taken in *all* directions, thereby gaining a cosmically broad view of life. As he sits on his ash heap "wasting away," Job is transported beyond his wounds, beyond his provincial world, into an experience of sublime, terrifying wonder. YHWH's answer constitutes Job's out-of-body, out-of-his-world, experience.

The second clause in Job's "confession" presents a double entendre, since the Hebrew verb "to comfort" *(nḥm)* exhibits a wide range of meaning, from "being sorry" to "being comforted." Fundamentally, the verb denotes a change of heart.[75] In the book of Job, this verb occurs seven other times and always with the sense of "comfort."[76] Furthermore, the theme of consolation is a prominent feature in Job. Job's friends come "to console and comfort him." But it is God's "rebuke" that has, in the end, assuaged Job's pain. Job's alleged repentance (so NRSV) was never an issue (except in the eyes of his friends). Moreover, two striking parallels are evident: Job's expectation of death in 42:6 corresponds to his death wish in ch. 3, and the final achievement of consolation recalls the friends' failed attempt to console him. In Job's last words the themes of comfort and death are once again conjoined. Repentance, on the other hand, is rendered irrelevant.

Upon the ash heap and before the grand sweep of the cosmos, in the throe of sublime wonder, Job has found comfort for his state of desolation.[77] In his very human and toilsome search for God and vindication,

---

75. Janzen, *At the Scent of Water*, 104-5.

76. See 2:11; 7:13; 15:11; 16:2; 21:34; 29:25; 42:11 (cf. the nominal form in 15:11).

77. The pairing of "dust and ashes" in 42:6b is also attested in Gen. 18:27, in which Abraham abases himself while challenging God's justice in connection with the fate of Sodom and Gomorrah. The phrase conveys diplomatic humility before YHWH. The pairing of "dust and ashes" finds its only other parallel in Job 30:19: "[God] has cast me into the mire, / and I have become like dust and ashes." The verse conveys the certain reality of defeat and death. Here God is depicted as Job's persecutor, who will bring about his death (30:23). The reference to "dust and ashes" connotes the evanescence of Job's fragile life. Likewise in Job 42:6.

Job encounters awe and a new-found knowledge, the wisdom of the wild. Job's restless heart finds resolution in revelation. In his final defense, Job sought the prospect of communion as he invited God to know his integrity and to permit him passage to YHWH's throne (31:6, 37). Access granted. Now death is anticipated.

The Epilogue: Job Restored

Job's response to YHWH in 42:2-6 gives stirring testimony that it is at the very limits of human knowledge and experience that God and the wonders that lie beyond come into view, however slight.[78] Such wonders have taken Job beyond his world, beyond himself, beyond life as he knew it. And the aftermath? Job can only imagine death. But what Job expected did not transpire. Far from it. The poet masterfully establishes a creative tension through the juxtaposition of poetry and prose, of discourse and narrative in ch. 42, comparable to the initial seam that divides chs. 2 and 3. Job does not expire as expected; he is not released from a life that had been consumed by finding resolution to his suffering. In the epilogue, consolation and restoration now become partners, replacing the former's old partner, death.

Many interpreters regard the epilogue as a "covenantal counterpoint,"[79] at best, to the dialogues or, at worst, a dramatic cop-out. Such judgments, however, are made external to the larger narrative. The primary frame of reference in which to discern the epilogue's significance must come from within Job's poetic character, where the reader has been all along. The reader of the dialogues has experienced firsthand Job's turmoil and distress, knowing all the while that Job is innocent of his friends' accusations. The empathic position of the reader is not meant to be jettisoned in the last chapter. The literary movement of the book raises the question of what Job must have felt in the transition to restoration, of what it meant for Job to be restored.

In the prologue, the reader viewed Job from the outside: Job's actions and responses outlined the external contours of his character. In the dialogues, however, Job's inner life is shamelessly laid bare; his character shifts from the stoically flat to the passionately complex. And there is no

78. Hankins, "Job and Limits of Knowledge," 407.
79. Levenson's phrase in *Creation and Persistence,* 156.

going back. While the epilogue undoubtedly recalls the story-world of the prologue, it cannot beat a path back to Job's flat character. By shifting the reader's perception, the dialogues have made sure that there is no return. Job now reenters his prosaic story-world fully fleshed, and the reader, having experienced the poetic depths of his travail, is beckoned to imagine the details of Job's life as the character of Job is restored. Unlike the prologue, the epilogue, thanks to the poetry preceding it, becomes fraught with pathos and grace.[80]

First, the divine act of restoration is not a response to Job's innocence, which would merely vindicate the friends' view of divine retribution. Rather, it is a "free gift from God,"[81] an act of divine gratuity as had been evident in God's work in the wild. What Job hears specifically is his vindication in God's address to Eliphaz. That Job has spoken rightly is repeated twice in the epilogue (42:7, 8).[82] Such vindication affirms that Job's relentless quest and protestations, culminating in his testimonial oath (chs. 29–31) and his awe-filled confession (42:1-6), have been deemed legitimate.[83] Throughout the dialogues, Job's character has progressed from resignation to defiant protest to deep yearning, acceptance, and new vision, a painful transformation of character, a journey from wound to wonder, now met with divine approbation and restoration. His friends, by contrast, never moved, stuck as they were in witnessing against Job throughout the course of the dialogues.

The epilogue adds a new virtue to Job's developing character: compassion for the other, even for his "friends." Job prays on their behalf, setting in motion the process of restoration (42:8-10). As in the YHWH speeches, the shackles of retributive justice are broken. Within this form of justice, Job's vindication would have come at the expense of his friends. They were wrong and therefore must be condemned, just as they condemned Job. Now the tables are turned. But Job's prayer undermines such necessity of reversal, as much as YHWH's presentation of creation over-

---

80. Erich Auerbach's analysis of Gen. 22 as a deceptively simple story "fraught with background" applies equally to the epilogue of Job (*Mimesis*, 5-10).

81. Krüger, "Did Job Repent?" 227.

82. The literal translation of 42:7 is "You have not spoken to (*'el*) me in the right way as my servant Job has." Evidently YHWH has in mind Job's oath in particular, the climax of his discourse, and Job's response in 42:2-6. See the discussion in Janzen, *At the Scent of Water*, 106-7.

83. This does not mean that YHWH approved of everything Job said, beginning in ch. 3, as clearly evident in YHWH's opening words in ch. 38 (see note 82).

comes the necessity of divine condemnation in light of Job's vindication (40:2, 8). The friends are restored as surely as Job is restored. The act of prayer, moreover, reveals something new about Job, specifically a *gratuitous* compassion that could only be found in the discovery of the God who takes gratuitous delight in manifold life. A suggestive counterpoint to Job's prayer for his friends is his sacrificial actions on behalf of his children in the prologue (1:4-5). There Job's actions were motivated by fear. Job's prayer on behalf of his friends is motivated by compassion.

What happens next in the epilogue poignantly conjoins consolation and restoration. Job's siblings and acquaintances succeed in what Job's friends had failed to do — offer effective consolation. Edwin Good has appropriately focused attention on the action of Job's family as providing a solution, perhaps the only solution, to the problem of evil.[84] In any case, their response is integrally related to Job's restoration; it marks the beginning of Job's reversal of misfortune.

The way in which Job gains a new family tugs at the stereotypical image of the patriarch. Yes, Job is doubly restored, and with the same number of children: seven sons and three daughters. This time, however, his daughters are specifically named: "Dove," "Cinnamon," and "Horn-of-Antimony," endearing titles that highlight their striking beauty. As YHWH took parental pride in the wondrous beauty of creation, there is a corresponding sense of pride shared by Job over his daughters.

What is more striking is that Job's last act involves granting his daughters an inheritance along with their brothers, an unprecedented move within Israel's legal traditions and unusual in the ancient Near East.[85] As Num. 27 and 36 suggest in the case of the daughters of Zelophehad, females can receive an inheritance only if there are no male siblings to carry on the father's lineage.[86] Though Job is restored as head of the household, he and his new family are cut from a different cloth. As his poetic words broke sapiential norms, Job breaks conventional social norms by granting his three daughters a share of the inheritance. In so doing, Job displays a boldness, a recklessness marked by compassion, perhaps the same compassion that Job received from his brothers and sisters and acquaintances four verses earlier. Job, patriarch that he is, breaks with conventional family values by dispensing material equality to his daughters, allowing them a degree of

---

84. Good, "Problem of Evil," 69.
85. See Westbrook and Wells, *Everyday Law in Biblical Israel,* 98-104.
86. See also 1 Chron. 2:34-36; Ezra 2:61; Neh. 7:63.

autonomy in a world steeped in patriarchal dependency.[87] Regarding Job's own character, he has a new "default drive": patriarchal prudence has been replaced by gratuitous compassion.

Equally suggestive is the very transition from Job's plight to his restoration. Literarily, it seems particularly abrupt, even artificial, as many have suggested. But in light of the continuity of Job's character, the sudden prospect of restoration takes on a different, more poignant dimension. From Job's angle, the epilogue is a portrait of tenacious hope.[88] Far from a mechanical reversal of fate, restoration for Job entails reentering the arena of civilized life. Just as he was thrown into the margins of life, where the periphery replaced the center, Job is now thrown back into the community with a new moral vision. On the one hand, Job's restoration requires nothing short of a bold reinvestment in family and communal life, along with the accompanying responsibilities and risks in a world that tragically lacks security and guarantees, ever potent with unpredictable mishap. On the other hand, Job's restoration requires a bold reinvestment on the part of his family and community in him to begin the process of healing, emotionally and materially. Job's refashioned integrity is met with a reconfiguration of the community's integrity.

Restoration requires risk, the risk to give and receive love in an ever-threatening, grief-dispensing world. For Job, such risk is evinced in raising a new family in just such a world, in facing the *rōgez* of raising children in a world of *rōgez*. It is a risk that Job accepts in grief over the loss of his children over forty chapters earlier, a grief that the God of the *whirlwind* cannot let him forget. But it is a risk that Job also exercises in courage, the same courage that took him to the courtroom seeking redress from God. Job has come to accept God's world on its own terms, a world of flux and tragedy, of ruin and restoration, a world of subversive vicissitudes and surprising gifts. In the end, the book of Job is not only about tenacious faith amid great suffering; it is also about the tenacious acceptance of blessing in a tragically fragile yet vibrantly wondrous world.

---

87. Job's personal motivation remains unspecified. Morrow suggests that the patriarchal view of female sexual power is what motivates Job to do what he does (*Protest against God*, 146). It remains unclear, however, why physical beauty alone would be the rationale in Job's redistribution of household wealth. Regardless of the motivation, Job has materially empowered a part of his family that would have typically remained dependent.

88. Davis is the only one I am aware of who has articulated this point, and it is from her discussion that I draw these conclusions ("Job and Jacob," 219-20).

A New Ecology of Character

The book of Job is about Job. Such an observation appears banal, obvious; but it is crucial to keep in mind that all other issues commonly associated with the book, including creation and theodicy, are of secondary importance to Job's character and his transformation. Job's character constitutes the bookends of the narrative but also remains central throughout. The satan's challenge to YHWH remains a constant query (1:9): "Does Job fear God for nothing?" And bound up with "fear" is the nature of integrity, as posed by Job's wife: "Do you still hold fast to your integrity?" (2:9). Together, these two questions present the dual foci of the book. What do "fear" and "integrity" look like now at the conclusion of the book?

Integrity Transformed

Within the book's overarching narrative, Job's integrity is more a process than a possession. Through the juxtaposition of the prologue and the poetry, Job's integrity begins its own remarkable transition. Job the stoic becomes Job the complainer. And for some forty chapters the poet renders in raw poetic discourse what is unspeakable in the prologue. Yet what binds the two vastly different characterizations of Job together is his integrity (tummâ). Integrity, or the coherence of character, oscillates between the stoic submissiveness of the prologue and the vulnerable tenacity of the dialogues. Job's integrity remains a work in progress until the very end, and the connecting thread through it all is that Job, as the reader fully knows but his friends strongly doubt, is innocent: Job knows he is not guilty of anything deserving of the calamities he has suffered. His unwavering belief in his innocence as the charges mount against him is what sustains him. But his integrity also renders him vulnerable. It is what launched the test in the first place; it is what makes him the target of his friends' "consolations"; it is what provokes God to meet him in theophany.

As depicted in the prologue, Job's character is initially shaped by the root values of emotional self-restraint, acceptance of one's fate, striving for honor, and submissive reverence. The dialogues, by contrast, deconstruct such virtues. Job's reconfigured character is marked by indignant tenacity, defiant honesty, righteous anger, and flagrant self-assertion, in short, chutzpah. Job's character has become shamefully "strange" and morally dissonant. Once his discourse gains momentum, the pathos of protest and grievance replaces the ethos of restraint and self-sacrifice. Job dares to assert his integrity in defiance of all the traditional metrics of good character, despite all appearances to the contrary, while his friends see only the hallmarks of folly and wickedness. It is these "unorthodox" traits, not the conventional virtues of reverence and deference, that provide the raw material for Job's transformation.

For all his strident honesty and wild tenacity, Job discovers a new aspect of his integrity when he encounters God in the shock and awe of divine discourse. In that encounter, Job finds himself in a state of fearful wonder. His integrity is once again reshaped, now that humility becomes its crowning mark. Job discovers that his tenacity is shared by the most alien of creatures and at the same time comes to understand his peripheral but critical place in God's wild kingdom. In his encounter with the wild, Job's integrity becomes decentered and shared with all of life. His humility too is a different beast altogether: humility without repentance, without need for forgiveness. In humility, Job accepts his place in God's expansive world as a subject among many. And beyond humility, it turns out, lies compassion. Job's intercession for the sake of his friends and his equitable delight in his daughters indicate a new kind of love: compassion without pity, love charged with respect for the other, love "for no reason."

"Fear" Transformed

In the heat of the rhetorical moment, Eliphaz indicts Job for undermining the "fear of God" (15:4), and for good reason. As Job's discourse recontextualizes his integrity, so it also refashions what it means to fear God. The "fear of the LORD" in proverbial wisdom profiles a relationship of openness and reverent receptivity to divine authority, a sense of awe and wonder about God that leads to wisdom. Job, however, perverts this notion, reducing it to divinely inspired terror. Rooted in his perception of divine capriciousness, such fear incapacitates Job, prompting him to seek shelter in Sheol. In time, however, Job comes to reject this paralyzing form of fear amid his sense of abandonment by God. Yet he still reveres God, but his reverence is now rooted in a *fearless* freedom, the audacious confidence to come before God "like a prince" (31:37).

According to Job's friends, godly fear should inspire confession, repentance, and ultimately praise and thanksgiving. If that were to be Job's proper stance before God, he would have aborted his quest for justice before he ever began. What motivates Job's resolve to pursue his case is not a terror-inspiring fear but a defiant trust that God will ultimately hear him out (see 23:6-7). Equally crucial is Job's *self*-trust. Despite severe doubts, Job refuses to give up on the veracity of his experience whose truth counters the narrow testimony of past tradition as represented by his friends. Without such trust, Job would not have gone beyond his birthday curse.

The divine discourse in chs. 38–41 adds a culminating dimension to this reformulation of fear. Whereas Job replaces submissive fear with defiant trust, God's discourse recaptures the awe-inspiring aspect of reverent fear. In YHWH's answer, Job confronts his "(e)strange(d)" character vis-à-vis a strange world filled with strange characters, objects of Job's fear and loathing. In creation's *Selbstoffenbarung,* or "self-revelation" (to borrow from von Rad), Job is reintroduced to fear, but this time to its affiliative side. With God's abiding astonishment, objects of revulsion turn into subjects of wonder, including Job himself! Among the creatures of the wild, Job finds himself in worthy company, worthy of his wide-eyed, jaw-dropping attention, worthy of wonder. YHWH's litany of the cosmos is not meant to terrify Job into submission, much less humiliate him, but to captivate him, to draw him into a "spiritual Copernican revolution" of wonder.[89] Amid the alien otherness of creation, YHWH unveils hints of common character between Job and the beasts of the wild. By proudly displaying the manifold forms of life on the margins and pushing them into the center of Job's purview, YHWH ushers Job into the cosmic community with all its privileges, responsibilities, and uncertainties.

In the end, Job is not left with his own experience, as important as it was in the necessary deconstruction of conventional norms and mores. He is also granted a glimpse of divine experience, of God's experience of the world. Rather than trumping Job's experience, YHWH explodes it. The divine answer is a shockwave that catapults Job into an experience of the sublime and thus toward a moral vision that takes him out of himself and yet brings him back into the community with a new sense of compassion and commitment that supersedes his patriarchal parameters. Such is the double movement of wonder: it "takes us out of the world only to put us back into the world, dismantling old possibilities to uncover new ones."[90] That is why the book of Job concludes as it does. The journey of wonder requires an epilogue.

89. Fontaine, "Wounded Hero," 83.
90. Rubenstein, *Strange Wonder,* 60.

"Return" to Wonder

Job's journey from wound to wonder is completed in his return. His passage from the whirlpool of torment to the whirlwind of wonder culminates, perhaps anticlimactically but also necessarily, in the epilogue. As the silent son in Prov. 1–9 successfully made the passage from home to the larger community as an adult, so too Job, who is driven from the confines of his all-too-familiar world and finds a cosmic community revealed to him by God, only to come home again. Like the son-turned-family-man at the conclusion of Proverbs, Job, the patriarch-turned-citizen of the cosmos, returns to his domicile.

What, then, are wonder's "new possibilities" for Job within his familial world? How does Job spend the rest of his life, all 140 years? One wonders. Still a man of integrity, Job, I suspect, was no longer the "serious man" he was in the prologue. I imagine him laughing, like the ostrich, as he boldly reinvested himself in raising a family. I doubt Job ever roused himself early in the morning to offer sacrifices for fear his children had sinned. Gratuitous delight, rather than honor and fear, motivated Job's care for his children. If Job got up at all in the early morning hours, he might have done so to see the sun rise and marvel at its restorative work as he began another day of work and play. He no longer needed the gestures of deference from young and old alike to sustain his way in the world. Job came to see beauty in the barrenness and dignity among the dispossessed. He no longer saw social outcasts as objects, whether of pity or of contempt. It took an alien world and a boastful God to show Job the common bond of life that embraces both ostriches and kings, the foolish and the wise, the stranger and the friend, the rich and the poor, monsters and daughters. God has made them all.

CHAPTER 5

Wandering among the Ruins: Ecclesiastes I

The whole temple of man's achievement must inevitably be buried
beneath the debris of a universe in ruins.

Bertrand Russell[1]

Ecclesiastes contains perhaps the most unconventional perspective on
wisdom and the moral life in the Bible. The entire book, except for the
epilogue (12:9-14), seems so unorthodox that it has been called the "strangest book in the Bible."[2] Others have deemed it the most pessimistic and/or
skeptical.[3] While granting the limited value of these assessments, I would
suggest that more fundamentally Ecclesiastes is the most enigmatic. The
book is littered with contradictions, paradoxes, and ambiguities. Yet for
all its hermeneutical challenges, the book bears a remarkably universal
appeal. It features an uncanny ability to speak to a wide range of readers across countless generations. Robert Gordis's assessment rings true:
"Whoever has dreamt great dreams in his youth and seen the vision flee,
or has loved and lost, or has beaten barehanded at the fortress of injustice
and come back bleeding and broken, has passed Koheleth's door."[4] Readers
past and present have passed through the book's threshold to find in Qo-

1. Quoted in Davies, *Last Three Minutes,* 13.
2. Scott, *Proverbs, Ecclesiastes,* 191; cf. Crenshaw, *Ecclesiastes,* 23.
3. Priest, "Humanism, Skepticism, and Pessimism"; Sneed, *Politics of Pessimism*; but
see the more nuanced discussion in Weeks, *Ecclesiastes and Scepticism,* esp. 132-69.
4. Gordis, *Koheleth,* 3.

heleth a kindred spirit in their disillusionment and in their joy, a figure cast partly, no doubt, in their own image. But such is the genius of Qoheleth's discourse: his words resonate on a variety of levels, addressing the needs and interests of a variety of readers, in every season.

Perhaps it is no surprise, then, that Qoheleth's historical identity remains shrouded in mystery. Indeed, Qoheleth is not even the author of Ecclesiastes. The sage is best considered the featured speaker of the book or its main character,[5] and the status of his discourse within the book remains a matter of dispute.[6] Properly speaking, the speaker bears no name. His allegedly royal pedigree ("son of David") fades largely after the first two chapters.[7] He "dons, as it were, the mask of Solomon, but does not cover with it every part of his face; one eye at least, and, of course, the mouth, are allowed to peek out."[8] Qoheleth, one could say, is a phantom of the royal opera. In any case, to speak of Qoheleth's character in the book is to speak not to his historical identity but to his literary profile and particularly to his monologic discourse.[9]

One clue to his literary identity comes from his self-designated title, *qōhelet,* which means something like "assembler." But here too ambiguity reigns. In context, the verbal root can mean one of two things, or perhaps both: convene an assembly consisting, perhaps, of students,[10] or "collect" things such as wisdom sayings and instructions (see 7:27).[11] Both roles seem to suit Qoheleth well. Like an auditor, Qoheleth takes an inventory of life by collecting and codifying the data of experience, both individual (his own) and collective (tradition). And like a teacher, Qoheleth candidly shares the results of his work with his expectant (or unsuspecting) audience.

---

5. I thus consider Qoheleth to be the speaker rather than the author, since his discourse, covering nearly all of 1:3–12:7, is framed by an introduction and two epilogues. The anonymous editors/epilogists are the ones responsible for Ecclesiastes as a book.

6. The two epilogues (12:9-11 and 12-14) reflect a divided opinion on Qoheleth's credibility as a sage. Not surprisingly, scholars are divided about the relationship between Qoheleth's words and those of the epilogists. See, e.g., Fox, "Frame-Narrative and Composition"; Sharp, "Ironic Representation"; Seow, "Beyond Them, My Son"; Shields, *End of Wisdom,* esp. 106-8, 236-39.

7. See Eccl. 1:1; cf. v. 12; 2:9. But see Christianson, who finds the Solomonic guise applicable to 7:25-29 and 12:9-11 (*Time to Tell,* 143-47).

8. Machinist, "Voice of the Historian," 134.

9. See Weeks, *Ecclesiastes and Scepticism,* 13-19.

10. Hence NRSV "Teacher."

11. The root of the term *(qhl)* tips the scales toward assembling people. See the extended discussion in Weeks, *Ecclesiastes and Scepticisim,* 180-96.

Qoheleth presents himself as the consummate examiner of life, perhaps the Bible's first and only "empiricist."[12]

> I, Qoheleth, was king over Israel in Jerusalem. And I applied my mind to inquire and to investigate through the faculty of wisdom all that goes on under heaven. It is an unhappy business that God has given to human beings to be occupied with. (1:12-13)

What is clear is that this sage, in the temporary guise of King Solomon, sets out to conduct an "analytical inquiry" of sorts,[13] or at least a probing, introspective one. Employing his intellect to examine all activity (1:13), the sage frames his insights largely as observations coupled with reflections.[14] Like Socrates, he is driven by the conviction that "the unexamined life is not worth living."[15] And who would be most qualified to examine life but the "Solomonic" Qoheleth! With the most qualified of credentials and the greatest of expectations, the sage begins his quest to determine meaning and purpose in life. He returns, however, empty-handed, much to his grave disappointment.[16] Like Saul Bellow, the ancient sage attaches an addendum to the Socratic motto: "But the examined life makes you wish you were dead."[17] Death looms large in Ecclesiastes.

At first glance, then, this somewhat deadening, melancholic book would seem to have little to do with wonder. One could easily make the case that Qoheleth's discourse comes close to writing wonder's obituary, and with it the death of character. The book revels in weariness and reeks with the stench of decay and disillusionment. Nevertheless, it is not the case that wonder flies out the door, but that it takes a decidedly philosophical, darker turn.

---

12. The term is used reservedly. See Fox, "Wisdom in Qoheleth," 119-21; idem, "Qoheleth's Epistemology"; cf. Crenshaw, "Qoheleth's Understanding of Intellectual Inquiry"; Schellenberg, *Erkenntnis als Problem,* 161-96; Weeks, *Ecclesiastes and Scepticism,* esp. 120-25. See chapter 1 above, wherein I refer to the biblical sages as "perceptionists," Qoheleth all the more so.

13. Machinist, "Voice of the Historian," 134.

14. E.g., 1:14; 2:13, 24; 3:16, 22; 4:1, 4, 7, 15; 8:9, 10, 17; 9:11.

15. *Apology* 38a.

16. Qoheleth's failed search for enduring meaning can be profitably compared to Gilgamesh's unsuccessful journey for immortal life. See Brown, *Ecclesiastes,* 1-7.

17. See Eccl. 4:2-3; 6:3 (but cf. 9:4). Quoted in Gussow, "For Saul Bellow."

Crisis: Social and Sapiential

In view of Qoheleth's numerous complaints, coupled with what little we know about the Second Temple period, particularly the Ptolemaic period, it is clear that much of the sage's discourse is a response to a deepening, multifaceted crisis, from economic to epistemological.[18] In light of it, Qoheleth's discourse could be regarded as a salvage operation for coping in an unprecedented age of turmoil.

Socioeconomic

Much of Qoheleth's discourse is cast in terms of profit and loss, touching upon the social and economic anxieties of his day and reflecting dramatic economic changes that began under Persian hegemony (ca. 539-333 BCE) and extended well into Ptolemaic rule in Palestine (ca. 319-200 BCE). In contrast to the largely subsistence, small-scale, agrarian-based economy of preexilic times, the economy of the Persian period became increasingly commercialized. A standardized monetary currency was established under Darius the Great (550-486 BCE) to facilitate commerce between Egypt and Persia. Some two centuries later, under Ptolemy II (283-246 BCE), coinage became firmly established in Yehud (as Israel was called in Persian times), yielding dramatic economic development.[19] In addition, an aggressive system of taxation was introduced by the Persians and continued to be enforced and developed throughout Hellenistic times.[20]

Consequently, a new market-driven economy of global proportions flourished, complete with myriad entrepreneurial opportunities and risks. Yet for many, such rapid growth was matched by devastating financial loss. While those who had extensive capital outlays possessed unprecedented opportunity for cultivating greater assets, those of lesser means were at a distinct disadvantage and suffered greatly. The prospect of financial gain was

18. It has been common for scholars to refer to Qoheleth's "crisis of wisdom." See, e.g., Lauha, "Krise des religiösen Glaubens"; Gese, "Crisis of Wisdom in Koheleth"; Crüsemann, "Unchangeable World"; Rose, "De la 'crise.'" Qoheleth's discourse is not itself the cause or representation of the "crisis of wisdom" but a response to it, namely to the failure of traditional wisdom to respond to the crisis of living under Ptolemaic rule (so Rose, "De la 'crise'"; Krüger, *Qoheleth*, 23; Sneed, *Politics of Pessimism*, 47).

19. Hengel, *Judaism and Hellenism*, 1:43-44.

20. Sneed, *Politics of Pessimism*, 91-98.

both alluring and elusive; the rewards were great but so were the risks.[21] One's earnings and possessions, Qoheleth observes, could easily be lost, turning gainful work into fruitless toil "under the sun." High risk/high reward was the name of the game played by many destined for great loss. The Persian system of property grants, moreover, undermined the traditional devolution of property, putting at risk the livelihood of families across generations. In short, the "entrepreneurial ethos" of Qoheleth's day was risky business, yielding wealth for some and misery for many (see, e.g., 2:18-23; 5:13-17).[22] In addition to the economic milieu of Qoheleth's day, an elaborate political bureaucracy was set in place under Persian hegemony and further developed under Ptolemaic rule to collect revenue through heavy taxation, exorbitant interest rates, and other means. "If you see the oppression of the poor and the violation of justice and righteousness in the province, do not be alarmed at the matter; for the high official[23] is watched by a higher, and there are yet higher ones over them" (5:7 [Eng. 8]). For Qoheleth, the call for justice plummets in a sea of bureaucratic diffusion.[24] The sage attributes the ubiquitous oppression of the poor to a top-heavy social hierarchy that diminishes communal responsibility. Qoheleth's social world was a highly stratified one in which wealth was gained sometimes easily, sometimes laboriously, depending on one's economic position, but in every case lost effortlessly. The diffusion of communal responsibility, moreover, constituted a debilitating social milieu that, in the sage's estimation, undermines wisdom's efficacy.

Sapiential

Qoheleth's crisis is not simply socioeconomic or political; it is also epistemological, a distinctly sapiential crisis.[25] The sage lived in a time of

21. For discussion of Yehud's economy in ancient Palestine, see Seow, "Socioeconomic Context"; under the Ptolemaic period, see Sneed, *Politics of Pessimism*, 91-120; Krüger, *Qoheleth*, 19-21.

22. See the discussion of socioeconomic context of the Ptolemaic period in Samuel Adams, *Wisdom in Transition*, 123-25. Stuart Weeks has argued that Qoheleth may have been a successful businessman fed up with the way wealth was distributed (*Ecclesiastes and Scepticism*, 34-37).

23. Heb. *gābōh* can also be translated as "arrogant one"; see Seow, *Ecclesiastes*, 201, 203.

24. See Sneed's discussion of a "layering of bureaucracy" under Ptolemaic rule (*Politics of Pessimism*, 91).

25. Relatedly, see Schellenberg, *Erkenntnis als Problem*, who casts the issue in terms of cognition (esp. 43-200).

free-flowing exchanges of ideas and perspectives from various cultures: Egyptian, Israelite, Persian, Hellenistic, all brought on by increased trade that began under the Persian Empire. Particularly after the completion of the Second Temple in 515 BCE, Yehud was no longer an isolated region but part of a major corridor for international commerce.[26] This continued into the Ptolemaic period as trade in perishable goods between Greece and Egypt increased further, and with them various nontangible items: ideas, perspectives, philosophies, cultural influences.[27] It was the business of sages/scribes to explore and mediate them within their own cultural context. Qoheleth found his own context parochial and inadequate.

The sapiential crisis that overshadows Qoheleth's observations is death. Not that death was suddenly discovered in the Second Temple period, but rather the distress of morbidity upon the individual, or what Robert Williamson aptly calls "death anxiety,"[28] reached unprecedented heights throughout the ancient cultures of the Eastern Mediterranean seaboard, and Qoheleth's discourse reflects this.[29] Traditional approaches that offered ways to ameliorate the existential distress of death collapse under Qoheleth's wary eye.[30] Qoheleth "consistently expresses his dissatisfaction with the world and human existence within that world through the idea, imagery, and fact of death."[31]

For Qoheleth, the leveling power of death, coupled with economic and social uncertainty, renders wisdom inefficacious, and with it all social striving, commercial venturing, and toiling. Before death's steely countenance, everything is rendered *hebel,* commonly translated "vanity." *Hebel* is the most significant motif in Ecclesiastes (repeated 38 times), the book's single-word thesis. "Vanity of vanities . . . vanity of vanities! All is vanity" (NRSV 1:2; see 12:8) is the book's motto, as much as the "fear of the LORD . . ." is Proverbs' motto. Qoheleth presents one example after another of life's *hebel,* from the cosmic to the personal. Paired frequently with

---

26. Berquist, *Judaism in Persia's Shadow,* 91-94.

27. Williamson, "Death and Symbolic Immortality," 187-89.

28. Williamson, "Death and Symbolic Immortality," 134 *et passim.* Williamson fruitfully applies the social-psychological discipline of Terror Management Theory to the texts of Proverbs, Ecclesiastes, and 4QInstruction.

29. See Burkes, *Death in Qoheleth.*

30. Burkes, *Death in Qoheleth,* 10-33.

31. Burkes, *Death in Qoheleth,* 35.

the expression "chasing wind" *(rĕʿût rûaḥ),*[32] the word itself conjures the image of "vapor," something ephemeral and insubstantial, perhaps even noxious.[33]

Nevertheless, *hebel* bears a rich and varied function in Qoheleth's discourse. As a metaphor, *hebel* wears many faces in Ecclesiastes, for the term can be translated in a variety of ways: "futility," "absurdity," "nothingness," "worthlessness," "transience," "ephemerality," "delusion," "insignificance," and "shit" all have been proposed, and no doubt a measure of translational flexibility is needed in each case.[34] But regardless of its specific nuance within each specific context, it is indubitable for Qoheleth that "*hebel* happens," inexorably so, and death is the stellar example. Put cosmically, *hebel* robs the world of moral coherence for Qoheleth as much as *rōgez* ("agitation") does for Job. Put personally, *hebel* drives a deep and permanent wedge between one's conduct and its expected consequence. In so doing, *hebel* signals the corrosive deconstruction of moral character.

Given the scourge of death and *hebel*'s all-encompassing reach, it is no surprise that the sage finds God remote, inscrutable, and largely indifferent to human plight, a far different Deity from the one who delivered a people from bondage. God is never addressed in the sage's discourse. Prayer is not part of his rhetoric. For Qoheleth, the acquisition of knowledge begins and ends with (frustrated) human inquiry; neither God nor a mediating link to God is available in the search for wisdom. While wisdom *(ḥokmâ)* is referenced repeatedly throughout the sage's discourse (29x), it lacks any hint of personification or transcendent nature (cf. Prov. 1:20-33; 8:1–9:6; Job 28:23-27). In Ecclesiastes *sapientia* is sapped of its potency and stripped of its subjectivity. All that is left are vestiges, inklings of insight of mere relative worth in a world that is largely irrational and uncontrollable.

---

32. See Eccl. 2:11, 17, 26; 4:4, 6; 6:9. The synonymous expression *raʿyôn rûaḥ* is paralleled with *hebel* in 4:16.

33. For an in-depth study of the various material nuances of "vapor" in Ecclesiastes, see Douglas Miller, *Symbol and Rhetoric*, esp. 91-156.

34. I agree with Fox that underlying most nuances of *hebel* is a measure of protest, pointing to the "tension between a certain reality and a framework of expectations" (Fox, *Qohelet and His Contradictions*, 31; see also idem, *Time to Tear Down*, 30-33, 48-49). That "framework" is the world according to sapiential tradition. Weeks has clarified the "tension" by arguing that the notion of *hebel* is not so much the failure of the world to meet human expectations as the "failure of human expectations to comprehend the realities of the world" (*Ecclesiastes and Scepticism*, 113).

Qoheleth's Self-Characterization

Unique to the Hebrew Scriptures, Ecclesiastes is essentially a self-presentation, primarily a monologue. What gives the book its overall coherence (in lieu of interspersed instructional material) are the various personal observations or confessions it contains. As Walther Zimmerli observed, the most characteristic speech form in Ecclesiastes is the "confessional" or "self-referential style."[35] Qoheleth's words are testimonial. His style reflects his epistemology: much of what he imparts is what he can personally verify.[36] It is he, and no one else, who undertakes the quest (1:13). Only toward the end of the book does the second person address surface, formally echoing the parent's address to his son in Prov. 1–9 but with an entirely different kind of counsel (see below). The bulk of the book, however, reflects a figure who, like Job, shares his personal experience and bares his soul, but unlike Job without external dialogic partners.[37] Qoheleth's "dialogue" comes from within as he recounts his quest to perceive and understand the world through wisdom, vacillating between various points of view and confessing his failure to find ultimate success in his pursuit. Yet it is precisely in his failure, in the transparency of his disillusionment, that Qoheleth attains his greatest authoritative status.[38] He is his own Socrates.

Crucial to understanding Qoheleth's character is his initial self-designation as king (1:12–2:26). The reasons behind the use of the royal metaphor are no doubt drawn from Solomon's legendary status as the wise king par excellence, which he exploits in order to deconstruct in ch. 2. Qoheleth reports on a series of grand "experiments" to test pleasure and its relationship to wisdom. Owing to his regal status, Qoheleth pulls out all the stops: nothing is spared, and all means are at his disposal (1:12-13a). Indeed, it is the sage's royal duty: "It is the glory of God to conceal things, but the glory of kings is to search things out" (Prov. 25:2). But such sapiential "glory" proves elusive for the royal sage.

---

35. My translation of *Bekenntnisstil* and *Ich-Stil* (Zimmerli, *Weisheit des Predigers Salomo*, 26; see Galling, "Kohelet-Studien," 280; Williams, "What Does It Profit?" 179.

36. See Adams, *Wisdom in Transition*, 141. Adams suggestively describes Qoheleth's way as a "personal experiment" (pp. 105-6). Schellenberg specifies "induction" and "falsification" as part of Qoheleth's "experimental" approach (*Erkenntnis als Problem*, 175-80).

37. Contrary to the claim that Ecclesiastes is a diatribe or disputation. See Fox's discussion in *Qohelet and His Contradictions*, 20-28 and 28 n. 11.

38. A telling contrast is the flat, parental figure in Proverbs. On one occasion, the father recounts his life as a boy, but avoids adopting a confessional tone (Prov. 4:3-9).

Qoheleth's self-declared status, his literary conceit, gives him regal recourse to search out everything. As king, Qoheleth is not bound to tradition, the corpus of conventional wisdom. Rather, he is in the unique position to confirm or disconfirm the veracity of conventional wisdom. So Qoheleth boldly embarks on an ambitious series of experiments or quests designed ultimately to do just that: discern and test the efficacy of wisdom. What follows is a veritable litany of accomplishments: "I made great," "I built" (Eccl. 2:4), "I planted" (vv. 4-5), "I made" (vv. 5, 6), "I acquired" (v. 7), "I gathered" (v. 8).

Qoheleth's self-introduction draws from the widespread genre of royal annals but in a way that is contrary to the genre's intent.[39] Essential to the genre is a listing of the king's great achievements, from success in battle to building monumental edifices, all for the purpose of immortalizing the king in memory.[40] By adopting this form of self-presentation, Qoheleth also intends to immortalize himself, not, however, by his (fictionalized) accomplishments but by his abysmal failures.

> I considered all that my hands had done and the toil I had spent in doing it, and again, all was futile *(hebel)* and chasing after wind, and there was nothing to be gained under the sun. (2:11)

All the king's accomplishments amount to nothing, the sage confesses. Qoheleth generalizes his failure elsewhere in his confession:

> All this I have tested by wisdom; I said, "I would be wise," but this was beyond me. That which is *(mâ-ššehāyâ)* is far off and very deep; who can discover it? (7:23-24)

> When I applied my mind to know wisdom and to observe the business that has been done on earth, . . . I saw all the work of God, that no one is able to discover what is happening under the sun. However much they may toil in seeking, they will not discover it. Even though those who are wise desire to know, they cannot discover it. (8:16-17)

For all his valiant efforts to understand it all and become supremely wise, Qoheleth casts himself as a royal failure. Like the heroic explorers of Job

---

39. Seow, "Qohelet's Autobiography."

40. E.g., West Semitic royal inscriptions such as the Mesha Inscription (*ANET*, 320-21) and the Kilamuwa Inscription (*ANET*, 654-55).

28, the sage's failed experiment subverts a familiar trope (see chapter 3 above): wisdom, it turns out, is not a matter of seeking, striving, or acquiring.

Although Qoheleth's regal caricature largely vanishes after ch. 2, the guise is not simply a foil to be shed and quickly forgotten. It serves as a critical point of departure for his self-characterization, namely his unchallenged, authoritative position of power and understanding. The figure of the king morphs into that of an elder sage with a keen familiarity with the business world. He has seen "everything," including the multitude of life's contradictions (7:15). He claims to have "acquired great wisdom," surpassing all before him (1:16a). No neophyte is he. In stark contrast to Elihu, Qoheleth exploits all the traditional motifs of journey, pursuit, search for wisdom, and social hierarchy to cement his position as the sage at the top of his game, as the one who has been at this business the longest and with the most means at his disposal. With the poignant treatise on the ravaging effects of death concluding his discourse to the "young man" in 12:1-8, Qoheleth presents himself not as the mere parental figure of Prov. 1–9, nor as the inspired youth in the character of Elihu, but as the great elder of wisdom. And so it is with the construction of such stature that Qoheleth is able to deconstruct so much sapientially.

Shaking the Foundations

While Qoheleth deconstructs wisdom's traditional ethos in a number of ways, he begins with creation, a testimony that the world as it is perceived has all to do with the self and its shaping.

The Static Cosmos: Ecclesiastes 1:3-11

For whatever reason, Qoheleth's opening words are not autobiographical but cosmological, prompted by his leading question about toil and gain (1:3). Although the answer is deferred for over a chapter (2:11), the sage builds up to it by offering his observations on creation followed by testimony of his personal quest. Not a creation account per se, 1:3-11 does provide a snapshot of the cosmos from Qoheleth's perspective. His words, moreover, conclude with further cosmological reflections in 12:2-7. Creation thus frames the sage's reflections in their entirety. Despite his predominantly dispassionate tone,[41] Qoheleth proves himself to be no disinterested observer. His opening question about material gain strikes at the heart of human purpose (1:3). "Gain" *(yitrôn)* is more than "a penny earned, a penny saved." Gain is what ensures one's legacy, extending it beyond one's fleeting life span. Toil is the effort exerted for gainful living, and questioning its value places all creation in question. In the sage's eyes, creation itself has a cosmic stake in the pursuit of gain, and Qoheleth, in turn, has a personal stake in creation's purpose.

> [2] "Futility of futilities,"[42] says Qoheleth,
>   "futility of futilities! All is futility!"
> [3] What gain[43] does one get from all the toil
>   at which one toils under the sun?
> [4] A generation goes, and a generation comes,
>   yet the earth remains ever the same.
> [5] The sun rises, and the sun sets,
>   panting[44] to the place where it rises.
> [6] Blowing[45] to the south and rounding to the north,
>   round and round goes the wind,
>   and on its rounds the wind returns.
> [7] All streams flow into the sea,
>   yet the sea is never full.
> To the place from which the streams flow,
>   there they flow again.
> [8] All words are wearisome,
>   more than one can express.
> The eye is not satisfied with seeing;
>   the ear is not filled with hearing.
> [9] What has been is what will be,
>   and what has been done is what will be done.

41. Except, evidently, when it comes to women; see 7:26.

42. Heb. *hābēl hăbālîm,* a poetic way of saying "utter futility."

43. Lit. "what is left over" *(yitrôn),* which can mean gain or advantage in the sense of surplus (3:9; 5:15 [Eng. 16]; cf. 5:7-8 [Eng. 8-9]). See Seow, *Ecclesiastes,* 103-4. But contra Seow, the term in this context does seem to take on commercial value in the sense of "profit." See Fox, *Time to Tear Down,* 112-13; Weeks, *Ecclesiastes and Scepticism,* 34-36.

44. Heb. *šô'ēp* (see, e.g., Jer. 2:24; 14:6; Isa. 42:14; Job 7:2). For a contrasting image of the sun, see Ps. 19:5b-7 (Eng. 4b-6).

45. Keeping the reader in poetic suspense, the subject of the verb is not divulged until the end of the line.

> There is nothing new under the sun.
> [10]If there is a thing of which it is said, "See this; it is new!"
>   it has already been, in the ages before us.
> [11]There is no remembrance of those who came before (us),
>   nor of those who will come after.
> There will be no remembrance of them
>   among those who will come afterward.

Generations come and go, the sun rises and sets, the wind blows hither and yon, and the streams flow perpetually, all the while both earth and sea remain unchanged. The sage observes the weary "revolutions" of the sun, whose "panting" to the place of its rising plays a part in the wind's unceasing circumambulations. Sun, wind, and streams are all in constant motion, all returning to where they began and continuing on, without pause. There is no breather for the sun. The perpetual cycles exhibit neither beginning nor ending, much less a new beginning.[46]

Although there seems to be something resonant of Heraclitus (ca. 535-475 BCE) here, who considered all things in constant flux and motion, the constant motion and effort that characterize the cosmos for this Israelite sage actually yields *no* change (1:4b).[47] Even as the millennia pass, any semblance of progress, any appearance of newness, is merely a mirage. Activity abounds, but nothing is achieved. Like a hamster spinning a wheel as it runs, no destination is ever reached. Such frenetic motion amounts to only running in place. All this cosmic kinesis is for naught. Ever in motion but never changing, the cosmos is uniformly indifferent to human living, from birth to death, a world without pause and effect, without history, and, as will be seen, without a future.

Nevertheless, such a world is far from chaotic. From Qoheleth's perspective, the world is perfectly orderly, even understandable; the sage simply understands it as perfectly indifferent to human need and desire, perfectly irrational to moral coherence.

> There is an evil that I have seen under the sun,
>   like an error stemming from a ruler:
> folly is set in many high places,
>   but the rich sit in low estate.

---

46. For a more optimistic, ecologically oriented reading particularly of Eccl. 1:4-7, see Dell, "Cycle of Life in Ecclesiastes."

47. Lit. "the earth stands forever."

I have seen slaves on horses,
    and princes walking on foot like slaves. (10:5-7)

Qoheleth's assessment of the social order is comparable to the numerical saying in Prov. 30:21-23. However, unlike the proverbial sage, Qoheleth does not see cosmic collapse or chaos as the result. Instead, he sees this as tragically "normal." Call it Qoheleth's "misanthropic principle."[48] Rather than chaos, the world according to Qoheleth is a distinctly alien order, quintessentially and cruelly strange.

As the sea is never filled, so human desire ("eye" and "ear") is never satisfied (1:8b). If the book of Proverbs is a "manual of desire," then Ecclesiastes is a "manual of disillusionment," a testimony to desire's insatiability and ultimately to the frustration of desire. For all their noble efforts, the people of past generations will be forgotten by those of subsequent generations (v. 11). Indeed, the same fate applies to every generation. Nothing of significance is left for posterity. Establishing a legacy is a futile venture. As the world turns, as the cosmic wheels grind on, life is, to quote the poet Edna St. Vincent Millay, not "one damn thing after another — it's one damn thing over and over."[49] Both natural and "man-made" history are doomed to repetition, much like the sun and the wind. The past is the future; "there is nothing new under the sun" (1:9). Any "new" thing is simply a variation of the past. Nothing is created out of nothing. The appearance of change lies only in the tunnel vision of the beholder. Whether true or not, Qoheleth's claim of life's seeming sameness indicates just how far the sage is able to step back and paint a picture of totality, a still life on a peeling canvas. In the role of the observing subject, Qoheleth has removed himself from a world that is not his to have or to master, a wholly estranged world. He is a stranger to the world.

By stepping back to gain the bigger picture, the sage sees the cosmos moving on its own frenetic inertia with human history mirroring its lifeless movements. Any sense of wonder passes as creation presses on in wearisome repetition. The music of the spheres is, in Qoheleth's ears, cosmically atonal and repetitive ad nauseum. No melody, no crescendo. For all the cosmic energy expended, nothing is gained and everything is lost.[50] The same goes for human striving: like cosmos, like humanity. According to

---

48. For more detail see Brown, *Seven Pillars of Creation*, 177-96.
49. Quoted in A. Adams, ed., *Home Book of Humorous Quotations*, 25.
50. See 2:22; 3:9; 6:11.

Qoheleth, creation is emptied of telos and filled with toil, a cosmos without direction and devoid even of its own genesis. There is nothing, properly speaking, *creative* about Qoheleth's cosmos. As there is no beginning, so there also is no point. The incessant motion of the cosmic elements is Qoheleth's stellar example of *hebel,* cosmic futility.

The Pit and the Pendulum: Ecclesiastes 3:1-9

Matching Qoheleth's opening poem is the best-known passage in Ecclesiastes on life's various "seasons":[51]

> [1] For everything there is a season,
>> and a time for every matter under the heavens:
>>
>>> [2] a time to bear[52] and a time to die;
>>>> a time to plant and a time to uproot what is planted;
>>> [3] a time to kill and a time to heal;
>>>> a time to break and a time to build;
>>> [4] a time to weep and a time to laugh;
>>>> a time to mourn and a time to dance;
>>> [5] a time to throw stones and a time to gather stones;
>>>> a time to embrace and a time to refrain from embracing;
>>> [6] a time to seek and a time to lose;
>>>> a time to keep and a time to throw away;
>>> [7] a time to tear and a time to sew;
>>>> a time to be silent and a time to speak;
>>> [8] a time to love and a time to hate;
>>>> a time of war and a time of peace.
>> [9] What gain does the worker have from toiling?

What Qoheleth does visually with his cosmological snapshot in 1:4-7, he now does from a singularly temporal standpoint in 3:1-8. Both poetic reflections step back to look at the larger picture, whether cosmologically or chronologically. This "seasonal" poem features fourteen antinomies or

---

51. It is important to note that Qoheleth's most famous passage is entirely descriptive, as opposed to prescriptive. The infinitives that populate the poem can just as easily be translated as gerunds: "a time of bearing and a time of dying."

52. The verb is likely transitive, given that all the following verbs are active (Krüger, *Qoheleth,* 75; Seow, *Ecclesiastes,* 160).

paired opposites. Being divisible by seven, this poetic catalogue conveys a sense of completion (cf. Gen. 1:1–2:3). Commenting on the symmetry of the poem, Crenshaw observes that "the effect . . . is mesmerizing like the ticking of a clock."[53] Like a grandfather clock, one might say, with its hypnotic pendulations. This symmetrical pairing of opposites, moreover, is resonant of Stoic philosophy, which viewed the universe in terms of perfectly balanced opposites (cf. Sir. 42:24-25).[54] But for Qoheleth, a cost comes with the elegance.

If the life of the cosmos in ch. 1 runs like a spinning wheel going nowhere, human life in ch. 3 resembles something of a swinging pendulum. Laughter and mourning, love and hate, war and peace are the poles within which life oscillates from birth to death and back again. In an age of peace, one can count on the advent of conflict, but also vice versa. Like the sun's "revolutions" and the wind's circumambulations, life swings incessantly back and forth, never stationary but never advancing. The modulated "swings" of human activity match the perpetual "cycles" of cosmic conduct. And so life oscillates indifferently between gain and loss, prosperity and adversity. The lesson for Qoheleth? "There is nothing new under the sun." Within the divinely modulated swings, a linear view of history, let alone of time, has no place. But there is also an admonition: "In the day of prosperity be joyful, and in the day of adversity consider. God has made the one as well as the other, so that mortals may not find out anything that will come after them" (7:14). Qoheleth concludes the poem by raising the same question posed at the beginning of his cosmic poem (3:9; 1:3): What gain is there in all the toiling, in all the oscillations? None.

Following the poem, Qoheleth provides theological commentary. Two verses in particular mark the sage's attempt to arrive at a comprehensively cosmic perspective.

> I have seen the business that God has given to everyone to be busy with. [God] has made everything exquisitely suitable *(yāpeh)* for its time. Moreover, [God] has put (a sense of) timelessness *(hā'ōlām)*[55]

---

53. Crenshaw, *Qoheleth*, 72.

54. Crenshaw, *Qoheleth*, 73.

55. The translation of *'ōlām* (commonly "eternity") in this verse has generated much discussion. See Whitley, *Koheleth*, 31-33; Murphy, *Ecclesiastes*, 34-35; Crenshaw, *Ecclesiastes*, 91, 97-98; Seow, *Ecclesiastes*, 163; Krüger, *Qoheleth*, 87-88. Parallel to v. 11a, the term maintains its temporal nuance, as evinced in the Greek translation *aiōna*. Attempts to render it with the meaning "hiddenness" or "unknown," though supportable contextually, fail in light

into their minds, such that they cannot determine what God has done from beginning to end. (3:10-11)

From the clockwork vagaries of human existence, coupled with the incessant cycles of creation, Qoheleth discerns an inscrutable elegance in the big picture of life. An entirely positive term, the Hebrew word for "exquisitely suitable" *(yāpeh)* elsewhere designates aesthetic approval of a person or thing, signifying beauty.[56] More than simply suitability or appropriateness, more a sense of pleasing perfection is meant here. Qoheleth deploys this loaded term in only one other place and in a very different context (see below), but here the sage finds an elegance that extends beyond human understanding. A generation comes, a generation goes, and it is all apt and elegant. Such balanced symmetry evokes even for a pessimistic sage a hint of mesmerizing wonder.

Perhaps just as wonder-provoking is a divinely endowed sense of timelessness or eternity *('ōlām)* in the human mind. Qoheleth contrasts punctiliar time (v. 11a; *'ēt*) with indefinite duration,[57] or the totality of time (v. 11b).[58] The overall temporal symmetry conveyed by the poem points to an abstracted sense of time, of time minus its arrow or direction, as any modern physicist would fully appreciate.[59] Qoheleth's mini-excursus on time illustrates well his remarkable facility to "step back" and gain a larger picture of the world and the self. In this self-transcending movement,[60] the sage is afforded a new vantage point. He comes to view the whole course of time and concludes that even though human beings have the ability to rise above the transient moments of their lives, there remains the impenetrable mystery of God's involvement in time. Only God holds the arrow, if there is one.

The swings and cycles of life and death, of generations passing and coming, are suitable only in God's mind, forever closed to human inquiry.

---

of Qoheleth's consistently temporal use of *'ōlām* elsewhere (1:4, 10; 2:16; 9:6; 12:5). Nevertheless, a wordplay may be at work (cf. Crenshaw, *Ecclesiastes*, 97-98; idem, *Qoheleth*, 64).

56. E.g., 1 Sam. 16:12; 2 Sam. 13:1; 1 Kgs 1:3-4; Cant. 1:16; Ezek. 33:32. See Crenshaw, *Ecclesiastes*, 91, 97; Krüger, *Qoheleth*, 85-86, who finds intertextual correspondence with "good" *(ṭôb)* in Gen. 1. Note also the pairing in Eccl. 5:17 (Eng. 18); see chapter 6 below.

57. So also Jenni, "Wort *'ōlām* im Alten Testament," 24-27; Murphy, *Ecclesiastes*, 34-35.

58. Podechard, *L'Ecclésiaste*, 295. His translation of the disputed term is "la durée entière" (292).

59. See Brown, *Seven Pillars of Creation*, 188-90.

60. See below for further discussion.

The beginning and the end lie beyond human ken. Hence the human sense of "timelessness" comes with a confounding limitation: it clouds the mind, preventing any hope of discerning God's purpose.[61] The wearying cycles of the cosmos described in ch. 1 and the unwavering swings of life and death delineated in ch. 3 together depict a sense of timelessness, of eternal repetition, that does more to obscure than to illumine, concealing what God is truly up to. Eventually, however, the clock must unwind. Enter the pit: "a time to die."

Death: Ecclesiastes 12:1-7

If the world in ch. 1 is a cosmos running in perpetuity, then the world according to ch. 12 is a cosmos running on empty. As generations come and go (1:5), so creation as a whole will eventually go, never to return. For Qoheleth, creation may not have had a beginning, but it surely has an ending.

> [1] Remember your creator[62] in the days of your youth,
>> before the days of trouble come,
> and the years draw near,
>> when you will say, "I have no pleasure in them";
> [2] before the sun darkens, even the light,[63] as well as the moon and the stars,
>> while the clouds return with rain;
> [3] in the day when the guards of the house tremble,
>> while the strong men cower,
> and the women who grind stop because they are few,
>> while those who look through the windows see dimly;
> [4] when the double doors on the street are shut,
>> while the sound of the mill is low,
> and one rises at the sound of a bird,
>> while all the daughters of song are brought low;
> [5] when one is afraid of heights,

---

61. Hence the possible wordplay. Cf. Crenshaw, *Ecclesiastes*, 97-98.

62. The word *bôrĕ'eykā* is ambiguous, including its variant plural form. It can also mean, in slightly variant form, "your pit" (i.e., grave) and "your cistern." See Crenshaw, *Qoheleth*, 66; Seow, *Ecclesiastes*, 351-52. Krüger, *Qoheleth*, 190.

63. The distinction between the "light" and the celestial bodies recalls the comparable distinction made in Gen. 1:3, 14-16. See Seow, *Ecclesiastes*, 353.

> and terrors are in the road;
> the almond tree blossoms,
>> the locust drags itself along and desire fails.
> Yes, humans go to their eternal home,
>> and the mourners will go about the streets;
> ⁶ before the silver cord is snapped,
>> and the golden bowl is broken,
> and the jar is broken at the fountain,
>> and the vessel⁶⁴ broken at the cistern,
> ⁷ and the dust returns to the earth as it was,
>> and the life-breath *(rûaḥ)* returns to God who gave it.

Creation's demise is marked by cosmic darkening (12:2) and the cessation of life (v. 7). The end of natural history marks a return to creation's preexistent state before the *'ādām* was created from "dust" and infused with God's breath (see Gen. 2:7). Between darkness and dust, the sage employs other images ranging from the domestic and the commercial to the natural. Some interpreters, from rabbinic times to the present, have understood these images as allegorical references to the aging body:⁶⁵ reference to grinding women (12:3) suggests tooth loss; the cowed "strong men" (v. 3) represent the bent back; the blossoming almond tree points to gray hair. Failing eyesight, insomnia, deafness, physical imbalance, and impotence are all considered to be allegorically featured in this narrative.

A strictly allegorical reading, however, poses the danger of dismissing the sheer variety of images Qoheleth employs, which itself is a marvel.⁶⁶ Most of these images can stand very well on their own even as some share metaphorical significance, particularly in v. 6. Qoheleth has chosen such a diverse array to demonstrate how death affects *all* areas of life, from the cosmic and the commercial to the domestic and the individual. The "panting" sun of 1:5 suffers burnout in 12:2. The toiling self of 4:8 is dead and buried in 12:5-7. The world's end is no apocalyptic overthrow.⁶⁷ Rather, it happens with gradual darkening and diminution. The perpetual cycles and swings of creation's regularities simply unwind. The world passes away

---

64. Or, much less likely, "wheel." See Seow, *Ecclesiastes*, 367.

65. See, e.g., Dulin, "How Sweet Is the Light," 267-69.

66. See Fox's insightful, albeit one-sided, treatment of 12:1-7 in "Aging and Death."

67. See Seow's discussion of the eschatological tenor of this section in *Ecclesiastes*, 372-82; idem, "Qohelet's Eschatological Poem."

in cosmic dissolution and bodily deterioration. The kinetic leads to the kenotic; energy expended is energy dissipated. Call it existential entropy or, simply, *hebel*.

In between these cosmic bookends (1:3-11; 12:2-7) are various reflections on creation. Qoheleth, for example, finds no ultimate distinction between animals and humans (3:18-21); he has no doctrine of the *imago Dei*. Humans are animals in life, if not in death. All share common breath *(rûaḥ)* in life, and their fate is equally sealed in death. As for any distinction emerging after death, Qoheleth remains uncommittedly agnostic (v. 21). Regardless, humans "have no advantage over the animals" (v. 19).

Life without human "advantage" is life beset by "time and accident," as the sage vividly illustrates in 9:11-12.

> Again I saw that under the sun the race does not belong to the swift, nor the battle to the strong, nor bread to the wise, nor wealth to the intelligent, nor favor to the skillful, for time and accident[68] befall them all. For, indeed, one cannot predict one's time. Like fish taken in a cruel net, and like birds caught in a snare, so humans are snared at a time of calamity, when it falls upon them suddenly.

Life thus cannot be planned, let alone controlled. Because of chance, life afflicts the living in ways that are cruelly unpredictable, irrespective of status and place.

Stepping Back in Self-Transcendence

Harmut Gese has noted that Qoheleth's wisdom is the product of a unique "mutation of structure" that stems from the author's relationship to his world.[69] By this Gese means that in the role of the observing subject Qoheleth has become estranged from the cosmos.[70] The sage's observations about the world reflect a perceptual posture that views the cosmos as a detached totality. The sage has stepped back and come to view the world in its seemingly pointless whole. While such a move carries with it an ethical

---

68. Heb. *'ēt wāpegaʿ*, which can be translated as a hendiadys: "(un)timely accident."

69. Gese, "Crisis of Wisdom in Koheleth," 142-43.

70. Gese, "Crisis of Wisdom in Koheleth," 143. See also Fisch, *Poetry with a Purpose*, 166.

as well as epistemological component, both lead to the same outcome: the apprehension of *hebel* (1:2; 12:8).[71]

The scope of "everything" in Qoheleth's thesis statements, however, is open to interpretation. For Fox, Qoheleth does not mean the "entirety of reality, but only of what happens in the realm of human existence, 'under the sun.'"[72] "Everything" is limited to life events "taken as a whole."[73] Fox's restriction, however, belies Qoheleth's cosmological observations that open the book (1:2-11).[74] *Hebel,* for example, includes the sun's perpetual cycling; it is as much a description of the absurdity of the cosmic condition as it is an indication of how the perceiving self is positioned in relation to the world.[75] *Hebel* acknowledges both the world's pointless absurdity and the individual's relationship to it, recognized in the act of "stepping back" and viewing the world and the self as a meaningless whole.[76] Qoheleth's notion of *hebel,* moreover, is forged not only from a collision between his expectations and the world around him, but also from a collision within himself.[77] In his study of the absurd, philosopher Thomas Nagel describes the human capacity of stepping back: "Humans have the special capacity to step back and survey themselves, and the lives to which they are committed, with that detached amazement which comes from watching an ant struggle up a heap of sand."[78] Or Sisyphus pushing his rock. Such "detached amazement" captures something of Qoheleth's critical perspective. Epistemologically, the sage removes himself from the world of toil and struggle, including his own, and is thereby able to question the point of *all* human and cosmological activity: detachment for the sake of deconstruction.

As ethicists have pointed out, this epistemological move constitutes

71. See Fox, "Meaning of *Hebel* for Qohelet"; idem, *Qohelet and His Contradictions,* 29-47; idem, *Time to Tear Down,* 30-33.

72. Fox, "Meaning of *Hebel* for Qohelet," 423.

73. Fox, "Meaning of *Hebel* for Qohelet," 424.

74. Fox's assertion that the natural phenomena described in 1:4-7 simply illustrate "the futility of human efforts" is too narrow ("Meaning of *Hebel* for Qohelet," 423). On the other hand, matters of cosmology are never divorced from issues of character; see Kamano, *Cosmology and Character,* esp. 43-150, 242-46.

75. Fox alludes to this dimension of the absurd when discussing the unique role wisdom plays in Qoheleth's thought: "Qohelet alone tries to think about life in its totality," which results in a "global judgment" (*Qohelet and His Contradictions,* 111).

76. See Nagel, "Absurd."

77. See Nagel, "Absurd," 722.

78. Nagel, "Absurd," 20.

an indispensable part of the moral discipline as a way of taking stock of one's conduct and discerning the "morally right thing."[79] By stepping back, by exercising the inherently human capacity to transcend the self, Qoheleth arrives at a new and profound knowledge of the world and his relationship to it. He perceives himself estranged from the world. Not only is the world a stranger to Qoheleth; he is a stranger unto himself. He sees himself consumed with the vocation of seeking out wisdom while knowing that he is doing nothing more than chasing wind. He observes himself like observing a rat scurrying in a maze full of dead ends. Yet strive he does; he can do no other. Qoheleth knows he toils for no one, let alone himself, yet finds himself unable to stop.[80] So also the human race. No matter how hard they strive to break out, human beings are caught in a vicious circle of limitation and ignorance.[81] By stepping back, Qoheleth nullifies the notion of moral purpose and thus moral character. Like Job, Qoheleth splits asunder what traditional wisdom had joined together: right character and blessing, conduct and consequence. *Ḥinnām* and *hebel*, instead, join hands.[82]

Wisdom's Demise?

By severing the causal connection between conduct and outcome, Qoheleth radically limits the scope and efficacy of wisdom.[83] His treatment of wisdom is remarkably diverse. Wisdom is characterized as vulnerable (e.g., 9:12-16),[84] inaccessible (7:23b-24), both a tool and a goal (e.g., 2:3, 9; 7:23a, 25; 8:17),[85] and perhaps even as a fickle woman (7:26-29).[86] There is, moreover, another aspect to wisdom that is quite formative for Qoheleth.

Qoheleth charges at the very outset in his confession that the pursuit of wisdom is an "unhappy business" (*'inyan rā'*) that has no ultimate pay-

79. Hauerwas, *Character and Christian Life*, 124.

80. Fox, "Meaning of *Hebel* for Qohelet," 426; idem, *Qohelet and His Contradictions*, 47.

81. O'Connor, *Wisdom Literature*, 122.

82. See Crenshaw's helpful comparison of *ḥinnām* and *hebel* in *Qoheleth*, 102, 107.

83. Murphy admits that Qoheleth "rejects traditional wisdom for the security it offers," but in so doing "purifies and extends it" (*Ecclesiastes*, lxiii, lxiv).

84. Fox, *Qohelet and His Contradictions*, 117; Murphy, *Ecclesiastes*, lxii.

85. For discussion of Qoheleth's treatment of wisdom as a methodology, see Fox, *Qohelet and His Contradictions*, 80-89.

86. Krüger, *Qoheleth*, 24, 146-47; but cf. Seow, *Ecclesiastes*, 262, who makes a case for the "foreign woman."

off (1:13-14; cf. v. 3). With such low commendation, Qoheleth likens the quest for wisdom to a failed business venture, giving wisdom a distinctive materialistic slant.[87] Such a construal is not unprecedented in traditional wisdom; material prosperity had long been considered a natural outcome of cultivating wisdom, even as wisdom was considered to surpass the value of wealth (see Prov. 3:14-17; 8:10, 18-19). However, Qoheleth goes further: he collapses wisdom's material blessings with wisdom itself only to find wisdom bankrupt.[88] Wisdom is inextricably tied to the question of material gain (1:3). The question of what kind of *yitrôn* ("net gain from an economic transaction")[89] results from labor is not simply a matter of curiosity by which wisdom is employed as a tool for inquiry. The very nature of wisdom is bound up with how one answers the question. Both the pursuit of wisdom and the pursuit of profit are business ventures: "When I applied my mind to know wisdom and to observe the business *(hā'inyān)* that is done on earth . . ." (8:16). "The protection[90] of wisdom is like the protection of money" (7:12), so Qoheleth intones. The pursuit of wisdom and the affairs of business go hand in hand (2:19-20).

Why does Qoheleth give wisdom such a materialistic slant? His treatment no doubt reflects the social climate of an aristocratic class, which shared in both the risks and gains of entrepreneurial opportunity and heavy taxation under Ptolemaic rule.[91] Encouraged by aggressive international trade and tight financial control imposed by a central bureaucracy, money rose to an unprecedented importance under the Ptolemies (see above).[92] Given such conditions, Qoheleth's answer to the question of lasting gain, namely that the pursuit of it is like chasing wind, reflects something of the pursuit of wisdom itself. As gain can be unwillingly handed over at a moment's notice to the "stranger," to one undeserving of the fruits of one's labors, wisdom too can slip easily through one's fingers. Wisdom is elusive, *sapientia abscondita* (7:23-24); it is the irretrievably lost coin.

Like the sage in Job 28, Qoheleth discerns wisdom as ever elusive and hidden. But there is more. Wisdom in Qoheleth's eyes is disenfranchised. On the one hand, it is metaphorically reduced to a material possession, a

---

87. See Crüsemann, "Unchangeable World," 65-66; Kugel, "Qohelet and Money."

88. Compare Solomon's prayer, which makes the distinction clear (1 Kgs. 3:9-14).

89. Galling, *Prediger*, 69.

90. Lit. "shadow" or "shelter" *(ṣēl)*.

91. See Crüsemann, "Unchangeable World," 66; Hengel, *Judaism and Hellenism*, 1:18-23, 126-27; Sneed, *Politics of Pessimism in Ecclesiastes*, 131-43.

92. See Whybray, *Ecclesiastes*, 10-11.

tangible means by which Qoheleth hoped to gain security and profit, but to no avail. Wisdom is an investment that guarantees no glorious return; its advantages are meager at best. On the other hand, wisdom is so abstracted and disembodied that it remains forever beyond the sage's reach. Quite in contrast to Wisdom in Proverbs, wisdom in Ecclesiastes lacks all person-ification; hence it cannot be embodied, let alone possessed.

With wisdom stripped of moral potency and material promise, wisdom without Wisdom, is there any place for wonder in Ecclesiastes? Gone, to be sure, is the rapturous amazement with which his sapiential predecessors viewed wisdom and the world. Gone is the kind of mystery that prompts astonishment and praise. While Qoheleth does acknowledge mystery, it is the kind that obscures rather than illumines. Yet wonder per-sists in Qoheleth's profile of God and life, more centrally than one might expect: a primal, aporetic form of wonder.

CHAPTER 6

Wondering among the Ruins: Ecclesiastes II

[Wonder] dismantles all subjective and otherworldly pretensions
and reveals the ordinary as strange, contingent, and, in many cases,
ethically insupportable.

Mary-Jane Rubenstein[1]

In one of the later Socratic dialogues, the prodigy Theaetetus finds himself at wit's end before Socrates' relentless questioning about the nature
of knowledge. Exasperated, the young man declares, "By the gods, Socrates, I am lost in wonder *(thaumazō)* when I think of all these things,
and sometimes when I regard them it really makes my head swim" (155c).
Socrates responds, "[T]his feeling of wonder *(to thaumazein)* shows that
you are a philosopher, since wonder is the only beginning of philosophy"
(155d).[2] The neophyte is at a loss to make sense of the "countless myri-
ads of . . . contradictions" that point to the elusive nature of knowledge
(155c). Or in the words of Mary-Jane Rubenstein, Theaetetus is bewildered by "the sudden insubstantiality of something he had held to be
self-evident" about the nature of knowledge itself.[3] "In freeing the young
philosopher from his own fledgling doctrines, Socrates has freed him
for the aporetic vertigo of wonder," of wonder at "the groundlessness

1. Rubenstein, *Strange Wonder*, 193.
2. Plato, *Theaetetus, Sophist*, 54-55.
3. Rubenstein, *Strange Wonder*, 4.

of things."[4] Call it deconstructive wonder. "Standing in *thaumazein,* the [young] philosopher stands exposed to that which he cannot master."[5]

Wonder Rising

Qoheleth, too, stands exposed to a world that he cannot master.[6] The sage's musings on the indifferent ordering of life, the inscrutability of God, the frustration of desire, and wisdom's unfathomability are debilitating conclusions to his attempt at discerning the "sum of things" (*ḥešbôn,* 7:25). He, too, is at a loss, and in more ways than one: economically, politically, theologically, sapientially. Qoheleth becomes lost in perplexity, the perplexity of *hebel.* Wickedness and justice trade places; death treats the wise and the foolish equally, even the animals; oppression is omnipresent; everything is in motion yet nothing ever changes; memory is an illusion; enjoyment is ever fleeting, yet it is the highest human good. *Hebel* exposes the groundlessness of things: futile and ephemeral, worthless and absurd. It is enough to make any sage's head swim in frustration, if not despair. The contradictions and complexities, paradoxes and perplexities, reduce the sage to a state of deconstructive wonder. In Qoheleth's hands, wonder turns at once philosophical and primal, emerging from the rubble of shaken foundations and prompting critical inquiry about human life and the world, on the one hand, and fearful awe about the God behind it all, on the other. Wonder is the beginning of wisdom, but it is according to Qoheleth also the ending of wisdom, of wisdom without Wisdom.

As noted in the previous chapter, wonder has specific iterations in Qoheleth's discernments. Amid the absurdities and paradoxes, amid the *hebel* of it all, Qoheleth finds that God "has made everything exquisitely suitable *(yāpeh)* for its time" (3:11a). As noted in the previous chapter, the sage discerns a transcendent, or at least a higher-order, symmetry that rises above the fray of life's vicissitudes. Amid the unpredictable events of human existence (e.g., 9:11-12), a larger scheme unfolds, an order of "seasonal" oscillations, a balancing of extremes (3:1-10), a cause for wonder. In addition, God "has placed (a sense of) timelessness *('ōlām)* into their minds, yet they cannot fathom what God has done from beginning to end"

---

4. Rubenstein, *Strange Wonder,* 7.
5. Rubenstein, *Strange Wonder,* 4.
6. See Seow, "Theology."

(v. 11b). In stepping back to survey all that he is able to perceive, Qoheleth discerns a kind of "perfection in the ordering of the world,"[7] but it is an ordering that is utterly indifferent, indeed alien, to human aspirations for gain, let alone mastery. Such ordering is God's alone, for God alone — a note of wonder evoked by the paradox of divine providence and human "imperception." This inscrutable aptness — the human inability to discern the direction of divine providence in light of the perceived symmetry of human events in God's created order — leads inexorably to the unsettling side of wonder.

God-Fearing

In all three wisdom books, "the fear of the LORD/God" is heavily referenced. Ecclesiastes is no exception. Fear of God for Qoheleth is a richly nuanced notion, ranging from a sense of foreboding to an acute awareness of mystery and reverence. Direct reference to "fear" in Ecclesiastes is found in five passages (3:14; 5:6 [Eng. 7]; 7:18; 8:12-13; 12:13). Fearing God is Qoheleth's chief virtue, a whole "new ethical category" according to Mark Sneed,[8] but what it means precisely is hard to determine.

First, who is God, the object of "fear," in Ecclesiastes? Qoheleth holds an immeasurably high view of the Deity, so high that God ordains everything yet remains ever remote and inscrutable (see, e.g., 3:14-15), and all attempts to grasp God, like grasping gain and chasing wind, result only in presumption. God is the quintessential Unknown, elusive and ineffable, placing impenetrable limits on all human inquiry. Neither bone-chilling terror nor benign indifference is Qoheleth's response to the inscrutable aptness and irrevocable power of God's ways (3:11, 14).

Qoheleth's most extensive injunction to fear God is found in an exhortation on religious observance (4:17–5:6 [Eng. 5:1-7]). Without using the term "fear" at the outset, Qoheleth conjures a sense of foreboding in the temple:

> Watch your steps[9] when you go to the house of God; to draw near to listen is more acceptable than fools offering sacrifice, for they do

---

7. To quote Deane-Drummond in her discussion of wonder, *Wonder and Wisdom.* See chapter 1 above.

8. Sneed, *Politics of Pessimism,* 201.

9. The Qere form (dual) is preferable.

not know that they are doing evil. Do not be rash with your mouth, nor let your heart be quick to utter a word before God, for God is in heaven, but you upon earth; therefore let your words be few. Indeed, dreams come with much preoccupation, and a fool's voice with many words. So when you make a vow to God, fulfill it without delay; for there is no pleasure in fools. Fulfill what you vow! Better that you not vow at all than that you vow and not fulfill it. Do not let your mouth lead your body into sin, and do not say before the messenger that it was a mistake. Why should God fume at your words and destroy the work of your hands? Vacuous dreams are in abundance, and words are aplenty.[10] *Fear God!*

With his wonderful wordplay on *šmr* ("watch/guard") and *šmʿ* ("listen") in the opening verse, Qoheleth seemingly depicts a God-haunted temple in which the worshiper must tiptoe around for fear of provoking God's wrath. But God does not lurk in the shadows; "God is in heaven," enthroned over all the earth (cf. Deut 4:39). Nevertheless, a sense of foreboding lingers within the hallowed walls. The upshot for Qoheleth is that such "fear" elicits obedience of a particular sort: the restraint of contrivance and, in turn, the opening of fearful receptivity: "watch" and "listen." Qoheleth conceives the temple as a conduit of communication, a typical view of the temple's function, but it is primarily one-way. Listening is preferred over sacrifice and supplication, humility over pride, and making vows is to be taken with utmost seriousness and as a last resort. It is not clear what is precisely meant by reference to dreams (5:2, 6 [Eng. 3, 7]),[11] but, regardless, Qoheleth associates dreams with obsessive concern and excessive verbiage.

Are these the outcomes of divinely induced terror, of paralyzing *theophobia?* Certainly not to the extreme that some have argued; otherwise, the sage would urge his audience to avoid the temple altogether! To be sure, Qoheleth acknowledges God's wrath, but the sage does not say that

---

10. See Seow, *Ecclesiastes*, 193, 200, for making sense of this final verse (i.e., taking *ḥălōmôt wahăbālîm* as a hendiadys).

11. The conceivable range of possibilities that fit the context extends from dreams that result in lack of sleep due to burdensome cares and worries (see 8:16) to prophetic incubation. I would suggest that Qoheleth is referring to (allegedly) divinely inspired dreams, since such an injunction against cultic (apocalyptic? see Joel 3:1 [Eng. 2:28]) reception of dreams accords well with his insistence upon the unsurpassable distance between God and humankind.

God will "destroy you," but rather that God will "destroy the work of your hands" in the case of careless vow making (5:5 [Eng. 6]). In any case, evidently not a fan of cultic poetry,[12] Qoheleth prefers a sanctuary of silence as the sign of authentic reverence, of true fear. For him, the temple is not a refuge in which God protects the steps of the righteous.[13] Rather, it is a place of caution and accountability, of "hesitant trepidation"[14] and reverent receptivity. Be still, and know that God is not to be trifled with.

To fear God, then, is to be fearfully receptive in the domain of the Holy, where human initiative is minimized and all scheming is eliminated. To fear God is to acknowledge the gulf between transcendent eminence and fragile creatureliness, the gulf between divine power and human frailty. Reverence is equated with utmost reticence in matters pertaining to the Divine, both discursive and performative.

Whereas Qoheleth highlights the anxious side of fear in ch. 5, which serves to cultivate restraint and humility before the Divine, in 3:14 the sage references fear in connection with the permanence of divine providence (v. 14a). God has made everything "exquisitely suitable" *(yāpeh)* for its time (v. 11), but humans cannot fathom, much less alter, what God has done. God's works are shrouded in mystery: humans cannot figure out what God is up to protologically or eschatologically. Such is the basis of godly "fear" for Qoheleth: an overweening sense of mystery and permanency in the ways of the divine. Such "fear" does not elicit paralyzing terror.[15] Nor does it affirm the educative value of the "fear of the LORD" in Proverbs.[16] A God whose work that cannot be changed (7:13b) yet has ordered life in elegant balance (3:11) is neither a terrifying tyrant nor a paternal pedagogue.

Qoheleth depicts a Deity that defies categorization, a God who is transcendentally remote and seemingly indifferent yet also generous, if discriminatory, when it comes to granting joy, as we shall see. Qoheleth's God has set limits to human discernment yet instilled in human beings the capacity to be painfully aware of those limitations. Qoheleth's fear of God is the appropriate response to God's unsearchable providence and the

12. Would Qoheleth consider the temple psalms (at least the long ones) to be the products of fools? Cf. Sir. 7:14.

13. Cf., e.g., Pss. 84:1-7; 91:11-12; 121:3. Williamson, "Death and Symbolic Immortality," 165; Fidler, "Qoheleth in 'the House of God,'" 12.

14. Williamson, "Death and Symbolic Immortality," 165.

15. Cf. Crenshaw, *Ecclesiastes*, 100.

16. Crenshaw, *Qoheleth*, 67.

permanency of divine action amid the impermanency of human activity (3:14). Human life and action pale against the work of the eternal God, whose plans, inscrutable as they are, are irrevocable. Such "fear" counsels acceptance (and action, as we shall see), not paralysis. To fear God is to embrace one's creaturely status, one's opportune chances for living, one's moment in time, all before the unfathomably enduring work of the Divine. Qoheleth's Deity is the unknown God, the wholly ineffable Other.[17]

The language of fear in Qoheleth's discourse is most heavily concentrated in the compact comparison between the God-fearers and the wicked in 8:12-13.[18]

> Though a sinner does evil a hundred times yet prolongs his life, I know that it is good for those who *fear God* when they (stand in) *fear before him.* But it is not good for the wicked. Like a shadow he will not prolong his days when he does not (stand in) *fear before God.*

Here Qoheleth contends that the God-fearers, literally those who "fear from before God" *(yārē' millipnê 'ĕlōhîm),* are "good" *(ṭôb),* both in a moral and salutary sense,[19] in contrast to the wicked, who act with impunity. The God-fearers see themselves standing ever *coram Deo.* Although "God is in heaven" (5:1 [Eng. 2]) to hold all humans on earth accountable, God's presence is somehow proximate and palpable for those who fear God. As Mark Sneed puts it, the God-fearers are "the new righteous."[20] Qoheleth does not attempt to soften the tension between the length of life of the wicked and his judgment on them in 8:13. Yet by bowing here to this tenet of traditional wisdom (i.e., divine retribution), Ecclesiastes recontextualizes the notion of well-being associated with reverent character. Well-being is not measured quantitatively by life span or by the number of achievements; it is evinced in the reverent acceptance of life on its own terms and the appropriateness of human conduct before God. In other words, well-being is measured qualitatively and morally. The wicked, notwithstanding their many schemes and many days, remain a mere shadow (cf. 6:12). Standing in awe before the might and mystery of the Creator, dwelling in the fearful

---

17. See also Sneed, *Politics of Pessimism,* 281.

18. Though possible, I am not convinced that 8:12b-13 is the work of a glossator, as many contend (e.g., Murphy, *Ecclesiastes,* 85, 87). See Sneed, "Note on Qoh 8, 12b-13"; Krüger, *Qoheleth,* 160-61.

19. As Krüger has argued, "good" here is primarily ethical in nuance (*Qoheleth,* 161).

20. Sneed, *Politics of Pessimism,* 62.

wonder of God, is the most fundamental life-affirming stance Qoheleth exhorts, irrespective of one's length of life.

To summarize, "fear of God" in Qoheleth covers the whole gamut from trepidation to reverence. In so doing, the sage shifts the focus of moral discourse away from specific maxims of conduct whose paths allegedly lead to success and reward. The "fear of God" is not so much a specific injunction for righteous living by which one receives just reward as it is an all-encompassing profile of character, of embodied wonder, of a way of living *coram Deo*. Standing in fear before God indicates a posture of utmost humility and surrender to the Mystery. In such wonder, nothing is presumed about God's ways, nothing is expected regarding specific outcomes in one's life. According to Proverbs, the fear of God is foundational for the myriad instructions and sayings that are meant to cultivate wisdom and foster righteousness. Qoheleth, however, recasts "fear" in a way that breaks the relentless striving for righteousness, which he considers a vicious, rather than virtuous, cycle (7:15-18). Such "fear," moreover, bursts wisdom's presumed outcomes, including the fame and glory that Wisdom promises in Proverbs 8.[21] Not only does fear of God eliminate the extremes of the sapiential enterprise; it also constitutes the source from which all conduct emerges. Qoheleth has given reverence its due without reducing it to primitive terror, on the one hand, or human confidence, on the other. For this sage, fear-filled wonder overcomes grand and glorious Wisdom. Wonder is more primal than wisdom, Qoheleth contends, and on the basis of such wonder a new way of navigating life is born.[22]

If anything, the ethical benchmarks of proper reverence, of fearful wonder, include a profound acceptance of life on its own terms, with both its absurd limitations and occasional redemptive joys (see below). Genuine "fear" rests on the acknowledgment of divine supremacy and transcendence and thus on the open reception of life's vicissitudes without manipulation or confident calculation. Qoheleth recognizes that joy and toil, life and death, are incalculable entities, unplanned except by the mysterious providence of God. Fear of God lies at the conclusion of Qoheleth's stepping back and discerning the irrelevance of striving for gain and glory. To fear God marks the active reshaping of desire: surrendering the desire to carve out a lasting, praiseworthy legacy and replacing it with a desire

---

21. See Krüger, *Qoheleth*, 24.

22. Contra Sneed, who unnecessarily (and artificially) polarizes ethics/piety and reverence/fear in Qoheleth's discourse (*Politics of Pessimism*, 149-50).

for simplicity and enjoyment. Proper reverence is rooted in a faith that is devoid of guarantees and high expectations and thus of ulterior motives, a faith in the transcendent Power that stands forever behind the irrational orderings of the cosmos, inaccessible to human inquiry.[23] Qoheleth has taken the reader trembling to the threshold of the Unknown to wonder in reverential perplexity, and it is out of such wonder that a new piety emerges, a piety that questions the morality of morality.

Character-Forming

What, then, is the shape of character for Qoheleth in the face of fearful wonder, in the light of human futility and transience? The sage has irreversibly dismantled the notion of moral character that binds together conduct and consequence, reward and virtue.[24] Nevertheless, the formation of character, the shaping of a way of life, remains a central concern.[25] The movement and structure of Ecclesiastes confirm this. The sage begins with his reflections on cosmology (1:1-11) and on his own life in pursuit of wisdom (1:12–2:26). He then slides seamlessly into further observations about life that become increasingly replete with proverbs[26] and instructions.[27] The latter half of Qoheleth's discourse is clearly weighted toward the didactic and concludes with a formal address to the "young man" in 11:9–12:8. The address appropriately, if not ironically, concludes his reflections by recalling a setting similar to that envisioned in Prov. 1–9. Qoheleth's rhetorical aim is to impart advice required for a reformulation of character. Qoheleth, in the end, proves himself to be no nihilist.

Qoheleth's reconfiguration of character is achieved by a dynamic movement of perspective comparable to that in Job. Both Job and Qoheleth are afforded the opportunity to step back and see the world in its

---

23. See Müller, "Wie sprach Qohälät von Gott?" 516; Michel, "Vom Gott," 286-87.

24. For a thorough discussion of the "act-consequence connection" in the wisdom literature (minus Job), see S. Adams, *Wisdom in Transition*, 53-100 (for Proverbs) and 101-52 (for Ecclesiastes).

25. So also Clements, *Wisdom in Theology*, 35. Contra Sneed, who erroneously identifies character formation with traditional *moral* character formation (*Politics of Pessimism*, 149-50). Sneed's apt description of "fear" in Qoheleth as a "new ethical category" and of the "God-fearers" as the "new righteous" belies his own claim (pp. 62, 201).

26. 3:1-8; 4:5-6, 13; 5:2, 9-11 (Eng. 3, 10-12); 7:1-13; 8:1-2; 9:17-18; 10:1-4, 8-20; 11:1-4.

27. 4:17–5:1 (Eng. 5:1-2); 5:3-5 (Eng. 4-6); 9:7-10; 11:5-10; 12:1-8, 13-14.

entirety. But, unlike Job, whose character is refashioned by the external dramatics of plot, dialogue, and most decisively by divine encounter, Qoheleth has no God-awful revelation about the world and himself. What he does have is the intellectual wherewithal to step back and observe human life and the cosmos as an estranged whole with a mixture of awe and disillusionment, bewilderment and resignation.

Ecclesiastes is in some sense a protest that all life is tainted with *hebel.* However, unlike Job, Qoheleth's protest is infused not with caustic blame or rancorous rhetoric but with observational rigor, resigned acceptance, and occasional wonder. On the one hand, the sage is resigned to oppression (5:7a [Eng. 8a]). On the other hand, he is amazed at the mystery of life in the womb and, by extension, the creative work of God (11:4-5). After concluding that there is nothing gained from pleasure and arduous toil (2:2-23), Qoheleth states, "There is nothing good for anyone (except) to eat and drink and come to find enjoyment in his work" (2:24). Ambitious goals, arrogant claims of knowledge, and singular striving for gain are all exposed for what they are in the face of *hebel:* delusions. Life's grand purposes are whittled down to simple, fleeting pleasures. With such a minimalist orientation, Qoheleth presents his own cardinal list of values and virtues, in addition to the root virtue of "fear" discussed above, each with a touch of wonder.

The Enigma of Enjoyment

Central to Qoheleth's reconstruction of character is his commendation of enjoyment manifest in eating, drinking, and finding pleasure in work. Qoheleth's commendation is given seven times. Throughout his discourse, enjoyment is sometimes considered a gift to be received, if and when it comes; elsewhere Qoheleth regards it as a duty. Enjoyment is God's gift to human beings, whose lives are brief and whose ignorance of the future is insurmountable. The sage's realistic assessments of the human condition highlight the serendipitous nature of enjoyment. Enjoyment, Qoheleth observes, has a mysteriously incidental quality to it, for it lies outside the domain of human achievement and design. Thus when and to whom the refreshing breezes of enjoyment blow no human being can determine. All the more reason to enjoy. By its divine origin and unbidden nature, enjoyment is an occasion of wonder for those able to partake.

The enigma of enjoyment, or paradox of joy, is highlighted as one charts the way the sage develops the theme throughout his discourse, from 2:24 to 11:7-10.

> There is nothing good for anyone (except) to eat and drink and come to find enjoyment in his work.[28] This also I have seen is from God's hand; for apart from [God][29] who eats and who gathers?[30] For God gives wisdom, knowledge, and joy to the one who is found worthy[31] before [God]. But to the offender [God] gives the work of gathering and collecting only to give to one whom God finds worthy. This is surely absurd *(hebel)* and wind-chasing. (2:24-26)

In his first reflection on joy, Qoheleth casts enjoyment as a divinely initiated act. Only God makes possible enjoyment to those whom God finds worthy, literally "good" *(ṭôb)*. Whether in enjoyment or in toil ("gathering and collecting"), God is the giver, and the sage finds such divine determination tantamount to *hebel,* in this case "absurdity." Humans have no say in this inequitable distribution. God's gift of joy is given discriminately. The following commendations similarly emphasize the giftedness of enjoyment but minus *hebel*'s condemnation.

> I know there is nothing good among [humans] except to rejoice and do well in their lifetime. Moreover, everyone who eats and drinks and finds enjoyment[32] in all their toil — that is God's gift. (3:12-13)

> So I have seen that there is nothing better than that a person rejoice in his activities, for that is his portion, for who can bring him to see what will happen after him? (3:22)

> This is what I have seen to be good *(ṭôb):* it is exquisitely fine *(yāpeh)* to eat and drink and find enjoyment in all the toil with which one toils under the sun the few days of life that God has given, for that is

28. Lit. "and let himself see good in his toil."

29. MT reads "from me" *(mimmenî),* but this makes little sense in context. Most likely this is a case of graphic confusion. See Seow, *Ecclesiastes,* 140-41.

30. The meaning of *yāḥûš* is disputed; it normally means "hasten." Given the Aramaic and Akkadian cognates, it could carry the meaning here of "worry" or "fret" (so Longman, *Book of Ecclesiastes,* 109). Seow, however, finds an Arabic cognate meaning "gather" *(Ecclesiastes,* 140), which in and of itself would be tenuous, but in light of the following verse fits perfectly.

31. Heb. *šeṭṭôb lĕpānāyw* ("who is good before him").

32. Lit. "see good" *(wĕrā'â ṭôb).*

one's portion *(ḥēleq)*. Likewise anyone to whom God gives wealth and assets and whom [God] permits to partake of them, to accept one's portion *(ḥēleq)*, and to find enjoyment in one's toil — this is God's gift *(mattat)*. For that person will scarcely brood over the days of his life, because God keeps him occupied with the joy of his heart. (5:17-19 [Eng. 18-20])

Implicit in this passage is Qoheleth's categorical distinction between enjoyment as one's "portion" *(ḥēleq)* and "gain" *(yitrôn)* as an object of striving (see 2:10). The former designates an expected share in one's work.[33] But it is not something for which one strives. Here the sage uses the term "portion" as a complement to the gifted nature of enjoyment (v. 19). There is something both natural and divinely serendipitous about joy, the sage contends.

Also striking in this passage is the appearance of *yāpeh*, which occurs elsewhere only in 3:11, concerning the divinely appointed times (see above). With this word, Qoheleth connects the divinely ordained events of human existence in their elegant symmetry with the simple pleasures of life, also granted by God. The momentous and the mundane are wedded under God's providential work and given unreserved affirmation, even as mystery about them both abounds. They too are instances of wonder.

So I extol enjoyment,[34] for there is nothing better for one under the sun than to eat, and drink, and enjoy oneself, for this can accompany him *(yilwennû)* in his toil throughout the days of his life that God has given him under the sun. (8:15)

Here the language becomes noticeably more commendatory, as indicated in the opening words. Moreover, enjoyment is no longer considered fleeting; it can "accompany" the life of the toiler. Note that such enjoyment is not cast as a product or result of striving, righteous or otherwise. Enjoyment, rather, joins the laborer in his/her laboring. Moreover, God's role lies in determining the extent of the toiler's life, but no mention is made of God determining who gets to receive enjoyment and when. That joy reaches beyond the momentary, that it has *lasting* efficacy for the individual, would suggest a cultivatable aspect to enjoyment, or in this next case at least, a dutiful side.

33. See also Krüger, *Qoheleth*, 3.
34. Lit. "praise enjoyment" *(wĕšibbaḥtî 'ănî 'et-haśśimḥâ)*.

Go, eat your bread with enjoyment, and drink your wine with a cheerful heart; for God has already approved what you do. Let your garments always be white; do not let oil be lacking on your head. Enjoy life with the woman you love, all the days of your fleeting life[35] (all your fleeting days),[36] that [God] has given you under the sun, because that is your portion in life and in your toil at which you toil under the sun. (9:7-9)

This commendation, as well as the final one, is cast not as an observation but as an imperative. Mimicking the advice of Siduri, the barmaid at the end of the universe who admonishes Gilgamesh concerning his heroic quest to gain immortality,[37] Qoheleth's commendation is, to state the obvious, commanding ("Go, eat, . . . drink. . . . Enjoy!"), directing the reader to experience enjoyment in simple sustenance and in love.

Qoheleth's final commendation is one that explicitly addresses a "young man" (bāḥûr), filled also with imperatival language.

Light is sweet, and it is pleasant for the eyes to see the sun. Even if one should live many years, let him rejoice in them all and remember that the days of darkness may be many. All that comes is fleeting (hebel). Rejoice, young man, while you remain young, and let your heart delight you in the days of your youth. Follow the ways of your heart and whatever your eyes see, and[38] know that for all these things God will bring you into judgment. Banish anxiety from your heart, and remove pain from your body; for youth and the dawn of life[39] are fleeting (hebel). (11:7-10).

In his address to a youth, much like the father's address to his son in Proverbs, Qoheleth issues another series of commands to experience joy. Now

---

35. Heb. ḥayyê heblekā. Here hebel refers to the brevity of life.

36. This parenthetical clause is possibly a case of inadvertent repetition (vertical dittography).

37. The parallel has long been recognized in Gilgamesh OB VA+BM iii 1-14. See the translations in *ANET*, 90; Dalley, *Myths from Mesopotamia*, 150; George, *Babylonian Gilgamesh Epic*, 1:278-79.

38. Syntactically, there is no indication that the *waw* in *wĕdā'* should be taken disjunctively ("but"), as most do by assuming that v. 9b is an "orthodox" gloss. Rather, the reference to divine judgment is intended to reinforce the exhortation in v. 9a, not contravene or temper it. See Towner, "Ecclesiastes," 353; Krüger, *Qoheleth*, 196-97.

39. The meaning of *šaḥărût* is unclear. For the etymology and interpretive possibilities, see Seow, *Ecclesiastes*, 350-51.

it is no longer a matter of eating and drinking but more broadly fulfilling the desires ("ways") of the heart. This final commendation constitutes a fitting crescendo to Qoheleth's series of commendations. The sage, in short, takes the issue of joy with dead seriousness, particularly in light of what follows in ch. 12.

The overall rhetorical movement of Qoheleth's reflections on enjoyment proceeds from observation ("I have seen . . .") to commendation and command ("go," "eat," drink," "rejoice," "follow"), from the divinely ordained (2:24-26; 3:13; 5:18-19 [Eng. 19-20]) to the humanly prescribed (9:7-9; 11:8-10), from reception to active agency.[40] Enjoyment comes unbidden, granted by God, but it is also realized with a change of heart, even as a matter of duty. For Qoheleth, enjoyment is both serendipitous and a matter of reshaping desire. Joy is never guaranteed, but it remains ever a possibility. Enjoyment thus is a wonder, a paradox in which the human encounters the Divine in mysterious interaction, a testimony both to the "hand of God" and to the human will. Joy is both gift and task, *Gabe* and *Aufgabe*.

Last, and by no means least, death constitutes the final motivation for joy in Qoheleth's commendations. Death inspires a profound acceptance of life on its own terms, and in the face of it Qoheleth does not espouse suicide as the final solution (cf. 6:3; 9:4), but instead commends the fleeting moments of joy,[41] moments that prove nothing less than redemptive in the "experiment" of living.

Joy and Fear

Also novel to Qoheleth's approach to joy is the connection joy has to fear. In her careful rhetorical study, Eunny Lee argues that fear and joy are by no means opposite poles in Qoheleth's discourse. Rather, they share an unlikely, somewhat enigmatic bond.[42] Case in point: the language of human incapacity before God's incomparable might and mystery (3:11b, 14) brackets one of Qoheleth's commendations of enjoyment (3:12-13).

---

40. Those who argue that Qoheleth considers enjoyment to be exclusively determined by God overlook the rhetorical buildup in his series of commendations, which concludes with strong exhortations and commands. For the sage, it is not a case of *either/or* — either determined by God or realized by human effort — but paradoxically *both/and,* as is the case with many of Qoheleth's reflections.

41. Cf. Crenshaw, "Shadow of Death in Qoheleth," 210-11.

42. Lee, *Vitality of Enjoyment.*

Moreover, [God] has put (a sense of) timelessness into their minds, such that they cannot determine what God has done from beginning to end. I know there is nothing good among [humans] except to rejoice and do well in their lifetime. Moreover, everyone who eats and drinks and finds enjoyment in all their toil — that is God's gift. *I know that whatever God does endures forever; nothing can be added to it, nor anything taken from it; God has done this, so that all should (stand in) fear before him.*

Because Qoheleth states elsewhere that enjoyment is the "hand of God" at work (2:24) and that God is the enabler of joy (5:18-19 [Eng. 19-20]), enjoyment is thus included among God's inalterable, mighty acts! God has "done this" (3:14), and what God has done includes, inter alia, the granting of joy. What, then, holds fear and joy together?

In 8:10-15 Qoheleth commends fear and enjoyment in parallel fashion. Both are invoked in the face of *hebel*. Again, as the wicked pursue evil with impunity, those who fear God are deemed qualitatively "good" (vv. 12-13). As the wicked are counted as righteous (and vice versa), Qoheleth commends the pleasure of eating and drinking (vv. 14-15). The rhetorical coordination is striking: fear and joy are complementary. So they are also, not coincidentally, within the rubric of wonder, as already noted in Proverbs (see chapter 1 above): "fear of the LORD" and Wisdom's transcendent "delight" in God and the world. But in Ecclesiastes, fear and joy are recast. As fear is given a more primal, visceral casting (see above), joy for Qoheleth is cast in more mundane terms.

Qoheleth's quest to know wisdom was to determine "what was good for mortals to do under heaven during the few days of their life" (2:3), and it is "to eat and drink, and find enjoyment in their toil" (v. 24). The simple, familiar act of eating, specifically eating with enjoyment, Qoheleth approaches with a sense of new-found awe. Wonder, exclaims Rubenstein, has the power to make the familiar strange, and in Qoheleth's case that would include the mundane meal.[43] With the loss of gain *(yitrôn)*, what is left are the grain and the grape: food and drink received from the hand of God in fear and wonder, all to enjoy.

What, then, to do with the last reference to "fear" in Ecclesiastes, found in the epilogue?

---

43. E.g., "Wonder wonders at the strangeness of the most familiar" (Rubenstein, *Strange Wonder*, 8).

> The end of the matter, all that has been heard:
> Fear God and keep his commandments;
> for that (applies) to all people. (12:13)

Although once described as the "kernel and the star of the whole book,"[44] the last reference in Ecclesiastes to "fear" ("fear God and keep his commandments") is halfway foreign to the tenor of Qoheleth's own reflections. The content and language is unmistakably distinct from Qoheleth's own discourse, not so much for what it emphasizes but for what it leaves out. Although the epilogist's injunction to "fear God" finds resonance with Qoheleth's own teaching, that is only half of it. Qoheleth makes no comment on Mosaic legislation in the book. Nowhere other than in 12:13b does the book mention "commandments" *(miṣwôt)* or make any allusion to torah.[45] The epilogist, on the other hand, like the Deuteronomist, finds fear and obedience as two sides of the same coin. A more complete summary, more fully in keeping with Qoheleth's teaching, would have been: "Fear God and, God-willing, enjoy a good meal!"[46] Clearly, the epilogist found "eating and drinking" either too banal or too controversial to even mention, let alone validate. Not so Qoheleth, preacher of fear and joy. The sage's reverence of God highlights not just the power of God's inscrutable work but also the splendor of the ordinary, those mundane marvels gratefully received at the table.[47]

Joy to the Work

On another enigmatic note, the relationship between joy and work is also something of a mystery. Given his predominantly negative assessment of toil, Qoheleth's insistence on the possibility of experiencing joy in one's labor is paradoxical at best. But in five out of the seven commendations, Qoheleth discerns an inextricable connection between toil and pleasure. Regardless of how this connection is worked out, it is to be sharply con-

---

44. Delitzsch, *Ecclesiastes*, 438.

45. For the final editor of the book, fearing God, along with keeping the commandments, was the key to appropriating Qoheleth's reflections. See Sheppard, *Wisdom as Hermeneutical Construct*, 120-29; idem, "Epilogue to Qoheleth," 182-89.

46. See Weeks, *Ecclesiastes and Scepticism*, 172, who also notes the lack of reference to joy in the epilogue.

47. See the discussion of "mundane wonder" in Keen, *Apology for Wonder*, 23-24.

trasted with Qoheleth's claim regarding the *lack* of connection between gain and toil (e.g., 1:3).[48] Enjoyment for Qoheleth has little to do with gain or profit *(yitrôn)*. That does not mean that Qoheleth gives up on work. Far from it, he places remarkably high value on it, but does so by reformulating its raison d'être.[49] He enjoins:

> Whatever your hand finds to do, do with your might;
>> for there is no work or thought or knowledge or wisdom in Sheol,
>> to which you are headed. (9:10)

Rather than urging divestment from work, Qoheleth urges wholehearted investment. The reason he provides is starkly simple: there is no work, let alone consciousness, after death. Conversely, something of the vitality of life pulses through the exertion of everyday work. Not for gain but for living does work have its legitimacy, Qoheleth concedes. His view of work is essentially nonutilitarian; work conducted simply as a means to a gainful end will lead to only frustration and disillusionment (see 4:8). But viewed as a way of life, as an essential exercise of living, work does have its fulfillment, even in the form of enjoyment, which can accompany one's toil at every step (8:15).[50]

Qoheleth's enigmatic take on work and joy offers an intriguing revision to Camus's interpretation of the Greek myth of Sisyphus. To be sure, both Qoheleth and Camus find much common ground with regard to their views about the absurd, as Fox and others have elucidated.[51] Sisyphus's pointless labor finds striking resonance with Qoheleth's view of arduous toil. But Camus and Qoheleth part company at the climactic mo-

---

48. Michel, "Vom Gott," 279.

49. For further discussion see Brown, "Whatever Your Hand Finds."

50. Contra Fox, who suggests that Qoheleth's use of *'āmāl* ("toil") in his reflections on pleasure implies that pleasure is simply "toil's product" (*Qohelet and His Contradictions,* 56). Fox is right to point out that Qoheleth is not preaching the intrinsic "joy of labor" (neither am I). However, the relationship between enjoyment and toil for Qoheleth is quite nuanced, if not enigmatic. Qoheleth certainly does not equate enjoyment with gain *(yitrôn)*; rather, pleasure *accompanies* a person in toil (8:15; see Fox, *Qohelet and His Contradictions,* 57). In so doing, Qoheleth acknowledges a distinction between oppressive, pointless work and the kind of labor that holds out the possibility of enjoyment. Sneed rightly points out that Qoheleth deconstructs "toil from nearly any angle," but fails to take into account the critically important passages of 8:15 and 9:10 (*Politics of Pessimism,* 248-51).

51. See Fox, *Time to Tear Down,* 8-11; Schwartz, "Koheleth and Camus"; Gordis, *Koheleth,* 112-21.

ment in the narrative when Sisyphus, condemned by the gods to futile labor, observes the boulder that he has pushed up nearly to the pinnacle of the mountain roll back into the valley. Camus states: "Sisyphus, proletarian of the gods, powerless and rebellious, knows the whole extent of his wretched condition: it is what he thinks of during his descent. The lucidity that was to constitute his torture at the same time crowns his victory. There is no fate that cannot be surmounted by scorn."[52] Both Camus and Qoheleth, in different ways, pose the question of what Sisyphus must have felt at the moment he knows he must descend once again to push his rock. Camus asks why at this very point in which Sisyphus realizes the futility of his labors a smile breaks out on his face, a "silent joy."[53] For Camus, it is a clever joy motivated by his defiance of the gods who have condemned him to such labor.

For Qoheleth, however, Sisyphus's smile would not be motivated by defiance. He no doubt feels resignation, even sorrow, in the realization that the activity itself is patently futile and thus absurd. But unlike Camus's Sisyphus, labor for Qoheleth can allow a person to cherish the few brief moments of rest with the cool breeze savored upon the sweaty brow before the descent begins again. The duration and quality of the rest are determined by God. Rest and sustenance are, or at least should be, integral parts of the daily rhythm of toil. But Qoheleth further claims that work is also an end in itself, as an integral part of the very exercise of life (9:10). The enjoyment found in work, whatever that is specifically, is understood to lie outside the domain of net gain. It is the toiler's gifted "portion." From a socioeconomic perspective, Qoheleth has taken toil out of the marketplace of entrepreneurial consumption and has lodged it squarely in the *living* room, which includes a table. The connection between joy and work is paradoxically, if not wondrously, serendipitous.

Simplicity Regained

Qoheleth's preference for reticence in speech, motivated by "fear," serves to impart many related values such as caution, self-restraint, and an acceptance of less (5:9 [Eng. 10]), that is, a life of simplicity. What a pow-

---

52. Camus, *Myth of Sisyphus*, 90.
53. Camus, *Myth of Sisyphus*, 91.

erfully ironic image Qoheleth has set up rhetorically: the Solomonic king unmatched in accomplishment and unsurpassed in glory finding himself envious of the common laborer, whose sleep is far more blissful than that of the wealthy (5:11 [Eng. 12])! A life devoid of great and glorious ambitions, however noble they may be, is Qoheleth's ideal, that is, a life of simple sufficiency in which constructive work and sufficient sustenance are all that is needed to live fully.[54]

In one of his most telling statements concerning the human condition, Qoheleth gives a common virtue a different twist:

> See, this alone I found,
>   that God made human beings straightforward *(yāšār)*,
>   but they have sought out myriad ingenuities. (7:29)

Within traditional wisdom, the adjective *yāšār* is aligned with "righteous" and "blameless" (Job 1:1). Here Qoheleth sharply delineates between *yāšār* and the multitude of ingenuities *(ḥiššĕḇōnôt)* humans have devised.[55] For the sage, an aspect of human "rightness" is straightforward simplicity. God created human beings simple, straightforward, and upright, but the pursuit of self-serving schemes has irreparably marred the human way.

The Death of Virtue-osity

Although Qoheleth espouses certain virtues, he does it in full recognition that there are severe limitations, even detriments, to leading a virtuous life. Ecclesiastes 7:15-18 crystallizes this point:

> Throughout my fleeting days *(bîmê heblî)* I have seen everything: righteous people who perish in their righteousness and wicked people who prolong their lives in their evildoing. Do not be too righteous, and do not act too wise; why desolate yourself? Do not be too wicked, and do not be a fool; why die before your time? It is good that you should take hold of the one, without letting go of the other; for the one who fears God shall go forth *(yēṣē')* with both of them.

---

54. O'Connor, *Wisdom Literature,* 130-31. See, similarly, Agur's prayer in Prov. 30:7-9.
55. For the etymology and nuance of this word, see Seow, *Ecclesiastes,* 265-66.

Is Qoheleth advocating a golden mean,[56] espousing an "ethic of moderation,"[57] counseling against excessive righteousness,[58] and/or critiquing hypocrisy?[59] Unlike Aristotle, Qoheleth is not contrasting opposing examples of human conduct in order to determine a moral mean.[60] Instead, he situates himself between the most fundamental categories of character, between the wicked and the righteous, between virtue and vice. Qoheleth observes with bitter irony that the social responses to the righteous and the wicked are far too easily reversed, reflecting moral blindness (7:15; 8:14).[61] The rhetorical questions in 7:16b and 17b indicate parallel fates: self-ruin and early death are the inevitable outcomes of the extremes of virtue and vice. Paradoxically, such extremes have much in common: shared destiny and perhaps also common motivation, namely the striving for self-gain, whether virtuously or duplicitously. Wickedness and extreme righteousness, it turns out, mirror each other. Both are forms of extremism, and either path leads to assured destruction.

But Qoheleth offers a third way, one that navigates between them by allowing one to cancel out the other yet both serving as urgent warnings from opposite sides. The sage subversively seeks a moderate way,[62] yes, but one that supersedes conventional moral categories, a way of living that moves beyond wickedness and righteousness, at least as traditionally conceived. Virtue-osity, in other words, is as ethically insupportable as wickedness.

The larger context of this passage fills out these ironic injunctions. Qoheleth observes that there is no righteous person who is without sin

---

56. Cf., e.g., Williams, "What Does It Profit a Man?" 186; Aristotle, *Nicomachean Ethics* 3.7–4.9.

57. Sneed, *Politics of Pessimism*, 62.

58. So Hertzberg, *Prediger*, 152-55; Strobel, *Buch Prediger*, 112-15; Zimmerli, *Buch des Predigers Salomo*, 209-10; Glasser, *Procès du bonheur par Qohelet*, 116-17.

59. So Whybray, "Qoheleth the Immoralist?" 191-204.

60. Identifying Aristotelian thought with Ecclesiastes is the result of confusing two different levels of abstraction regarding moral categories. Aristotle located virtue between the opposite extremes of concrete action (*Nicomachean Ethics* 2.7). Courage, for example, is the mean between cowardice and recklessness, while self-control is situated between self-indulgence and insensitivity. Qoheleth, on the other hand, attempts to establish an ethical way between the abstract categories of righteousness and wickedness (7:16-17).

61. Elsewhere Qoheleth concludes that the wicked and the righteous suffer the same fate (2:14; 3:17-19).

62. The subversive element involves setting extreme virtue in parallel with wickedness, thereby undercutting the value of the former.

(7:20; cf. v. 22; 8:11). Strident righteousness is an unattainable ideal and nothing more than an illusion, a matter of arrogant presumption.[63] Like wisdom, righteousness is unreachable (7:23-24), and to think otherwise betrays an exalted estimation of one's moral faculties. The extremes of virtue and vice are exposed for what they are: elusive quests for self-gain, analogous to unremitting toil. Extreme righteousness is unable to ensure long life and happiness; indeed, just the opposite. The pretense of blamelessness accompanied by the expectations of reward will only result in self-ruin.[64]

In his warning against being overly righteous, Qoheleth attacks the causal nexus between righteousness and fortune, countering the logical conclusion that super-righteousness will afford ultimate fulfillment. Implicit is the recognition that all efforts that strive to fulfill the pure ideals of righteousness ultimately stem from the self-serving desire to reap ideal rewards. Yet to caution against consideration of the other extreme, Qoheleth immediately points out that wickedness will result in untimely death. Given the parallel with excessive righteousness, wickedness is itself defined as an extreme form of conduct.

The key to understanding the relationship between these two extremes and the alternative that Qoheleth suggests is found in the concluding positive statement, "One who fears God shall go forth with both of them" (7:18b). The precise nuance of "go forth" ($y\bar{e}\d{s}\bar{e}$') is a matter of dispute.[65] Some have taken it to mean to "escape, avoid."[66] However, rendered this way the verse simply repeats what has already been stated. More commonly accepted is Robert Gordis's rendering of the verb with a legal nuance akin to the mishnaic formula "will do his duty by both."[67]

This generic verb, however, need not have such a restricted legal focus. In conjunction with v. 18a, the conveyed image is a physical one of carrying the two precepts in vv. 16-17, one in each hand. "Going forth" denotes general conduct in life, guided by the balance, or better the cancellation, between wickedness and super-righteousness. The traditional association of moral conduct with the "way" of wisdom remains ever in the background.[68] Hence Qoheleth is not against traveling along the path

---

63. Qoheleth highlights the presumption of the wise in 8:17.

64. See 4:7-8; 5:12-16 (Eng. 13-17); cf. 6:1-6.

65. See Whybray's discussion of the options ("Qoheleth the Immoralist?" 200-201).

66. E.g., Zimmerli, *Buch des Predigers Salomo,* 209-10.

67. Gordis, *Koheleth,* 267-68.

68. See chapter 2 above.

of life; rather, he suggests a new set of guidelines that dismantles obsessive practices based on the presumption that such a path will lead to full knowledge and abundant reward.

In a passage strikingly similar to 7:15-18, Qoheleth again notes the travesty of justice that afflicts the righteous and concludes with recommending enjoyment:

> There is an absurdity *(hebel)* that takes place on earth: there are righteous people who are treated according to the conduct of the wicked, and there are wicked people who are treated according to the conduct of the righteous. I said that this is also absurd *(hebel)*. So I extol enjoyment, for there is nothing better for one under the sun than to eat, and drink, and enjoy oneself, for this can accompany him in his toil throughout the days of his life that God has given him under the sun. (8:14-15)

Similar to 7:14, the wicked and the righteous have traded places in the eyes of society, warranting Qoheleth's verdict of *hebel*. Together, these two passages suggest that the path Qoheleth commends amid moral absurdity is one that engenders enjoyment.

All in all, Qoheleth pointedly exposes the dangers brought on by a kind of "works righteousness," for lack of a better phrase, namely the obsessive striving to outdo oneself in virtue-osity. Excessive righteousness is rooted in the pretension of thinking that one can discern and even direct the work of God (8:16-17). The unknowable future and the lack of moral retribution are inescapable realities that shatter once and for all grandiose claims concerning the rewards of righteousness. In the end, Qoheleth does not so much forge a middle way or golden mean between practical alternatives (à la Aristotle) as he sees the way of the righteous and that of the wicked as a zero-sum game. Extremes on both sides, held together even as they are held apart, yield a golden zero. But it is precisely there that freedom and enjoyment are found, freedom from the strictures of ethical extremism and enjoyment of simple pleasures that cannot be earned. Moreover, the one who successfully goes forth is one who fears God (7:18), "the highest accolade of moral virtue that can be bestowed."[69] Indeed, it is precisely the "fear of God" that counters the temptation to go to such moral (and immoral) extremes.

---

69. Whybray, "Qoheleth the Immoralist?" 201.

Carpe Diem and the Reshaping of Desire

Divine reverence cultivates, inter alia, a receptive openness to serendipity. Faced with the fact that human striving cannot provide the means for self-gain, Qoheleth encourages one to receive each moment that life (i.e., God) offers. The sage's resolute focus on the moment leads him to condemn wallowing in nostalgia (7:10). For Qoheleth, the present, not the past or the future, carries the precedent for living; it is all that is available. The past is dead and forgotten, and except for the certitude of death, the future is ever cloaked in uncertainty. Only the present warrants attention.

It is no accident, then, that Qoheleth in the end identifies the figure of the young man as his intended audience (11:9). Youth serves as a fitting context and metaphor to illustrate the importance of living in the present. For the elder sage, youth incarnates such an approach to life, the robust embodiment of carpe diem in contrast to the silent and submissive son in Proverbs. Motivated, perhaps even emboldened,[70] by divine judgment, Qoheleth urges the youth to revel in joy and banish anxiety and pain (11:9-10). Far from being a parental figure, Qoheleth gives permission for the youth to fulfill his deepest desires (contra Num. 15:39) in the face of *hebel*, as manifest in impending decrepitude and death (12:1-7). Though perhaps one could accuse Qoheleth of romanticizing youth, he is not giving license to a reckless life of self-gratification that would cause pain and endangerment to self and others. But neither is he encouraging a life of submission and striving.[71] The sage is advocating the fulfillment of desire, informed by divine judgment. His counsel to the youth is founded upon the profound recognition that the absurdity of human life requires nothing less, and nothing more, than exhausting every present moment as a gift rather than as a task. Carpe diem is all about reshaping desire to what is given, not to what one strives for.[72]

---

70. Again, see Towner, "Ecclesiastes," 353.

71. Again, the sage is forging a middle path, one that is both liberating and yet not irresponsible. See Brown, *Ecclesiastes*, 104-7.

72. Sneed talks of carpe diem as exclusively a matter of "lowering expectations" and "passive acceptance" of life's pleasures (*Politics of Pessimism*, e.g., 174-76, 201). Overlooked, however, is the concerted effort needed to redirect desire away from the powerful allure of striving for gain at all costs to accepting and savoring what is given, away from "heroic," self-serving goals to simple, everyday delights.

Aporetic Probing and Pleasure

The "strangest book in the Bible" proves to be the most enigmatic and intellectually challenging. Its perplexing nature both beckons and bewilders readers (at least this one), and for all that has been said by way of commentary and reflection, I am not at all sure if any of it (or any other interpretation) is on target. Such is the enigmatic power of Ecclesiastes. The book is both a puzzle and an invitation, prompting constant wondering, as evinced in the divergent interpretations it has generated in scholarship, let alone throughout the history of interpretation. Despite the attempts to contain it in epilogues or commentaries, Ecclesiastes defies easy categorization: Is it pessimistic or is it ironically playful? Is it dark and dour or joyful and life-affirming? Is it deconstructive or instructive? Yes.

The probative nature of Qoheleth's reflections invites the reader's probing. As the ancient sage tried to make sense of life, so the reader must try to make sense of his words and in their light make sense of her own life, perhaps the ultimate aim of the book. The book's paradoxes and contradictions, ambiguities and complexities, reveal not a clumsy mishmash of conflicting opinions but an active, probing, evolving intellect at work. Crenshaw appropriately celebrates Qoheleth's courage and curiosity, his honesty and openness to alter his views and stretch his mind.[73] And stretch Qoheleth does as he attempts to bring into his purview everything done "under the sun" in order to test and question, to seek and search out wisdom.

But to no avail. Like Socrates (who is thought to have said, "I know one thing, that I know nothing"),[74] Qoheleth comes up against the impenetrable limits of human knowledge to encounter mystery. Discernment leads to bewilderment. Like Theaetetus besieged by Socrates' probing questions, Qoheleth is "lost" in aporetic wonder at the tenuous nature of wisdom itself. This is not the wonder that lifts the soul to heights of ecstasy or arrives at serene certitude. Rather, it is the kind of wonder that questions, deconstructs, and ultimately surrenders to the Unknown.[75] Qoheleth's "fear seeking understanding" turns into "fear accepting the unknown."

But this sage of sages does not simply wallow in aporia, in utter confusion. While casting into question traditional profiles of wisdom and char-

73. Crenshaw, *Qoheleth*, 115.

74. This famous line is actually nowhere said by Socrates in Plato's works. See Fine, "Does Socrates Claim?"

75. This troubling side of wonder is emphasized by Rubenstein and Miller. See chapter 1 above and chapter 4 above.

acter, including the efficacy of accumulated wisdom, Qoheleth begins to construct a new way of living. Like Job, Qoheleth places enough weight on his own experience to counter many of the "truths" of inherited tradition. Beyond Job, however, Qoheleth has turned his experience into an epistemological vantage point lodged in his autobiographical, analytical style. The sage revels in "introspective reporting."[76] Despite the deconstructive consequences, Qoheleth's style places high value on the definitive role of individual perception and personal intellect to make sense of life and world, moral and otherwise.

While Wisdom remains unreachable for Qoheleth, the very failure of his pursuit affords him a view of the world and the human condition in their irrational totalities. It is in the failed nature of the quest (not unlike the failure of exploration described in Job 28) that the contours of character become subversively reshaped. Qoheleth does not condemn his search as a trail of tears, though it does have its share of disillusionment and frustration. Instead, as the model sage he is, Qoheleth commends the examined life come what may: full awareness of life's absurdities and tragedies, including particularly death, as well as life's small graces. It is from his step back that Qoheleth reenters changed. The profile of this new character is only faintly sketched, but it is one fashioned from a fearful acceptance of life received from the hand of God. It is this attitude of fearful receptivity that also enables him to accept enjoyment as it is given and to cultivate it. By plumbing the depths of finitude, Qoheleth comes to espouse a radical openness to life, a life lived without certitude, except for the certitude of death, and thus without pretense, free from delusions of gain and grandeur, royal or commercial, moral or selfish.

The book of Ecclesiastes is, on the one hand, a lament of resignation about life and the frustration of work and economic practices in particular. For an achievement-driven, entrepreneurial society, Qoheleth's message speaks to those who with ambitious plans for success are ripe for disillusionment. Qoheleth's instruction is of universal import, made more urgent in a highly commercialized age, as it was in the monetized age of his time. In almost Humean fashion,[77] Qoheleth demonstrates that the means and the end, effort and result, work and gain, conduct and consequence, bear no necessary connection in the real world.

---

76. Fox, *Qohelet and His Contradictions,* 93.

77. I refer to the Scottish philosopher David Hume, who argued against the philosophical claim that material cause and effect bore a necessary connection.

On the other hand, the book is an invitation to a "nonprofit" existence. In probing life's disillusionments, all examples of *hebel,* Qoheleth finds an answer, and it lies in the emergent desire to live into the present. The sage's answer is admittedly anticlimactic: eat, drink, and find enjoyment in one's labors. All noble and honorable goals and ideals are whittled down to simple pleasures received in gratitude. Some would say that such values are hedonistic, and rightly so. But Qoheleth is no hedonist, for he is no seeker of or striver after pleasure. He counts himself as a receiver. The elusive enjoyment Qoheleth commends, and commends he does, is one that thrives not on the accomplishment, not on the goals achieved, but on the very doing, thinking, toiling, and, most importantly, receiving (9:10). Faced with a world that cannot be mastered, Qoheleth urges his readers to go forth freed from obsession and extremism, freed from illusions of grandeur, freed from compulsive striving, yet filled with fear and wonder in the receiving and in the doing, with wonder minus the glory, with wisdom minus Wisdom.

CHAPTER 7

Conclusion: Trembling at the Threshold

Wonder prevents us from living inside our little worlds.

Jerome Miller[1]

The diversity of the wisdom corpus is so striking that it is difficult to see how these three books of the Hebrew Bible hang together canonically, let alone thematically. According to rabbinic tradition, Proverbs was written by Solomon in his prime, while the book of Ecclesiastes was codified in his old age.[2] Historical naiveté aside, the rabbis appropriately recognized wisdom's ever-evolving nature by setting wisdom within the context of the ever-forming self. In other words, the complexity of the wisdom corpus ultimately comes down to the complexity of the human self. To include under wisdom's umbrella the elements of perception, intention, virtue, emotion, and desire is to acknowledge the complexity of *embodied* wisdom, of wisdom vis-à-vis the self. In biblical wisdom, the polarities of reason and emotion, passion and intellect, mind and heart, body and soul (i.e., *nepeš*) are complementary rather than opposing; they are complementary aspects of the whole self.

As a complement to its complexity, wisdom's open-ended, dynamic character is grounded in wonder. According to Jerome Miller, wonder

1. Miller, *In the Throe of Wonder,* 35.
2. And Solomon wrote Song of Songs in his youth (Song of Songs Rabbah I:VI.17.H; Jacob Neusner, *Song of Songs Rabbah,* 1:50).

contains its own polarity, and by way of illustration he lifts up an archetypal childhood experience: the child who is "transfixed by wonder before the door to a secret room."[3]

> Perhaps the child gets the courage to raise her hand toward the latch — and then, just as she is about to lift it, she stops her hand under the influence of a final, unnerving premonition. She pulls back from the door, surprised that she could have come so close to opening it; she is ready to turn and run back. . . . And yet she does not flee but advances again. For wonder puts into motion precisely this dreadful play between withdrawal and venturing, retreat and longing, reluctance and urgency, delay and hastening. When caught in its sway we do not stand motionless; we are held fast in the throe of an ambivalence between the known and the unknown, the same and the other, the past and the future.[4]

The child, Miller observes, is held in the grip of "fascination and terror,"[5] but it is in the sway of wonder that fascination tips the scale toward approaching rather than retreating, prompting her to open the door. Miller concludes: "As children, we do not know what is hidden behind the doors we are on the verge of opening. We stand there on the verge, on the threshold of a forbidden place we are sure it is dangerous to enter."[6]

Each in its own way, Proverbs, Job, and Ecclesiastes place the reader on the threshold of wonder: the silent son before the powerfully desirable figure of Wisdom, who shares common domain with the seductive Stranger; Job before the transcendentally powerful God of the whirlwind displaying an alien world of brutal beauty; Qoheleth before the long shadow of death, the inscrutable elegance of life, and a transcendentally mysterious God. While each book has its share of *tremendum,* the approach taken by each is different, so also the threshold. The son ventures forth to open the door beyond which Wisdom awaits to welcome him. Job is catapulted through the threshold into a world he regarded with horror and revulsion. Qoheleth's door, however, remains locked, but after using all the keys at his disposal he discovers a small slot.

---

3. Miller, *In the Throe of Wonder,* 33.

4. Miller, *In the Throe of Wonder,* 36.

5. Miller, *In the Throe of Wonder,* 35. Again, an analogy can be made with the dialectic of *mysterium* and *fascinans* in Rudolf Otto, *Idea of the Holy,* esp. 12-40.

6. Miller, *In the Throe of Wonder,* 34.

Simplistic, yes, but I hope suggestive. Each book is complex, literarily and intellectually, and increasingly so as one reads them in the order of presentation in this study. Whereas much of Proverbs was designed for the education of youth, directing their passions toward Wisdom, Job and Ecclesiastes were clearly intended for more advanced levels of intellectual engagement. But even Proverbs has its challenging material, with its generous share of "enigmas" and subtle sayings, not to mention the damning, puzzling words of Agur. Taken together, all three books encourage approaches to life marked by "intellectual, moral, and aesthetic growth over the course of the human life span," the business of wonder. Such also is the business of wisdom. Wonder animates the desire to affiliate and explore. Amid the temptation of withdrawal and retreat, it is the desire for affiliation, the eros of inquiry, that ultimately wins, that moves the formation of character along, even in painful fits and starts. If the son had spurned Wisdom, if Job had died on his ash heap, if Qoheleth had given up his inquiry at the outset, then wisdom's winding way would never have inched forward.

Saving Fear, Shaping Desire

All three wisdom books have much to do with identifying worthy objects of wonder. And many such objects, it turns out, are subjects in their own right, dreadful yet desirable subjects. A hermeneutic of wonder highlights, among other things, the role of awe and eros in the self's formation, in the self's growth in wisdom. What, then, do these books regard as worthy of wonder, as vital desiderata in the matrix of human agency?

In Proverbs desire is frequently, but not exclusively, cast erotically, hence Wisdom's distinctly feminine personification for a predominantly male readership.[8] More broadly, the power of desire is manifest in many ways: the desire for wealth, for sex, for violence, for marital intimacy, for Wisdom, for family, for righteousness and justice. Through the respective speeches of the parent and Wisdom, the framers of Proverbs attempt to redirect desire toward what is good and life-giving while exposing false

---

7. Fuller, *Wonder*, 2.

8. See Yoder, "Shaping of Erotic Desire"; Murphy, "Wisdom and Eros." More recently, Yoder has widened the notion of desire beyond its typically erotic associations to include, fundamentally, the appetites ("Contours of Desire").

desires and their objects for what they are: objects of revulsion, death-inducing desires.

Whereas the strange woman reflects illicit desire, sapiential desire in Proverbs remains safely within bounds, as powerfully illustrated in Wisdom's personification in the first nine chapters and in the concluding homage to the "woman of strength." But there is more to Wisdom than what appears to be a domestication of desire on the part of anxious sages. Wisdom, in addition to being feminine, is cosmic and transcendent. She is the cosmic child, God's only begotten daughter, delight of the world and of God (Prov. 8:22-31), homebuilder and host (9:1-6). Her attraction reaches beyond the erotic;[9] it is thoroughly cosmic and transcendent. She is wondrous. To affiliate with Wisdom is to do what she does. And what would wisdom do (WWWD)? She would walk the paths of righteousness and justice (8:20) and joyfully engage creation and God (8:30-31).

While initially fearsome (1:20-33), Wisdom's depiction as God's cosmic child in 8:30-31 marks a high point in her own rhetorical formation in Proverbs. In her cosmic, most transcendent profile, Wisdom casts herself as a child at play, establishing a familial bond of identity with her children. She is also "sister," a term of endearment (7:4; cf. Song 4:9-12), and mother (Prov. 8:32). Her final and fitting act is extending hospitality to all who would sit at her table to partake of her sapiential fare (9:5). Wisdom is a wonder; she is wholly Other yet wholly familiar. In Wisdom, "fear seeking understanding" finds its fulfillment. In Wisdom, the hunger for wonder is satisfied beyond measure.

In Job wonder takes a strange turn, and so also desire. Job himself becomes the quintessential stranger, a decentered, peripheralized character. Deemed outcast and a purveyor of moral chaos, Job is an alien to his community and even to himself (e.g., 19:13-19). His desire for esteem and social recognition, for the honor and glory due an upstanding paterfamilias, has failed him. Job has become a patriarch's nightmare, or a dark fantasy. Sitting on his ash heap, suffering the insults of his "friends," Job yearns for death. His first poetic words declare death as his fondest desire. But to no avail. Job's death wish becomes displaced with an all-consuming desire for vindication, desire fueled by righteous anger and formalized in litigation, giving him reason to live and confidence to venture forth "like a prince," lawsuit in hand, and approach the very throne of God (31:37).

---

9. Similarly, the appeal of the "woman of strength" builds on her works and her strength rather than on her erotic attraction (Yoder, "Shaping of Erotic Desire," 158).

YHWH, however, meets Job not in a throne room or in a courtroom but outside in a death-dealing whirlwind. Spared from death, Job is imprinted with a frighteningly wondrous vision of life, specifically of creation's raging, sublime beauty. In Job's eyes, creation itself becomes "other," no longer an object of dread and contempt but a source of fearful wonder, wholly alien but, on closer inspection, strangely familiar. Creation is revealed as a community of free subjects, not objects of revulsion, and their habits and demeanors bear a strange symmetry with Job's. In the whirlwind, shock turns toward awe, and chaos becomes sublime. God compels Job to see creation as God sees it, with admiration and awe. This God sustains the world gratuitously, not retributively. And Job is left not to die but to raise a new family, but this time sustained by the gratuitous extravagance of love, of love "for nothing." Job's desire? It is for his children, daughters as well as sons, and by extension friends and foreigners alike. Job's fear? Freed from debilitating anxiety and loathsome terror, Job's fear is refined into formative awe.

Qoheleth is the one who most rigorously embodies the eros of inquiry. His life is consumed with seeking out wisdom and seeking with wisdom, with attempting to render a summary account of it all, albeit more as an accountant than as an empiricist (7:25). But Wisdom proves far too elusive, the future remains far too uncertain, life proceeds without guarantees, and death rules over all. All hope for enduring accomplishments, royal and otherwise, is laid to rest at death's door. Immortalizing the self through reputation is found to be a lost cause. Any hope of lasting gain is gone with the wind. All is *hebel*, and consequently "the appetite is never filled" (6:7b).

Qoheleth's desire for wisdom is, to be sure, tied to his personal desire to enhance the self. Yes, Qoheleth is a selfish sage. "Nothing in Ecclesiastes ever indicates that Qoheleth was able to rise above self-absorption."[10] Although this is nothing new among sages, the great frequency of Qoheleth's self-referencing, matched by his largely dispassionate tone, could easily be read as narcissistic, indicating an inordinate desire for self-preservation.[11] In any case, Qoheleth presents himself as the measure of all things (à la Protagoras). Thus of all the sapiential figures in the wisdom corpus, Qoheleth suffers the most from frustrated desire: the door to Wisdom remains under lock and key, try as he might to open it. God remains shrouded in

---

10. Crenshaw, *Qoheleth*, 86.

11. See the description of narcissism in the context of a highly commercialized culture (i.e., North American) in Lowen, *Narcissism*, 6-46, 213-16.

mystery, separated from human life by a yawning chasm (5:2 [Eng. 1]). Fear thus resides in the impenetrable mystery that is God; and in the realm of fearful mystery, high expectations are undercut, high-minded virtues are deemed dangerous, and the desire for self-glory is stifled. By relativizing wisdom, Qoheleth has returned fear to its numinous roots.

Near the conclusion of his discourse, Qoheleth encourages the young man to "follow the ways of your heart and whatever your eyes see, and know that for all these things God will bring you into judgment" (11:9). Passionate desire remains a staple of wonder (see also 9:9). But more broadly, for the old as well as for the young, the simple savoring of food and drink marks the reshaping of desire toward the mundane. That food and drink are deemed the very gifts of God, evidence of the "hand of God" at work, claims such simple pleasures as worthy of wonder, worthy objects of desire. They are, after all, what Wisdom offers at her spacious home (Prov. 9:4).

Forming Character

What is found worthy of wonder is found worthy of desire, and the cultivation of wonder and the shaping of desire have all to do with the formation of character. As wonder is formative and dynamic, so also is character. All three wisdom books depict the formation of character as a process, as an "emplotment" of the self.[12] The narrative nature of character (i.e., character's formation) is indicated in the repeated motif of the pathway throughout the wisdom corpus, such as the "way" of wisdom or the "way" of the wicked. And things are bound to happen along the "way," surprising detours and unexpected junctures that deconstruct old convictions and reach toward new insights. Such is the way of wisdom's wonder, that which keeps the self in motion and ever in the throe of inquiry.

The Self Turning Outward

As noted in chapter 1, the double movement of wonder "takes us out of the world only to put us back into the world, dismantling old possibil-

---

12. See Ricoeur's investigation of narrative "emplotment" in relation to character in *Time and Narrative*, 1:31-51.

ities."[13] Out and back. Each book traces the self starting from a central, familiar setting and then moving into liminal realms, which can engender fear and, ultimately, wonder.

The character of the silent son sitting deferentially at the feet of his elders is oriented toward a community sharply divided between the righteous and the wicked, between foreign women and woman Wisdom, a world rife with conflict, temptation, terror, and wonder. The father commends the way of prudence and warns his son against his violently rapacious friends (Prov. 1:8-19). He or the mother details the tragic story of a young man dragged down to his death by the femme fatale (Prov. 7:6-23).[14] In both cases, the parental voice paints a picture of terror and compels the son to step back and look at the motivations and consequences of disastrous actions. The parent presents a rhetorically persuasive case for maintaining the familiar and the familial.

Nevertheless, the familial gives way to the cosmic and the communal in the son's rite of passage. Guided by Wisdom, his "sister," he is instructed to avoid all that is strange and wicked as he makes his way through the winding streets, city gates, and market squares of public engagement. Wisdom, the cosmic child, reveals her own family of origin in a way that inspires awe and delight. She is the bridge between family and community, youth and age, and the self and creation, even God. For the son, Wisdom is the liminal link to his maturity. She replaces the parental hand of guidance by guiding the son through the threshold of adulthood. The book of Proverbs is about letting go as much as it is about holding firm.

Similar to Proverbs, the book of Job is about leaving the security and sentiment of the patriarchal household. But unlike the proverbial son's journey, the movement of Job's anomalous character is much more subversive, requiring a deconstruction of the traditional norms and marks of patriarchal character. Through circuitous deliberations, Job replaces his initially submissive posture with one of grievance and bitter protest. Job's chutzpah becomes a crowning mark of his integrity in transition. Yet his journey does not end with impassioned protests against his friends and God. Like Wisdom leading the son outward into the community, YHWH leads Job into a frighteningly wondrous, quintessentially strange cosmic community. Estranged from family and friends, Job finds himself in a world whose horizons embrace the very margins of the perceived orders of cre-

---

13. Rubenstein, *Strange Wonder*, 60.
14. See Brenner, "Proverbs 1-9."

ation, far beyond human control. As the periphery becomes the center, Job finds himself on the edge. The strange, wild creatures become his new community, and in them Job is afforded a new moral vision that embraces the margins, as humanly perceived, of the cosmic community. No longer based on mechanical laws of reaction and retribution, creation is the Creator's cosmic ark, with all creatures living fully and freely. Job's odyssey deliberately blurs the boundaries between the familiar and the strange in wonder's liminality.

Qoheleth's odyssey is much less dramatic yet equally profound. Qoheleth, too, attempts to penetrate the secrets of the cosmos but, unlike Job, gets lost in utter mystery and disillusionment in realizing the groundlessness of gain and the tenuousness of wisdom. His journey takes him to the void rather than to the sublime. There is no God or Wisdom to lead Qoheleth to new visions of moral engagement. He has no revelation from on high, only a revelation of himself from below. His journey cuts to the core of conscious existence. Driven by disillusionment, Qoheleth steps back and transcends the self that is consumed with toil and transcends the world that is filled with futility, and he finds it all *hebel*. Here wonder is the window into absurdity. Through it, the sage discerns a world of elegance and beauty, on the one hand, and frustration and despair, on the other. Qoheleth journeys from self to non-self, a search ostensibly for wisdom that leads not to a renewal of life but to an acute awareness of death's unassailable power and the futility of toiling for gain. Qoheleth's step back is his *via negativa*, an exercise of wonder's deconstructive power. Unlike Job, Qoheleth cannot identify himself with creation's strangeness and thereby find some sense of resolution. Instead, this sage of sages finds himself intractably out of sync with creation's irrational, mysterious orderliness; he is forever estranged from the world he sees around him, a world of *hebel* in a handbasket held by God.

The Self's Return

Each of the wisdom books, however, does not conclude with the self in limbo. With the turning outward there is the turning back, a reentry into the context from which the self first departed. It is in this return that the development of character reaches its conclusive formation. Proverbs concludes with a return to family life, the point of departure for the silent son. Navigating his way through a divided community, through the competing voices that vie for his allegiance, into the cosmic delight of Wisdom's way in the world, the would-be patriarch establishes himself as one who has fulfilled his deepest desire, desire shaped by his encounters with various voices along the way. He marries a "woman of strength" — Wisdom's incarnation in the household — and raises a prosperous family, securing the community's esteem. Proverbs begins and ends in the familial context. The danger of the strange is both acknowledged and avoided.

The familial that the former "son" and the "woman of strength" embody serves to maintain the moral structures of the community. The latter provides not only for the welfare of the family but also for the well-being of the community. In consort, the couple leads a life of service and security. Although their household might seem like a fortress, impregnable to the ravages of climate and chaos (Prov. 31:17, 21, 25), the door of this domicile remains ever open as the matriarch conducts commerce and extends her hand to the poor, while her spouse takes his seat among the elders, exercising his communal duties. This is a far cry from "amoral familism," in which the family becomes the exclusive context of moral agency.[15]

Job's rite of passage moves him beyond an ethos of grievance, which he had perfected to an art form in the dialogues, and toward a life of passionate reinvestment in family and community. Job has discovered God's gratuitous delight in a tragic yet vibrant creation characterized by fiercely dynamic, competing forces. And so Job attends to his family, fully aware that security is never guaranteed, even amid restoration. By raising a family, Job takes on a life of risk, uncalculating and undaunted, a life of gratuitous giving.

Having encountered the void of disillusionment, Qoheleth also makes his return to the vicissitudes of everyday existence. And indeed, like Job, his reentry comes at the cost of new orientation. Whereas Job returns with renewed vision, ready to embrace the risks of life with new attentiveness, Qoheleth returns with a sigh of resignation mixed with bewilderment, a surrender to wonder's deconstructive side. It is precisely through the veil of cosmic indifference and vocational despair that Qoheleth arrives at an unconditional acceptance of life on its own minimalist terms. Only within the absurd confinements of life, sustained by an inscrutable God, is Qoheleth able to commend a life of enjoyment exercised in simplicity.

15. This phrase is borrowed from Wilson's reference to E. C. Banfield's study of a southern Italian village, whose extreme poverty is attributable to an intractable unwillingness to cooperate beyond each family's own material interests (*Moral Sense*, 228).

Qoheleth reenters the self, having stepped back from the self that constituted him and the world that he expected would yield grand results from his royally grand experiment.

He has no other choice. One cannot live fractured, forever split between a life consumed with the desire to understand and achieve great things and a life resigned to unmitigated futility. Qoheleth does not, in the end, find death as the solution to a divided, disillusioned life. "A living dog," after all, "is better than a dead lion" (9:4). Without satisfying answers, without the fulfillment of deep desire, Qoheleth reinvests in the self by focusing on life's fleeting yet redemptive moments of joy and the vital constancy of work. His character is reoriented to enjoy them, his desire reshaped to relish them, receiving them as incalculable gifts of God, as ordinary wonders in a hopelessly estranged world.

A Synthesis of Character?

If the central figures of these three books were seated together at table, no doubt enjoying food and wine, they undoubtedly would have much to say to each other in rebuke as well as in approval. All would argue, no doubt, over who — the aged or youth, the established or the dispossessed — could lay claim to the lion's share of wisdom (particularly if Elihu were invited). In addition, Job would chide Qoheleth for being so melancholic about such matters, while Qoheleth would point out that Job's revelational experience was hopelessly privileged. To be sure, both Job and Qoheleth would rebuke the proverbial grown-up "son" for his naiveté and simplistic worldview (though he could respond with the words of Agur). But perhaps the proverbial sage would have the last word by pointing out that fearful reverence remains formative for every profile of normative character.

All would recognize that the way of wisdom, the pathway of formation, is a rugged road of crisis and wonder. The youth must sever his familial ties in order to embark upon an uncharted, conflict-filled landscape beyond the security of hearth and home, while Job and Qoheleth must let go of preconceived notions of moral coherence and ethical practice. Dead ends are inevitably encountered on their respective journeys. To pose the question of a standard profile of right character is analogous to asking a chess master for the best move. Any answer must be framed relative to every step in which the game progresses. And as the game proceeds in a way that defines it as chess and not "Chutes and Ladders," so there is a common thread that connects the wisdom books: their concern for making sense of life and living fully. Each book features snapshot profiles of works in progress, configured in response to social challenges and perceived crises.

Whether painted with the tidy strokes of proverbial wisdom or with Qoheleth's impressionistic brush, these various portraits of wise character form part of an even larger canvas that features the litany of God's salvific acts and the giving of Torah, the impassioned words of temple worship and the commanding words of the prophets. And in it all and through it all the beloved community continues its struggle for "righteousness, justice, and equity" on God's cosmic canvas. For this, wisdom offers an enduring sense of mystery of all that is, of all that is *Other*: the reverberating laughter of Wisdom's cosmic delight, the inalienable dignity of creation's denizens, and the unfathomable nature of the God behind it all. Creation remains a central feature of biblical wisdom, but never in isolation. Lodged in the eye of the beholder, the cosmic perspective is lived out in conduct. Creation and character find their nexus in perception, whether revelatory or realistic, conventional or subversive, and perception has all to do with wonder.

Is biblical wisdom, then, simply "advice literature"?[16] There is, to be sure, plenty of advice given, and the genres the sages employ betray their strong didactic interests. But the sages went after something deeper, as is clear from the various "texts of *tremendum*," some verging on "texts of terror," they included within their scribal works, their textual tableaus of creation and life. Such passages lift wisdom above the level of mere guidance counseling; they extend wisdom far beyond training exercises on writing tablets. With these texts, the sages proved themselves to be not only counselors and teachers but also, and most fundamentally, *thaumaturgists*. The sages who gathered around the table for dialogue and debate were wielders of wonder, for they knew all too well that without wonder wisdom withers.

---

16. Weeks, *Introduction*, 1-5. See also Sneed, "Is the 'Wisdom Tradition' a Tradition?" 68-69.

Works Cited

Abrams, M. H. *A Glossary of Literary Terms*. 4th ed. New York: Holt, Rinehart, Winston, 1981.

Adams, A. K., ed. *The Home Book of Humorous Quotations*. New York: Dodd, Mead, 1969.

Adams, Samuel L. *Wisdom in Transition: Act and Consequence in Second Temple Instructions*. JSJSup 125. Leiden: Brill, 2008.

Allen, Diogenes. *The Traces of God in a Frequently Hostile World*. Cambridge, MA: Cowley, 1981.

Alonso Schöckel, Luis, and José Luis Sicre Díaz. *Job: Comentario teológico y literario*. Nueva Biblia Española. Madrid: Cristiandad, 1983.

Alter, Robert. *The Art of Biblical Narrative*. New York: Basic Books, 1981.

———. *The Art of Biblical Poetry*. New York: Basic Books, 1985.

Aristotle. *Nicomachean Ethics*. Trans. Martin Ostwald. LLA 75. Indianapolis: Bobbs-Merrill, 1962.

Auerbach, Erich. *Mimesis: The Representation of Reality in Western Literature*. Trans. Willard R. Trask. Garden City, NY: Doubleday, 1957.

Baechler, Jean. "Virtue: Its Nature, Exigency, and Acquisition." Pages 2-48 in *Virtue*. Ed. John W. Chapman and William A. Galston. Nomos 34. New York: New York University Press, 1991.

Balentine, Samuel E. *Job*. Smyth & Helwys Commentary. Macon, GA: Smyth & Helwys, 2006.

Bar-Efrat, Shim'on. *The Art of the Biblical Story*. Tel Aviv: Sifriat Hapoalim, 1979.

Baskin, Judith R. "Rabbinic Interpretations of Job." Pages 101-10 in *The Voice from the Whirlwind: Interpreting the Book of Job*. Ed. Leo G. Perdue and W. Clark Gilpin. Nashville: Abingdon, 1992.

Becker, Joachim. *Gottesfurcht im Alten Testament*. Analecta biblica 25. Rome: Pontifical Biblical Institute, 1965.

Bennett, William J., ed. *The Book of Virtues: A Treasury of Great Moral Stories.* New York: Simon & Schuster, 1993.

Berlin, Adele. *Poetics and Interpretation of Biblical Narrative.* BLS 9. Sheffield: Almond, 1983.

Berquist, Jon L. *Judaism in Persia's Shadow: A Social and Historical Approach.* Minneapolis: Fortress, 1995.

Birch, Bruce. *Let Justice Roll Down.* Louisville: Westminster John Knox, 1991.

———, and Larry Rasmussen. *Bible and Ethics in the Christian Life.* Rev. ed. Minneapolis: Augsburg, 1989.

Blanchard, Kenneth H., and Norman Vincent Peale. *The Power of Ethical Management.* New York: William Morrow, 1988.

Blenkinsopp, Joseph. "The Social Context of the 'Outsider Woman' in Prov 1–9." *Bib* 72 (1991): 457-73.

Boecker, Hans-Jochen. *Law and the Administration of Justice in the Old Testament and Ancient East.* Trans. Jeremy Moiser. Minneapolis: Augsburg, 1980.

Bondi, Richard. "Character." Pages 82-84 in *Westminster Dictionary of Christian Ethics.* Ed. James F. Childress and John Macquarrie. Philadelphia: Westminster, 1986.

———. "The Elements of Character." *JRE* 12 (1984): 201-18.

Brenner, Athalya. "God's Answer to Job." *VT* 31 (1981): 129-37.

———. "Proverbs 1–9: An F Voice?" Pages 113-30 in *On Gendering Texts: Female and Male Voices in the Hebrew Bible.* Ed. Athalya Brenner and Fokkelien Dijk-Hemmes. Leiden: Brill, 1993.

Brown, William P. *Character in Crisis: A Fresh Approach to the Wisdom Literature of the Bible.* Grand Rapids: Eerdmans, 1996.

———. " 'Come, O Children . . . I Will Teach You the Fear of the LORD' (Psalm 34:12): Comparing Psalms and Proverbs." Pages 85-102 in *Seeking Out the Wisdom of the Ancients: Essays Offered to Honor Michael V. Fox on the Occasion of His Sixty-Fifth Birthday.* Ed. Ronald L. Troxel, Kelvin G. Freibel, and Dennis R. Magary. Winona Lake, IN: Eisenbrauns, 2005.

———. "The Didactic Power of Metaphor in the Aphoristic Sayings of Proverbs." *JSOT* 29 (2004): 133-54.

———. *Ecclesiastes.* IBC. Louisville: Westminster John Knox, 2000.

———. *The Ethos of the Cosmos: The Genesis of Moral Imagination in the Bible.* Grand Rapids: Eerdmans, 1999.

———. "The Law and the Sages: A Reexamination of *Tôrâ* in the Book of Proverbs." Pages 251-80 in *Constituting the Community: Studies on the Polity of Ancient Israel in Honor of S. Dean McBride Jr.* Ed. John T. Strong and Steven S. Tuell. Winona Lake, IN: Eisenbrauns, 2005.

———. "The Pedagogy of Proverbs 10:1–31:9." Pages 150-82 in *Character and Scripture: Moral Formation, Community, and Biblical Interpretation.* Ed. William P. Brown. Grand Rapids: Eerdmans, 2002.

———. *The Seven Pillars of Creation: The Bible, Science, and the Ecology of Wonder.* New York: Oxford University Press, 2010.

———. "To Discipline without Destruction: The Multifaceted Profile of the Child in Proverbs." Pages 63-81 in *The Child in the Bible*. Ed. Marcia J. Bunge. Grand Rapids: Eerdmans, 2008.

———. " 'Whatever Your Hand Finds to Do': Qoheleth's Work Ethic." *Int* 55 (2001): 271-84.

Brueggemann, Walter. *Abiding Astonishment: Psalms, Modernity, and the Making of History*. Louisville: Westminster John Knox, 1991.

———. *In Man We Trust*. Richmond: John Knox, 1972.

———. "Scripture and an Ecumenical Life-Style: A Study in Wisdom Theology." *Int* 34 (1970): 3-19.

———. "The Social Significance of Solomon as a Patron of Wisdom." Pages 117-32 in *The Sage in Israel and the Ancient Near East*. Ed. John G. Gammie and Leo G. Perdue. Winona Lake, IN: Eisenbrauns, 1990.

Budziszewski, J. "Religion and Civic Virtue." Pages 49-68 in *Virtue*. Ed. John W. Chapman and William A. Galston. Nomos 34. New York: New York University Press, 1991.

Bulkeley, Kelly. *The Wondering Brain: Thinking about Religion with and beyond Cognitive Neuroscience*. New York: Routledge, 2005.

Burkes, Shannon. *Death in Qoheleth and Egyptian Biographies of the Late Period*. SBLDS 170. Atlanta: Society of Biblical Literature, 1999.

Camp, Claudia V. "What's So Strange about the Strange Woman?" Pages 17-31 in *The Bible and the Politics of Exegesis: Essays in Honor of Norman K. Gottwald*. Ed. David Jobling, Peggy L. Day, and Gerald T. Sheppard. Cleveland: Pilgrim, 1991.

———. *Wisdom and the Feminine in the Book of Proverbs*. BLS 11. Sheffield: Almond, 1985.

Campbell, Mary Bruce. *Wonder and Science: Imagining Worlds in Early Modern Europe*. Ithaca: Cornell University Press, 1999.

Camus, Albert. *The Myth of Sisyphus and Other Essays*. Trans. Justin O'Brien. New York: Knopf, 1955.

Cessario, Romanus. *The Moral Virtues and Theological Ethics*. Notre Dame: University of Notre Dame Press, 1991.

Chatman, Seymour B. *Story and Discourse: Narrative Structure in Fiction and Film*. Ithaca, NY: Cornell University Press, 1978.

Chitando, Ezra. "The Good Wife: A Phenomenological Rereading of Proverbs 31:10-31 in the Contexts of HIV/AIDS in Zimbabwe." *Scriptura* 86 (2004): 151-59.

Christianson, Eric S. *A Time to Tell: Narrative Strategies in Ecclesiastes*. JSOTSup 280. Sheffield: Sheffield Academic Press, 1998.

Clements, Ronald E. *Wisdom in Theology*. Grand Rapids: Eerdmans, 1992.

Clifford, Richard J., S.J. *The Book of Proverbs and Our Search for Wisdom*. Milwaukee: Marquette University Press, 1995.

Clines, David J. A. "False Naivety in the Prologue to Job." *HAR* 9 (1985): 127-36.

———. " 'The Fear of the Lord Is Wisdom' (Job 28:28): A Semantic and Contextual Study." Pages 57-92 in *Job 28: Cognition in Context*. Ed. Ellen van Wolde. BIS 64. Leiden: Brill, 2003.

———. *Job 1–20*. WBC 17. Waco: Word, 1989.

———. "Job's Fifth Friend: An Ethical Critique of the Book of Job." *BI* 12 (2004): 233-50.

———. "Putting Elihu in His Place: A Proposal for the Relocation of Job 32-37." *JSOT* 29 (2004): 243-53.

Collins, John J. "Wisdom Reconsidered, in Light of the Scrolls." *DSD* 4 (1997): 265-81.

Cooper, Alan. "Reading and Misreading the Prologue of Job." *JSOT* 46 (1990): 67-79.

———. "The Sense of the Book of Job." *Prooftexts* 17 (1997): 227-44.

Covey, Stephen R. *The Seven Habits of Highly Effective People: Restoring the Character Ethic*. New York: Simon & Schuster, 1990.

Crenshaw, James L. "Clanging Symbols." Pages 51-64 in *Justice and the Holy: Essays in Honor of Walter Harrelson*. Ed. Douglas A. Knight and Peter J. Paris. Atlanta: Scholars Press, 1989. Repr. as pages 371-82 in *Urgent Advice and Probing Questions: Collected Writings on Old Testament Wisdom*. Macon, GA: Mercer University Press, 1995.

———. *Ecclesiastes*. OTL. Philadelphia: Westminster, 1987.

———. "Ecclesiastes: Odd Book In." *BibRev* 31 (1990): 28-33.

———. *Education in Ancient Israel: Across the Deadening Silence*. ABRL. New York: Doubleday, 1998.

———. *Old Testament Wisdom: An Introduction*. 2nd ed. Louisville: Westminster John Knox, 1998.

———. *Qoheleth: The Ironic Wink*. SPOT. Columbia: University of South Carolina Press, 2013.

———. "Qoheleth's Understanding of Intellectual Inquiry." Pages 205-24 in *Qohelet in the Context of Wisdom*. Ed. A. Schoors. BETL 136. Leuven: Leuven University Press, 1998.

———. *Reading Job: A Literary and Theological Commentary*. Macon, GA: Smyth & Helwys, 2011.

———. "The Shadow of Death in Qoheleth." Pages 205-16 in *Israelite Wisdom: Theological and Literary Essays in Honor of Samuel Terrien*. Ed. John G. Gammie et al. Missoula, MT: Scholars Press, 1978. Repr. as pages 573-85 in *Urgent Advice and Probing Questions: Collected Writings on Old Testament Wisdom*. Macon, GA: Mercer University Press, 1995.

———. "Wisdom and Authority: Sapiential Rhetoric and Its Warrants." Pages 10-29 in *Congress Volume, Vienna, 1980*. Ed. J. A. Emerton. VTSup 32. Leiden: Brill, 1981. Repr. as pages 326-43 in *Urgent Advice and Probing Questions: Collected Writings on Old Testament Wisdom*. Macon, GA: Mercer University Press, 1995.

Crüsemann, Frank. "The Unchangeable World: The 'Crisis of Wisdom' in Koheleth." Pages 57-77 in *God of the Lowly: Socio-Historical Interpretations of the Bible.* Ed. Willy Schottroff and Wolfgang Stegemann. Trans. Matthew J. O'Connell. Maryknoll, NY: Orbis, 1984.

Curtis, John Briggs. "On Job's Response to Yahweh." *JBL* 98 (1979): 497-511.

Dahood, Mitchell. "*Mišmār* 'Muzzle' in Job 7:12." *JBL* 90 (1961): 270-71.

Dalley, Stephanie. *Myths from Mesopotamia: Creation, the Flood, Gilgamesh, and Others,* 2nd ed. Oxford World's Classics. Oxford: Oxford University Press, 2000.

Daston, Lorraine, and Katherine Park. *Wonders and the Order of Nature.* New York: Zone, 1998.

Davies, Paul. *The Last Three Minutes: Conjectures about the Ultimate Fate of the Universe.* New York: Basic Books, 1994.

Davis, Ellen F. *Getting Involved with God: Rediscovering the Old Testament.* Cambridge, MA: Cowley, 2001.

———. "Job and Jacob: The Integrity of Faith." Pages 203-24 in *Reading Between Texts: Intertextuality and the Hebrew Bible.* Ed. Danna Nolan Fewell. Louisville: Westminster John Knox, 1992.

———. "Preserving Virtues: Renewing the Tradition of the Sages." Pages 183-201 in *Character and Scripture: Moral Formation, Community, and Biblical Interpretation.* Ed. William P. Brown. Grand Rapids: Eerdmans, 2002.

———. *Proverbs, Ecclesiastes, and the Song of Songs.* Westminster Bible Companion. Louisville: Westminster John Knox, 2000.

Day, Peggy L. *An Adversary in Heaven: śāṭān in the Hebrew Bible.* HSM 43. Atlanta: Scholars Press, 1988.

Deane-Drummond, Celia. *Wonder and Wisdom: Conversations in Science, Spirituality, and Theology.* Philadelphia: Templeton Foundation Press, 2005.

Delitzsch, Franz. *Ecclesiastes.* Pages 177-442 in *Proverbs, Ecclesiastes, Song of Solomon.* 1872. Trans. M. G. Easton. Repr. Grand Rapids: Eerdmans, 1984.

Dell, Katharine J. *The Book of Job as Sceptical Literature.* BZAW 197. Berlin: de Gruyter, 1991.

———. *The Book of Proverbs in Social and Theological Context.* Cambridge: Cambridge University Press, 2006.

———. "The Cycle of Life in Ecclesiastes." *VT* 59 (2009): 181-89.

———. *"Get Wisdom, Get Insight": An Introduction to Israel's Wisdom Literature.* Macon, GA: Smyth & Helwys, 2000.

———. "Job: Sceptics, Philosophers and Tragedians." Pages 1-20 in *Das Buch Hiob und seine Interpretationen: Beiträge zum Hiob-Symposium auf dem Monte Verità vom 14.-19. August 2005.* Ed. Thomas Krüger et al. Zurich: Theologischer Verlag, 2007.

Dick, Michael B. "The Neo-Assyrian Royal Lion Hunt and Yahweh's Answer to Job." *JBL* 125 (2006): 243-70.

Doll, Jen. "The Moral Decline in the Words We Use." *Atlantic Wire* (24 August 2012). Accessed on 17 September 2012 at http://www.theatlanticwire.com/entertainment/2012/08/moral-decline-words-we-use/56142/.

Douglas, Mary. *Purity and Danger: An Analysis of the Concepts of Pollution and Taboo*. London: Routledge and Kegan Paul, 1966.

Dulin, Rachel Z. " 'How Sweet Is the Light': Qoheleth's Age-Centered Teachings." *Int* 55 (2001): 260-70.

Ellul, Jacques. *The Reason for Being: A Meditation on Ecclesiastes*. Trans. Joyce Main Hanks. Grand Rapids: Eerdmans, 1990.

Engel, Helmut. *Die Susanna-Erzählung: Einleitung, Übersetzung und Kommentar zum Septuaginta-Text und zur Theodotion-Bearbeitung*. OBO 61. Freiburg: Universitätsverlag, 1985.

Fidler, Ruth. "Qoheleth in 'the House of God': Text and Intertext in Qoh 4:17–5:6 (Eng. 5:1-7)." *HS* 47 (2006): 7-21.

Fine, Gail. "Does Socrates Claim to Know That He Knows Nothing?" *Oxford Studies in Ancient Philosophy* 35 (2008): 49-88.

Fisch, Harold. *Poetry with a Purpose: Biblical Poetics and Interpretation*. Indiana Studies in Biblical Literature. Bloomington: Indiana University Press, 1988.

Fishbane, Michael. "The Book of Job and Inner-Biblical Discourse." Pages 86-98 in *The Voice from the Whirlwind: Interpreting the Book of Job*. Ed. Leo G. Perdue and W. Clark Gilpin. Nashville: Abingdon, 1992.

Fohrer, Georg. "The Righteous Man in Job 31." Pages 1-22 in *Essays in Old Testament Ethics (J. Philip Hyatt, In Memoriam)*. Ed. James L. Crenshaw and John T. Willis. New York: Ktav, 1974.

Fontaine, Carole R. *Traditional Sayings in the Old Testament*. BLS 5. Sheffield: Almond, 1982.

―――. "Wounded Hero on a Shaman's Quest." Pages 70-85 in *The Voice from the Whirlwind: Interpreting the Book of Job*. Ed. Leo G. Perdue and W. Clark Gilpin. Nashville: Abingdon, 1992.

Forster, E. M. *Aspects of the Novel*. Harmondsworth: Penguin, 1963.

Forti, Tova. "The *Isha Zara* in Proverbs 1–9: Allegory and Allegorization." *HS* 48 (2007): 89-100.

Fowl, Stephen E., and L. Gregory Jones. *Reading in Communion: Scripture and Ethics in Christian Life*. Grand Rapids: Eerdmans, 1991.

Fox, Michael V. "Aging and Death in Qoheleth 12." *JSOT* 42 (1988): 55-77.

―――. " '*Amon* Again." *JBL* 115 (1996): 699-702.

―――. "Frame-Narrative and Composition in the Book of Qohelet." *HUCA* 48 (1977): 83-106.

―――. "Job the Pious." *ZAW* 117 (2005): 351-66.

―――. "The Meaning of *Hebel* for Qohelet." *JBL* 105 (1986): 409-27.

―――. "The Pedagogy of Proverbs 2." *JBL* 113 (1994): 233-43.

―――. *Proverbs 1–9: A New Translation with Introduction and Commentary*. AB 18A. New York: Doubleday, 2000.

―――. *Proverbs 10–31: A New Translation with Introduction and Commentary*. Anchor Yale Bible 18B. New Haven: Yale University Press, 2009.

―――. *Qohelet and His Contradictions*. BLS 18. JSOTSup 71. Sheffield: Almond Press, 1989.

———. "Qohelet's Epistemology." *HUCA* 58 (1987): 137-55.

———. *A Time to Tear Down and a Time to Build Up: A Rereading of Ecclesiastes.* Grand Rapids: Eerdmans, 1999.

———. "Wisdom in Qoheleth." Pages 115-31 in *In Search of Wisdom: Essays in Memory of John G. Gammie.* Ed. Leo G. Perdue, Bernard Brandon Scott, and William Johnston Wiseman. Louisville: Westminster John Knox, 1993.

Frankena, William K. *Ethics.* 2nd ed. Foundations of Philosophy. Englewood Cliffs, NJ: Prentice-Hall, 1973.

Freedman, David Noel. "The Elihu Speeches in the Book of Job: A Hypothetical Episode in the Literary History of the Work." *HTR* 61 (1968): 51-59.

Fretheim, Terence E. *God and World in the Old Testament: A Relational Theology of Creation.* Nashville: Abingdon, 2005.

Fuchs, Gisela. *Mythos und Hiobdictung, Aufnahme und Umdeutung altorientalischer Vorstellungen.* Stuttgart: Kohlhammer, 1993.

Fuller, Robert C. *Wonder: From Emotion to Spirituality.* Chapel Hill: University of North Carolina Press, 2006.

Galling, Kurt. "Kohelet-Studien." *ZAW* 50 (1932): 276-99.

———. *Der Prediger.* HAT 18. Tübingen: Mohr (Siebeck), 1969.

Galston, William A. "Introduction: The Revival of the Virtues." Pages 1-22 in *Virtue.* Ed. John W. Chapman and William A. Galston. Nomos 34. New York: New York University Press, 1991.

Gammie, John G. "Behemoth and Leviathan: On the Didactic and Theological Significance of Job 40:15–41:26." Pages 217-31 in *Israelite Wisdom: Theological and Literary Essays in Honor of Samuel Terrien.* Ed. John G. Gammie et al. Missoula, MT: Scholars Press, 1978.

Garrett, Susan R. "The 'Weaker Sex' in the *Testament of Job.*" *JBL* 112 (1993): 55-70.

Geeraerts, Dirk. "Caught in a Web of Irony: Job and His Embarrassed God." Pages 37-56 in *Job 28: Cognition in Context.* Ed. Ellen van Wolde. BIS 64. Leiden: Brill, 2003.

George, A. R. *The Babylonian Gilgamesh Epic: Introduction, Critical Edition and Cuneiform Texts.* 2 vols. Oxford: Oxford University Press, 2003.

Gerstenberger, Erhard S. *Israel in the Persian Period: The Fifth and Fourth Centuries B.C.E.* Trans. Siegfried S. Schatzmann. SBLBE 8. Atlanta: Society of Biblical Literature, 2011.

Gese, Hartmut. "The Crisis of Wisdom in Koheleth." Trans. Lester L. Grabbe. Pages 141-53 in *Theodicy in the Old Testament.* Ed. James L. Crenshaw. IRT 4. Philadelphia: Fortress, 1983.

———. *Lehre und Wirklichkeit in der alten Weisheit.* Tübingen: Mohr, 1958.

Gilkey, Langdon. "Power, Order, Justice, and Redemption: Theological Comments on Job." Pages 159-71 in *The Voice from the Whirlwind: Interpreting the Book of Job.* Ed. Leo G. Perdue and W. Clark Gilpin. Nashville: Abingdon, 1992.

Girard, René. *Job, the Victim of His People.* Trans. Yvonne Freccero. Stanford: Stanford University Press, 1987.

Glasser, E. *Le procès du bonheur par Qohelet.* LD 61. Paris: Cerf, 1970.

Good, Edwin M. *In Turns of Tempest: A Reading of Job*. Stanford: Stanford University Press, 1990.

———. "Job." Pages 407-32 in *Harper's Bible Commentary*. Ed. James L. Mays. San Francisco: Harper & Row, 1988.

———. "Job and the Literary Task: A Response." *Soundings* 56 (1973): 470-84.

———. "The Problem of Evil in the Book of Job." Pages 50-69 in *The Voice from the Whirlwind: Interpreting the Book of Job*. Ed. Leo G. Perdue and W. Clark Gilpin. Nashville: Abingdon, 1992.

Gordis, Robert. *Koheleth — The Man and His World: A Study of Ecclesiastes*. 3rd ed. New York: Schocken, 1968.

Greenstein, Edward L. "The Poem on Wisdom in Job 28 in Its Conceptual and Literary Contexts." Pages 253-80 in *Job 28: Cognition in Context*. Ed. Ellen van Wolde. BIS 64. Leiden: Brill, 2003.

Gunn, David M. *The Fate of King Saul: Interpretation of a Biblical Story*. JSOTSup 14. Sheffield: JSOT Press, 1980.

———. *The Story of King David: Genre and Interpretation*. JSOTSup 6. Sheffield: JSOT Press, 1978.

Gussow, Mel. "For Saul Bellow, Seeing the Earth with Fresh Eyes." *New York Times* (26 May 1997). Accessed on 17 September 2012 at http://www.nytimes .com/1997/05/26/books/for-saul-bellow-seeing-the-earth-with-fresh-eyes .html?scp=1&sq=Gussow%20%22Seeing%20the%20Earth%22&st=cse.

Habel, Norman C. *The Book of Job*. OTL. Philadelphia: Westminster, 1985.

———. "In Defense of God the Sage." Pages 21-38 in *The Voice from the Whirlwind: Interpreting the Book of Job*. Ed. Leo G. Perdue and W. Clark Gilpin. Nashville: Abingdon, 1992.

———. "The Role of Elihu in the Design of the Book of Job." Pages 81-98 in *In the Shelter of Elyon: Essays on Ancient Palestinian Life and Literature in Honor of G. W. Ahlström*. Ed. W. Boyd Barrick and John R. Spencer. JSOTSup 31. Sheffield: JSOT Press, 1984.

Hall, Stephen S. *Wisdom: From Philosophy to Neuroscience*. New York: Knopf, 2010.

Hankins, Charles Davis. "Job and the Limits of Wisdom." Ph.D. diss. Emory University, 2011.

Hauerwas, Stanley. *Character and the Christian Life: A Study in Theological Ethics*. TUMSR 3. San Antonio: Trinity University Press, 1975.

———. *A Community of Character: Toward a Constructive Christian Social Ethic*. Notre Dame: University of Notre Dame Press, 1981.

———. *The Peaceable Kingdom: A Primer in Christian Ethics*. Notre Dame: University of Notre Dame Press, 1983.

———. "The Self as Story: A Reconsideration of the Relation of Religion and Morality from the Agent's Perspective." Pages 68-89 in *Vision and Virtue: Essays in Christian Ethical Reflection*. Notre Dame: Fides, 1974.

Heim, Knute M. *Like Grapes of Gold Set in Silver: Proverbial Clusters in Proverbs 10:1–21:16*. BZAW 273. Berlin: de Gruyter, 2001.

Hengel, Martin. *Judaism and Hellenism: Studies in Their Encounter in Palestine during the Early Hellenistic Period.* Trans. John Bowden. 1974. Repr. 2 vols. in 1. Philadelphia: Fortress, 1981.

Henriksen, Jan-Olav. "Desire: Gift and Giving." Pages 1-30 in *Saving Desire: The Seduction of Christian Theology.* Ed. F. LeRon Shults and Jan-Olav Henriksen. Grand Rapids: Eerdmans, 2011.

Hermisson, Hans-Jürgen. "Observations on the Creation Theology in Wisdom." Pages 43-57 in *Israelite Wisdom: Theological and Literary Essays in Honor of Samuel Terrien.* Ed. John G. Gammie et al. Missoula, MT: Scholars Press, 1978.

Hertzberg, Hans Wilhelm. *Der Prediger.* KAT 17.4. Gütersloh: Mohn, 1963.

Heschel, Abraham Joshua. *God in Search of Man: A Philosophy of Judaism.* New York: Farrar, Straus and Giroux, 1955.

Hinman, Lawrence M. "Seeing Wisely — Learning to Become Wise." Pages 413-24 in *Understanding Wisdom: Sources, Science, and Society.* Ed. Warren S. Brown. Philadelphia: Templeton Foundation Press, 2000.

Holmes, Richard. *The Age of Wonder: How the Romantic Generation Discovered the Beauty and Terror of Science.* New York: Vintage, 2010.

Impey, Chris. *The Living Cosmos: Our Search for Life in the Universe.* New York: Random House, 2007.

Jaeger, Werner. *Paideia: The Ideals of Greek Culture.* Trans. Gilbert Highet. 2nd ed. 3 vols. Oxford: Blackwell, 1939-1944.

Janowski, Bernd. *Rettungsgewissheit und Epiphanie des Heils.* WMANT 59. Neukirchen-Vluyn: Neukirchener Verlag, 1989.

Janzen, J. Gerald. *At the Scent of Water: The Ground of Hope in the Book of Job.* Grand Rapids: Eerdmans, 2009.

———. "Creation and the Human Predicament in Job 1:9-11 and 38–41." *Ex Auditu* 3 (1987): 45-53.

———. *Job.* IBC. Atlanta: John Knox, 1985.

Janzen, Waldemar. *Old Testament Ethics: A Paradigmatic Approach.* Louisville: Westminster John Knox, 1994.

Jenni, Ernst. "Das Wort ʿōlām im Alten Testament." *ZAW* 65 (1953): 1-35.

Jones, Scott C. *Rumors of Wisdom: Job 28 as Poetry.* BZAW 398. Berlin: de Gruyter, 2009.

Kamano, Naoto. *Cosmology and Character: Qoheleth's Pedagogy from a Rhetorical-Critical Perspective.* BZAW 312. Berlin: de Gruyter, 2002.

Kant, Immanuel. *Critique of Practical Reason.* Trans. and ed. Mary Gregor. Cambridge: Cambridge University Press, 1997.

Kaplan, L. J. "Maimonides, Dale Patrick, and Job XLI 6." *VT* 28 (1978): 356-58.

Kass, Leon R. *The Hungry Soul: Eating and the Perfecting of Our Nature.* New York: Free Press, 1994.

———. "The Wisdom of Repugnance." *The New Republic* 216, no. 22, issue 4, 298 (1997): 17-26.

Kayatz, Christa. *Studien zu Proverbien 1-9.* WMANT 22. Neukirchen-Vluyn: Neukirchener Verlag, 1966.

Keel, Othmar. *Jahwes Entgegnung an Ijob*. FRLANT 121. Göttingen: Vandenhoeck & Ruprecht, 1978.

Keen, Sam. *Apology for Wonder*. New York: Harper & Row, 1969.

Kermode, Frank. *The Genesis of Secrecy: On the Interpretation of Narrative*. Cambridge: Harvard University Press, 1979.

Kesebir, Pelin, and Selin Kesebir. "The Cultural Salience of Moral Character and Virtue Declined in Twentieth Century America." *Journal of Positive Psychology* (2012). Available at Social Science Research Network: http://ssrn.com/abstract=2120724. Accessed on 17 September 2012 at http://papers.ssrn.com/sol3/papers.cfm?abstract_id=2120724.

Koch, Klaus. "Is There a Doctrine of Retribution in the Old Testament?" Trans. Thomas H. Trapp. Pages 57-87 in *Theodicy in the Old Testament*. Ed. James L. Crenshaw. IRT 4. Philadelphia: Fortress, 1983.

Konner, Melvin. *The Tangled Wing: Biological Constraints on the Human Spirit*. 2nd ed. New York: Henry Holt, 2002.

Kovacs, Brian W. "Is There a Class-Ethic in Proverbs?" Pages 171-89 in *Essays in Old Testament Ethics (J. Philip Hyatt, In Memoriam)*. Ed. James L. Crenshaw and John T. Willis. New York: Ktav, 1974.

Krüger, Thomas. "Did Job Repent?" Pages 217-29 in *Das Buch Hiob und Seine Interpretationen. Beiträge zum Hiob-Symposium auf dem Monte Verità vom 14.-19. August 2005*. Ed. Thomas Krüger. ATANT 88. Zurich: Theologischer Verlag, 2007.

———. *Qoheleth: A Commentary*. Trans. O. C. Dean Jr. Hermeneia. Minneapolis: Fortress, 2004.

Kugel, James L. "Qohelet and Money." *CBQ* 51 (1989): 32-49.

Kuhn, Thomas S. *The Structure of Scientific Revolutions*. Chicago: University of Chicago Press, 1970.

Kunstler, James Howard. *The Long Emergency: Surviving the Converging Catastrophes of the Twenty-First Century*. New York: Atlantic Monthly Press, 2005.

Lang, Bernhard. *Wisdom and the Book of Proverbs: An Israelite Goddess Redefined*. New York: Pilgrim, 1986.

Lauha, Aarre. "Die Krise des religiösen Glaubens bei Kohelet." Pages 183-91 in *Wisdom in Israel and in the Ancient Near East*. Ed. Martin Noth and D. Winton Thomas. VTSup 3. Leiden: Brill, 1955.

Lee, Eunny P. *The Vitality of Enjoyment in Qohelet's Theological Rhetoric*. BZAW 353. Berlin: de Gruyter, 2005.

Leeuwen, Raymond C. van. "Liminality and Worldview in Proverbs 1-9." *Semeia* 50 (1990): 111-44.

Levenson, Jon D. *Creation and the Persistence of Evil*. San Francisco: Harper & Row, 1988.

Lichtheim, Miriam. *Ancient Egyptian Literature*. 3 vols. Berkeley: University of California Press, 1973-1980.

Lonergan, Bernard J. F. *Insight: A Study of Human Understanding*. 3rd ed. New York: Philosophical Library, 1970.

Longinus, Cassius. *On the Sublime.* Trans. W. Hamilton Frye. LCL. Cambridge: Harvard University Press, 1982.

Longman, Tremper, III. *The Book of Ecclesiastes.* NICOT. Grand Rapids: Eerdmans, 1998.

Loretz, Oswald. *Qohelet und der alte Orient: Untersuchungen zu Stil und theologischer Thematik des Buches Qohelet.* Freiburg: Herder, 1964.

Lowen, Alexander. *Narcissism: Denial of the True Self.* New York: Touchstone, 1997.

MacDonald, Duncan B. *The Hebrew Literary Genius: An Interpretation.* Princeton: Princeton University Press, 1933.

Machinist, Peter. "The Voice of the Historian in the Ancient Near Eastern and Mediterranean World." *Int* 57 (2003): 117-37.

MacIntyre, Alasdair. *After Virtue: A Study in Moral Theory.* Notre Dame: University of Notre Dame Press, 1981.

Masenya, Madipoane. "Proverbs 31:10-31 in a South African Context: A Reading for the Liberation of African (Northern Sotho) Women." *Semeia* 78 (1997): 56-68.

McKane, William. *Proverbs: A New Approach.* OTL. Philadelphia: Westminster, 1970.

McKibben, Bill. *The Comforting Whirlwind: God, Job and the Scale of Creation.* Cambridge, MA: Cowley, 2005.

Mettinger, Tryggve N. D. "The God of Job: Avenger, Tyrant, or Victor?" Pages 39-49 in *The Voice from the Whirlwind: Interpreting the Book of Job.* Ed. Leo G. Perdue and W. Clark Gilpin. Nashville: Abingdon, 1992.

Michel, Diethelm. *Untersuchungen zur Eigenart des Buches Qoheleth.* BZAW 183. Berlin: de Gruyter, 1989.

———. "Vom Gott, der im Himmel ist (Reden von Gott bei Qohelet)." Pages 274-89 in *Untersuchungen zur Eigenart des Buches Qohelet.* Berlin: de Gruyter, 1989. Repr. from *ThViat* 12 (1975): 87-100.

Miller, Douglas B. *Symbol and Rhetoric in Ecclesiastes: The Place of Hebel in Qohelet's Work.* SBL Academia Biblica 2. Atlanta: Society of Biblical Literature, 2002.

Miller, Jerome A. *In the Throe of Wonder: Intimations of the Sacred in a Post-Modern World.* New York: SUNY, 1992.

Moore, Rick D. "The Integrity of Job." *CBQ* 45 (1983): 17-31.

Morrow, William S. "Consolation, Rejection, and Repentance in Job 42:6." *JBL* 105 (1986): 211-25.

———. *Protest against God: The Eclipse of a Biblical Tradition.* HBM 4. Sheffield: Sheffield Phoenix, 2006.

Müller, Hans-Peter."Der unheimliche Gast: Zum Denken Kohelets." *ZTK* 84 (1987): 440-64.

———. "Wie sprach Qohälät von Gott?" *VT* 18 (1968): 507-21.

Murphy, Roland E. *Ecclesiastes.* WBC 23A. Waco: Word, 1992.

———. "Qoheleth's 'Quarrel' with the Fathers." Pages 235-45 in *From Faith to*

Faith: Essays to Honor Donald G. Miller. Ed. Dikran Y. Hadidian. Pittsburgh Theological Monograph Series 31. Pittsburgh: Pickwick, 1979.

———. *Responses to 101 Questions on the Psalms and Other Writings.* New York: Paulist Press, 1994.

———. "Wisdom and Creation." *JBL* 104 (1985): 3-11.

———. "Wisdom and Eros in Proverbs 1–9." *CBQ* 50 (1988): 600-603.

Nagel, Thomas. "The Absurd." *Journal of Philosophy* 68 (1971): 716-27.

Nelson, Daniel M. *The Priority of Prudence: Virtue and Natural Law in Thomas Aquinas and the Implications for Modern Ethics.* University Park: Pennsylvania State University Press, 1992.

Neusner, Jacob. *Song of Songs Rabbah: An Analytical Translation.* 2 vols. BJS 197, 198. Atlanta: Scholars Press, 1989.

Newsom, Carol A. "The Book of Job." *NIB* 4:317-637.

———. *The Book of Job: A Contest of Moral Imaginations.* Oxford: Oxford University Press, 2003.

———. "Dialogue and Allegorical Hermeneutics in Job 28:28." Pages 299-305 in *Job 28: Cognition in Context.* Ed. Ellen van Wolde. BIS 64. Leiden: Brill, 2003.

———. "Job." Pages 130-36 in *The Women's Bible Commentary.* Ed. Carol A. Newsom and Sharon H. Ringe. Louisville: Westminster John Knox, 1992.

———. "The Moral Sense of Nature: Ethics in the Light of God's Speech to Job." *PSB* n.s. 15 (1994): 9-27.

———. "Woman and the Discourse of Patriarchal Wisdom: A Study of Proverbs 1–9." Pages 142-60 in *Gender and Difference in Ancient Israel.* Ed. Peggy L. Day. Minneapolis: Fortress, 1989.

Nussbaum, Martha C. *Upheavals of Thought: The Intelligence of Emotions.* New York: Cambridge University Press, 2001.

O'Connor, Kathleen M. "Wild, Raging Creativity: Job in the Whirlwind." Pages 48-56 in *Earth, Wind, and Fire: Biblical and Theological Perspectives on Creation.* Ed. Carol J. Dempsey and Mary Margaret Pazdan. Collegeville, MN: Liturgical Press, 2004.

———. *The Wisdom Literature.* MBS 5. Wilmington, DL: Glazier, 1988.

Otto, Rudolf. *The Idea of the Holy: An Inquiry into the Non-rational Factor in the Idea of the Divine and Its Relation to the Rational.* Trans. John W. Harvey. 2nd ed. 1958. Repr. London: Oxford University Press, 1969.

Patrick, Dale. "Job's Address of God." *ZAW* 91 (1979): 268-82.

———. "The Translation of Job XLII 6." *VT* 26 (1971): 369-71.

Paul, Shalom M. "An Unrecognized Medical Idiom in Canticles 6,12 and Job 9,21." *Bib* 59 (1978): 545-47.

Penchansky, David. *Understanding Wisdom Literature: Conflict and Dissonance in the Hebrew Text.* Grand Rapids: Eerdmans, 2012.

Perdue, Leo G. "Cosmology and the Social Order in the Wisdom Tradition." Pages 457-78 in *The Sage in Israel and the Ancient Near East.* Ed. John G. Gammie and Leo G. Perdue. Winona Lake, IN: Eisenbrauns, 1990.

———. "Job's Assault on Creation." *HAR* 10 (1986): 295-315.

———. *Proverbs.* IBC. Louisville: Westminster John Knox, 2000.

———. *The Sword and the Stylus: An Introduction to Wisdom in the Age of Empires.* Grand Rapids: Eerdmans, 2008.

———. *Wisdom and Creation: The Theology of Wisdom Literature.* Nashville: Abingdon, 1994.

———. *Wisdom and Cult: A Critical Analysis of the Views of Cult in the Wisdom Literatures of Israel and the Ancient Near East.* SBLDS 30. Missoula, MT: Scholars Press, 1977.

———. *Wisdom in Revolt: Metaphorical Theology in the Book of Job.* JSOTSup 112. BLS 29. Sheffield: Almond, 1991.

———. *Wisdom Literature: A Theological History.* Louisville: Westminster John Knox, 2007.

Peters, Thomas J., and Robert H. Waterman Jr. *In Search of Excellence.* New York: Harper & Row, 1982.

Pinckaers, Servais. "Virtue Is Not a Habit." *Cross Currents* 12 (1962): 65-81.

Pincoffs, Edmund L. *Quandaries and Virtues: Against Reductivism in Ethics.* Lawrence: University Press of Kansas, 1986.

Plato. *Theaetetus, Sophist.* Trans. Harold North Fowler. LCL. Cambridge: Harvard University Press, 1967.

Pleins, John David. "Poverty in the Social World of the Wise." *JSOT* 37 (1987): 61-78.

Plotkin, Henry. *Darwin Machines and the Nature of Knowledge.* Cambridge: Harvard University Press, 1993.

Podechard, Emmanuel. *L'Ecclésiaste.* Ebib. Paris: Gabalda, 1912.

Pope, Marvin H. *Job.* AB 15. Garden City, NY: Doubleday, 1965.

Priest, John F. "Humanism, Skepticism, and Pessimism in Israel." *JAAR* 36 (1968): 311-26.

———. "Where Is Wisdom to Be Placed?" Pages 281-88 in *Studies in Ancient Israelite Wisdom.* Ed. James L. Crenshaw. LBS. New York: Ktav, 1976. Repr. from *JBR* 31 (1963): 275-82.

Rad, Gerhard von. *Old Testament Theology.* Vol. 1: *The Theology of Israel's Historical Traditions.* Trans. D. M. G. Stalker. New York: Harper & Row, 1962.

———. *Weisheit in Israel.* Neukirchen-Vluyn: Neukirchener Verlag, 1970.

———. *Wisdom in Israel.* Trans. James D. Martin. 1972. Repr. Nashville: Abingdon, 1988.

Ricoeur, Paul. *Time and Narrative.* Trans. Kathleen McLaughlin and David Pellauer. 3 vols. Chicago: University of Chicago Press, 1984-1988.

Riess, Jana. "The Woman of Worth: Impressions on Proverbs 31:10-31." *Dialogue: A Journal of Mormon Thought* 30 (1997): 141-51.

Rimmon-Kennan, Shlomith. *Narrative Fiction: Contemporary Poetics.* New Accents. London: Methuen. 1983.

Ringgren, Helmer. *Sprüche/Prediger.* ATD 16.1. Göttingen: Vandenhoeck & Ruprecht, 1962.

Roberts, Robert C. *Emotions: An Essay in Aid of Moral Psychology.* Cambridge: Cambridge University Press, 2003.

Rose, Martin. "De la 'crise de la sagesse' à la 'sagesse de la crise.'" *Revue de théologie et de philosophie* 131 (1999): 115-34.

Rubenstein, Mary-Jane. *Strange Wonder: The Closure of Metaphysics and the Opening of Awe.* New York: Columbia University Press, 2008.

Safire, William. *The First Dissident: The Book of Job in Today's Politics.* New York: Random House, 1992.

Sandoval, Timothy J. *The Discourse of Wealth and Poverty in the Book of Proverbs.* BIS 77. Leiden: Brill, 2006.

———. "Revisiting the Prologue of Proverbs." *JBL* 126 (2007): 455-73.

Sawyer, John F. A. "The Authorship and Structure of the Book of Job." Pages 253-57 in *Studia Biblica 1978.* Vol. 1: *Papers on Old Testament and Related Themes.* Ed. E. A. Livingston. JSOTSup 11. Sheffield: JSOT Press, 1979.

Schäfer, Rolf. *Die Poesie der Weisen: Dichotomie als Grundstruktur der Lehr- und Weisheitsgedichte in Proverbien 1–9.* WMANT 77. Neukirchen-Vluyn: Neukirchener Verlag, 1999.

Schellenberg, Annette. *Erkenntnis als Problem: Qohelet und die alttestamentliche Diskussion um das menschliche Erkennen.* OBO 188. Freiburg: Universitätsverlag, 2002.

Schifferdecker, Kathryn. *Out of the Whirlwind: Creation Theology in the Book of Job.* HTS 61. Cambridge: Harvard University Press, 2008.

Schmid, Hans Heinrich. "Creation, Righteousness, and Salvation: 'Creation Theology' as the Broad Horizon of Biblical Theology." Trans. Bernhard W. Anderson and Dan G. Johnson. Pages 102-17 in *Creation in the Old Testament.* Ed. Bernhard W. Anderson. IRT 6. Philadelphia: Fortress, 1984.

———. *Gerechtigkeit als Weltordnung.* BHT 40. Tübingen: Mohr (Siebeck), 1968.

Schwartz, Matthew J. "Koheleth and Camus: Two Views of Achievement." *Judaism* 35 (1986): 29-34.

Scott, R. B. Y. "Wisdom in Creation: The *'ĀMÔN* of Proverbs VIII 30." *VT* 10 (1960): 213-23.

Seow, Choon-Leong. "'Beyond Them, My Son, Be Warned': The Epilogue of Qoheleth Revisited." Pages 125-41 in *Wisdom, You Are My Sister: Studies in Honor of Roland E. Murphy, O.Carm., on the Occasion of His Eightieth Birthday.* Ed. Michael L. Barré. CBQMS 29. Washington, D.C.: Catholic Biblical Association of America, 1997.

———. *Commentary on Job 1–21.* Illuminations Commentaries. Grand Rapids: Eerdmans, 2013.

———. *Ecclesiastes.* AB 18C. New York: Doubleday, 1997.

———. "Job's Wife, with Due Respect." Pages 351-74 in *Das Buch Hiob und seine Interpretationen: Beiträge zum Hiob-Symposium auf dem Monte Verità vom 14.-19. August 2005.* Ed. Thomas Krüger et al. Zurich: Theologischer Verlag, 2007.

———. "Qohelet's Autobiography." Pages 275-87 in *Fortunate the Eyes That See:*

Essays in Honor of David Noel Freedman in Celebration of His Seventieth Birthday. Ed. Astrid B. Beck et al. Grand Rapids: Eerdmans, 1995.

―――. "Qohelet's Eschatological Poem." *JBL* 118 (1999): 209-34.

―――. "The Socioeconomic Context of 'the Preacher's' Hermeneutic." *PSB* n.s. 17 (1996): 168-95.

―――. "Theology When Everything Is Out of Control." *Int* 55 (2001): 237-49.

Sharp, Carolyn J. "Ironic Representation, Authorial Voice, and Meaning in Qohelet." *BI* 12 (2004): 37-68.

Sheppard, Gerald T. "The Epilogue to Qoheleth as Theological Commentary." *CBQ* 39 (1977): 182-89.

―――. *Wisdom as a Hermeneutical Construct.* BZAW 151. Berlin: de Gruyter, 1980.

Sherman, Nancy. "Wise Emotions." Pages 319-38 in *Understanding Wisdom: Sources, Science, and Society.* Ed. Warren S. Brown. Philadelphia: Templeton Foundation Press, 2000.

Shields, Martin A. *The End of Wisdom: A Reappraisal of the Historical and Canonical Function of Ecclesiastes.* Winona Lake, IN: Eisenbrauns, 2006.

Simon, Yves R. *The Definition of Moral Virtue.* Ed. Vukan Juic. New York: Fordham University Press, 1986.

Simpson, Mona. "A Sister's Eulogy for Steve Jobs." *New York Times,* Op-Ed. 30. October 2011. Accessed 10 July 2012 at http://www.nytimes.com/2011/10/30/opinion/mona-simpsons-eulogy-for-steve-jobs.html?_r=1&pagewanted=all.

Smith, Mark S. "The Divine Family at Ugarit and Israelite Monotheism." Pages 40-68 in *The Whirlwind: Essays on Job, Hermeneutics and Theology in Memory of Jane Morse.* Ed. Stephen L. Cook, Corrine L. Patton, and James W. Watts. JSOTSup 336. London: Sheffield Academic Press, 2001.

Sneed, Mark R. "Is the 'Wisdom Tradition' a Tradition?" *CBQ* 73 (2011): 50-71.

―――. "A Note on Qoh 8,12b-13." *Bib* 84 (2003): 412-16.

―――. *The Politics of Pessimism in Ecclesiastes: A Social-Science Perspective.* SBLAIL 12. Atlanta: Society of Biblical Literature, 2012.

Southgate, Christopher. *The Groaning of Creation: God, Evolution, and the Problem of Evil.* Louisville: Westminster John Knox, 2008.

Spittler, Russell P. "Testament of Job." *OTP* 1:829-58.

Sternberg, Meir. *The Poetics of Biblical Narrative.* Bloomington: Indiana University Press, 1987.

Stevens, Marty E. *Leadership Roles of the Old Testament: King, Prophet, Priest, and Sage.* Eugene, OR: Cascade, 2012.

Stewart, Anne. "A Honeyed Cup: Poetry, Pedagogy, and Ethos in the Book of Proverbs." Ph.D diss., Emory University, 2013.

Strawn, Brent A. *What Is Stronger than a Lion? Leonine Image and Metaphor in the Hebrew Bible and the Ancient Near East.* OBO 212. Fribourg: Academic Press, 2005.

Strobel, Albert. *Das Buch Prediger (Kohelet).* Die Welt der Bibel. Düsseldorf: Patmos, 1967.

Tan, Nancy Nam Hoon. *The "Foreignness" of the Foreign Woman in Proverbs 1–9: A Study of the Origin and Development of a Biblical Motif.* BZAW 381. Berlin: de Gruyter, 2008.

Terrien, Samuel. "The Play of Wisdom: Turning Point in Biblical Theology." *HBT* 3 (1981): 125-53.

Thomas Aquinas. *Virtue.* Vol. 23 of *Summa Theologiæ.* Trans. W. D. Hughes. New York: McGraw-Hill, 1969.

Tough, Paul. *How Children Succeed: Grit, Curiosity, and the Hidden Power of Character.* New York: Houghton Mifflin Harcourt, 2012.

Towner, W. Sibley. "Ecclesiastes." *NIB* 5:265-360.

———. "The Renewed Authority of Old Testament Wisdom for Contemporary Faith." Pages 132-47 in *Canon and Authority: Essays in Old Testament Religion and Theology.* Ed. George W. Coats and Burke O. Long. Philadelphia: Fortress, 1977.

Tsevat, Matitiahu. "The Meaning of the Book of Job." *HUCA* 37 (1966): 73-106. Repr. as pages 1-38 in *The Meaning of the Book of Job and Other Biblical Studies.* New York: Ktav, 1980.

van der Ven, Johannes A. *Formation of the Moral Self.* Studies in Practical Theology. Grand Rapids: Eerdmans, 1998.

Washington, Harold C. *Wealth and Poverty in the Instruction of Amenemope and the Hebrew Proverbs.* SBLDS 142. Atlanta: Scholars Press, 1994.

Weeks, Stuart. "The Context and Meaning of Proverbs 8:30a." *JBL* 125 (2006): 433-42.

———. *Early Israelite Wisdom.* Oxford: Oxford University Press, 1994.

———. *Ecclesiastes and Scepticism.* LHB/OTS 541. New York: T&T Clark, 2012.

———. *The Introduction to the Study of Wisdom Literature.* London: T&T Clark, 2010.

Westbrook, Raymond, and Bruce Wells. *Everyday Law in Biblical Israel: An Introduction.* Louisville: Westminster John Knox, 2009.

Westermann, Claus. "The Two Faces of Job." Trans. Graham Harrison. Pages 15-22 in *Job and the Silence of God.* Ed. Christian Duquoc and Casiano Floristan. Concilium. New York: Seabury, 1983.

Whitley, Charles F. *Koheleth: His Language and Thought.* BZAW 148. Berlin: de Gruyter, 1979.

Whybray, R. N. *The Composition of the Book of Proverbs.* JSOTSup 168. Sheffield: Sheffield Academic Press, 1994.

———. *Ecclesiastes.* NCBC. Grand Rapids: Eerdmans, 1989.

———. *Proverbs.* NCBC. Grand Rapids: Eerdmans, 1994.

———. "Qoheleth, Preacher of Joy." *JSOT* 23 (1982): 87-98.

———. "Qoheleth the Immoralist? (Qoh 7:16-17)." Pages 191-204 in *Israelite Wisdom: Theological and Literary Essays in Honor of Samuel Terrien.* Ed. John G. Gammie et al. Missoula, MT: Scholars Press, 1978.

———. *Wisdom in Proverbs: The Concept of Wisdom in Proverbs 1–9.* SBT 1/45. Naperville, IL: Allenson, 1965.

Williams, James G. "Job and the God of Victims." Pages 208-31 in *The Voice from the Whirlwind: Interpreting the Book of Job*. Ed. Leo G. Perdue and W. Clark Gilpin. Nashville: Abingdon, 1992.

———. "Job's Vision: The Dialectic of Person and Presence." *HAR* 8 (1984): 259-72.

———. "What Does It Profit a Man? The Wisdom of Koheleth." *Judaism* 20 (1971): 179-93. Repr. as pages 375-89 in *The Sage in Israel and the Ancient Near East*. Ed. John G. Gammie and Leo G. Perdue. Winona Lake, IN: Eisenbrauns, 1990.

Williamson, Robert, Jr. "Death and Symbolic Immortality in Second Temple Wisdom Instruction." Ph.D. diss., Emory University, 2011.

Wilson, Edward O. *The Creation: An Appeal to Save Life on Earth*. New York: Norton, 2006.

Wilson, James Q. *The Moral Sense*. New York: Free Press, 1993.

———. *On Character: Essays*. Lanham, MD: AEI Press, 1991.

Wintermute, Orval S. "Jubilees." *OTP* 2:35-142.

Wolde, Ellen J. van. "Job 42:1-6: The Reversal of Job." Pages 223-50 in *The Book of Job*. Ed. W. A. M. Beuken. BETL 114. Leuven: Leuven University Press, 1994.

———. "Wisdom, Who Can Find It? A Non-Cognitive and Cognitive Study of Job 28:1-11." Pages 1-36 in *Job 28: Cognition in Context*. Ed. Ellen van Wolde. BIS 64. Leiden: Brill, 2003.

Wolters, Al. "Proverbs XXXI 10-31 as Heroic Hymn: A Form-Critical Analysis." *VT* 38 (1988): 446-57.

Yee, Gale A. " 'I Have Perfumed My Bed with Myrrh': The Foreign Woman (*'iššâ zārâ*) in Proverbs 1–9." *JSOT* 48 (1989): 53-68.

Yoder, Christine Roy. "Contours of Desire in Israelite Wisdom Literature." Paper read at the SBL annual meeting, Chicago, November 2012.

———. "Forming 'Fearers of Yahweh': Repetition and Contradiction as Pedagogy in Proverbs." Pages 167-83 in *Seeking Out the Wisdom of the Ancients: Essays Offered to Honor Michael V. Fox on the Occasion of His Sixty-Fifth Birthday*. Ed. Ronald L. Troxel, Kelvin G. Freibel, and Dennis R. Magary. Winona Lake, IN: Eisenbrauns, 2005.

———. "The Objects of Our Affections: Emotions and the Moral Life in Proverbs 1–9." Pages 73-88 in *Shaking Heaven and Earth: Essays in Honor of Walter Brueggemann and Charles B. Cousar*. Ed. C. Roy Yoder et al. Louisville: Westminster John Knox, 2005.

———. "On the Threshold of Kingship: A Study of Agur (Proverbs 30)." *Int* 63 (2009): 254-63.

———. *Proverbs*. AOTC. Nashville: Abingdon, 2009.

———. "The Shaping of Erotic Desire in Proverbs 1–9." Pages 148-63 in *Saving Desire: The Seduction of Christian Theology*. Ed. F. LeRon Shults and Jan-Olav Henriksen. Grand Rapids: Eerdmans, 2011.

———. *Wisdom as a Woman of Substance: A Socioeconomic Reading of Proverbs 1–9 and 31:10-31*. BZAW 304. Berlin: de Gruyter, 2001.

————. "The Woman of Substance *('ēšet ḥayil):* A Socioeconomic Reading of Proverbs 31:10-31." *JBL* 122 (2003): 427-47.

Ziegler, J. "Die Hilfe Gottes am Morgen." Pages 281-88 in *Alttestamentliche Studien.* BBB 1. Bonn: Peter Hanstein, 1950.

Zimmerli, Walther. *Das Buch des Predigers Salomo.* ATD 16.1. Göttingen: Vandenhoeck & Ruprecht, 1962.

————. "Concerning the Structure of Old Testament Wisdom." Trans. Brian W. Kovacs. Pages 175-207 in *Studies in Ancient Israelite Wisdom.* Ed. James L. Crenshaw. LBS. New York: Ktav 1976.

————. "The Place and Limit of the Wisdom in the Framework of the Old Testament Theology." Pages 314-26 in *Studies in Ancient Israelite Wisdom.* Ed. James L. Crenshaw. LBS. New York: Ktav, 1976. Repr. from *SJT* 17 (1964): 146-58.

————. *Die Weisheit des Predigers Salomo.* Aus der Welt der Religion, Biblische Reihe 11. Berlin: Töpelmann, 1936.

Zuckerman, Bruce. *Job the Silent: A Study in Historical Counterpoint.* New York: Oxford University Press, 1991.

Subject and Name Index

Index of Scripture and Other Ancient Literature